RUMANIA

Black Sea

YUGOSLAVIA

BULGARIA

Salonika

Ita. Brindisi
Ita.
Taranto
Ita.

Ita.

ALBANIA

GREECE

TURKEY

Piraeus

Ita. Leros

Ita.
Rhodes

SYRIA

CYPRUS

Fr. Beirut
LEBANON

CRETE

Haifa
Br.

*Mediterranean
Sea*

Port Said Br.

PALESTINIA

Benghazi

Tobruk

Ita.
Bardia Sidi Barrani

Br.
Alexandria

Br.

LIBYA

4 July 1940
British Naval Fleet
disarmed French Fleet in
Alexandria harbour French
ships were attached to
British Fleet against the enemy
(Vichy Government, Germany Italy)

EGYPT

This book belongs
to:—
IAN HARVIE

THE RELUCTANT ENEMIES

By the same author

NOVELS

The Felthams
Lady in Thin Armour
Gentlemen in Pink Uniform
The Younger Felthams
Girl in the Limelight
The Cruiser
The Rock
Leviathan
The Golden Creek
The Admiral
A Matter of Diplomacy
The Powder Train
The Tarnham Connection
The Resident
Next Saturday in Milan
Honours of War and Peace
The Cairo Sleeper

HISTORY

The Grey Top Hat
Atlantic Conquest
Cochrane
Escape Route Green
The Deadly Stroke
Hitler – The Last Ten Days
D Day
The North African War
The True Glory: The Story of the
Royal Navy over a Thousand Years

PLAYS

Jessica
A Time to be Born
Frost at Midnight
Quartet for Five
A Few Days in Greece

WARREN TUTE

THE RELUCTANT ENEMIES

*The story of the last war between
Britain and France
1940 – 1942*

COLLINS
8 Grafton Street, London W1
1990

William Collins Sons and Co. Ltd
London · Glasgow · Sydney · Auckland
Toronto · Johannesburg

British Library Cataloguing in Publication Data
Tute, Warren, *1914*–
The reluctant enemies: the Story of the Last War between Britain
and France, 1940–1942.
1. Great Britain. Foreign relations with France, 1939–1945
2. France. Foreign relations with Great Britain, 1939–1945
I. Title
940.53'22'41

ISBN 0 00 215318 1

© Warren Tute 1989

Photoset in Linotron Trump Medieval by
The Spartan Press Ltd
Lymington, Hants
Printed and bound in Great Britain by
William Collins Sons and Co. Ltd, Glasgow

CONTENTS

Contents

Contents

LIST OF MAPS

PREFACE

I doubt if the English and the French will ever understand each other. They may pretend to do so now but the premiss scarcely stands up to examination. This does not, of course, preclude their being good neighbours which at present they are. Understanding is something else.

The two nations certainly did not comprehend one another during the war years of 1940–44 which form the matter of this book. There are obvious and complex reasons for this but, of course, the root of misunderstanding lies naturally in the different language each nation speaks and also in the fact that comparatively few Englishmen even today can carry on a conversation in French beyond, say, the ability to ask the way or order a meal and even fewer educated Frenchmen can do the same in English which, privately, they resent as the world language richer in every respect than their own.

And this is 1989 in the satellite world of instant communication. In 1940 language links between the two great nations were by comparison primordial. They also lay necessarily in the hands of a few professionals such as statesmen, diplomats, press and business men to which were added those of the leisured classes who travelled. How else could it be? In 1939 those were the conditions of ordinary social life in Europe which for the second time in the twentieth century was about to embark on a catastrophic war.

Except for a few films, newsreels, occasional press features and books neither the French nor the Anglo-Saxons had any real conception of the values, of the way of life, of the spiritual texture, if you like, of the other nation.

Indeed they disliked and distrusted each other in a 'Dad's Army' way which had been inculcated in them generation after generation over the centuries and which still exists to this day. There were exceptions, of course, at the top. The generality, however, was nowhere in the running.

Small wonder, therefore, that the events this book recounts resulted more often than not from tragic misunderstandings which hindsight shows to have been possibly avoidable but which at the time were beyond the capacity of the actors in this particular historical drama.

I say all this to explain in some little way a number of harsh things I have felt I had to set out about the men of Vichy France and to a certain extent also of the French hierarchy of the time. I have loved and respected the French all my life and I now live with pleasure and contentment in a village in south-west France, in what was once 'la France anglaise'. Why then am I prefacing the book in this way?

—Nowadays those of us who lived through the war years are thinning out on the ground. Memories fade: emotions dry up. However, I think there would still be unanimous agreement that the torrid summer of 1940, when France collapsed was to all of us the worst year of the war. The unthinkable had happened. Our ally had gone. No one knew where they stood nor what might next occur. 'La belle France' lay in ruins, the Nazi flag fluttering over Paris and eight million starving refugees cluttering the roads of what had long been considered by intelligent people to be the most civilized country in the world. Chaos reigned. It was Nemesis. And Pétain was all they had.

I think the unending horror of this epoch should be borne continuously in mind as you read the story of this shabby little war. A friend of mine, a distinguished Admiral, with whom I served on Eisenhower's staff in the Mediterranean through the events described and who later on served as Naval Attaché in Rome, then as Naval Deputy to the Supreme Allied Commander in Paris and still later as Chairman of the NATO Chiefs of Staff Committee in

Brussels, has given me what is perhaps the kindest introduction this book can have:

'Whilst I do not disagree with the view that most of the
French leaders were weak and corrupt after the surrender
of France, I wonder if enough is made of their extremely
difficult position. We as a country have never been invaded
or forced to surrender (since 1066) and I sometimes wonder
how we would behave if this were ever to happen. I think
somewhere in the book more should be made of the
extreme difficulties facing the defeated French and sympathy for them in their difficulties. I think this is important if
French people are to understand the book.'

What better place to put this suggestion than here and
now before the story begins? I can only add that for myself I
am of exactly the same mind as the Admiral. There but for
the Grace of God . . .

Floreat, floreat, Marianne.

I

The auguries of conflict

'God created nothing, neither man nor beast to which He did not set its opposite in order to hold it in fear and humility. That is why he made France and England neighbours.' So said Philippe de Commynes who lived at the end of the fifteenth century, and indeed for the next 400 years these contrary neighbours were to be intermittently but frequently at war with each other. This book is the story of the last hostilities to take place during World War II between France and her 'hereditary enemy'.

The two countries had entered the war against Nazi Germany in September 1939 firmly allied, although there were private and professional jealousies, doubts and anxieties on either side. Both countries then further cemented this alliance in April 1940 by a pact specifying that neither would seek or conclude a separate peace with the enemy. Almost immediately this was to be put to the test. A few days later Hitler invaded Denmark and Norway and the blitzkrieg leading to the fall of France began.

On 14 June 1940 the German Army entered Paris. On 22 June an Armistice between France and the Reich was asked for and granted. Consent to this action had been grudgingly given by the British subject to a guarantee that the French fleet would never fall into the enemy's hands. The dynamic François Darlan, Admiral of the Fleet and head of the French Navy had given his promise to this effect and this was believed by the British War Cabinet. However when the Armistice terms became known, French ability to keep this promise under *force majeure* came into doubt, since

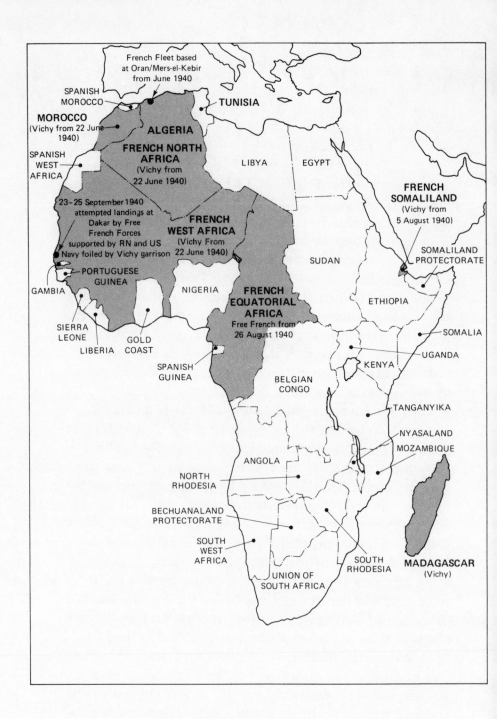

French Fleet based
at Oran/Mers-el-Kebir
from June 1940

SPANISH
MOROCCO

MOROCCO
(Vichy from 22 June
1940)

TUNISIA

ALGERIA

FRENCH NORTH
AFRICA
(Vichy from
22 June 1940)

SPANISH
WEST
AFRICA

LIBYA

EGYPT

FRENCH
SOMALILAND
(Vichy from
5 August 1940)

23–25 September 1940
attempted landings at
Dakar by Free
French Forces
supported by RN and US
Navy foiled by Vichy garrison

FRENCH
WEST AFRICA
(Vichy From
22 June 1940)

SUDAN

SOMALILAND
PROTECTORATE

PORTUGUESE
GUINEA

GAMBIA

NIGERIA

FRENCH
EQUATORIAL
AFRICA
Free French from
26 August 1940

ETHIOPIA

SOMALIA

SIERRA
LEONE

LIBERIA

GOLD
COAST

UGANDA

KENYA

SPANISH
GUINEA

BELGIAN
CONGO

TANGANYIKA

NYASALAND

MOZAMBIQUE

ANGOLA

NORTH
RHODESIA

BECHUANALAND
PROTECTORATE

SOUTH
WEST
AFRICA

SOUTH
RHODESIA

MADAGASCAR
(Vichy)

UNION OF
SOUTH AFRICA

Hitler had decreed that the ships of the French Navy were to be demobilized in their home ports, some of which were already under direct German occupation and control. So could Hitler be trusted? And if not what was then to be done?

Advice was not lacking on the British side: 'Dear Prime Minister', George Bernard Shaw wrote on 25 June, 'why not declare war on France and capture her fleet (which would gladly strike its colors to us) before A.H. recovers his breath? Surely this is the logic of the situation?' The old fool might be senile but he had a point, although his assumption about the fleet revealed a sad and dangerous naivety. After all, the stupendous idea of politically uniting the two great nations had astonishingly been proposed by the British only two days after the fall of Paris and six days before the Armistice itself, but had been curtly brushed aside by the tatterdemalion French Government on the run as merely an attempt to reduce France to the status of a British dominion. However great the fall, French pride stuck out of the wreckage like a jagged rock. The auguries were sinister and the predicament of the United Kingdom at once became acute.

In simple terms, by the end of June 1940 Hitler had overrun Europe. The British and their Empire now stood alone as the only organized force opposing the Axis powers. The British Army or rather the British Expedition-ary Force in Europe had been rescued at Dunkirk but needed desperately to be re-equipped. The Battle of Britain in the air lay a few weeks ahead. Were that to be lost, invasion would become certain. British sea lifelines were threatened by German submarines in the Atlantic, soon to be operating from French ports, and by Italian submarines and aircraft in the Mediterranean.

As against these dire threats Churchill and the War Cabinet could oppose two matchless resources, the Royal Navy's command of the sea and the R.A.F. Fighter Comm-and's control of the air space of south-east England. In addition and in the shadows they had the tacit backing of the President of the United States although not, as yet, of the American nation itself. Meanwhile the British remained determined and undefeated. Time now was of the essence and the survival of the free world had come to depend solely and simply on British supremacy at sea. For that reason the French Navy, fourth in strength after the navies of the British Empire, the United States and Japan, assumed overnight a paramount importance. The French Navy was both powerful and intact. It had fought well during what they nicknamed the 'drôle de guerre' from September 1939 till the summer of 1940. There had been no phoney war at sea. Moreover the French fleet had not been impaired by the *débâcle* in mainland France. Its morale was high. In the Mediterranean it more than balanced the Italian fleet. The French fleet continued to be very much in being and therefore to count as a cardinal factor in the balance sheet of power. So what was next to be done? The world was not to be kept waiting for long.

On 3 July 1940 and on the specific orders of the British War Cabinet, the Royal Navy took over, neutralized or sank the entire French fleet in European and Mediterranean waters, except for those units in French metropolitan ports. Surprise was total and in naval terms success was almost complete. This swift action was considered by the French, however, as mean, underhand and treacherous. The blow was struck without loss of life (the French submarine *Surcouf* excepted) in British and British-controlled ports such as Alexandria in Egypt. However at Mers-el-Kébir in French North Africa, where the great French Atlantic Fleet lay moored, the toll was severe: 1297 French naval officers and men were killed and a further 351 wounded. This proved to be, as Churchill dubbed it, a deadly stroke in deed and effect and it was these tragic events at Mers-el-Kébir which provoked this last Franco-British conflict – reluctant, undeclared and abhorred by both sides.

Reactions were instant. Darlan in Vichy furiously claimed betrayal by his brothers-in-arms and that this meant war with England. Vice-President Laval said attack would be met with attack. De Gaulle in London, desperately trying to muster support for the Free French, came near to despair. Hitler, of course, was delighted and began at once working towards persuading the French Navy into prompt and active support of the Axis now certain to defeat the British, his propaganda gave out, in a matter of weeks. Only Roosevelt saw Mers-el-Kébir for what it was – a precautionary measure and a clear indication that the British had no intention whatever of suing for peace. The perfidious war had begun.

2

The background

Vichy France broke off diplomatic relations with the United Kingdom on 5 July 1940. At that time Albert Lebrun, elected in 1933, still remained President of France and the 666 deputies (an unfortunate number had anyone referred to the Book of Revelation) had comprised the French equivalent of the House of Commons since before the war. Harried from Paris to Bordeaux and then on to Vichy, the nation's elected representatives moved about the quiet inland spa, dazed with shock, appalled by what had happened to France, uncertain, ill-informed and virtually leaderless. The 84-year-old Marshal Pétain, summoned back from Madrid where he had been the French Ambassador at the start of the rout, waited in the wings until Laval, the Deputy from the Auvergne with his white tie and drooping cigarette, could manipulate the puppet, for whom he had the most scathing private contempt, into the position of Head of State with quasi-totalitarian powers similar to those of the German and Italian dictators he so admired and with whom he was determined to align his stricken country. Thus was a seedbed prepared for civil war.

To set the scene for the drama which unfolded half a century ago it is necessary to establish the personalities involved, the ideas they held, the conditions in which they worked and the means they had at their disposal or which they lacked. To understand what happened it is further necessary to visualize essential differences in the character, values and outlook of the French and the British (whom the French like to call 'the Anglo-Saxons') and how these applied at the time. Moreover since this turned out to be basically a naval war, the being and status of the two navies also enter the reckoning.

History, as American author William Pfaff points out, is an insistent force affecting what currently goes on at any particular time because the past is what put us where we all are. The past has always to be reconciled with the present life of a nation since the bill presented by history requires payment. What happened, therefore, between July 1940 and November 1942 when what might be described as 'the shooting war' between Britain and Vichy France took place is intelligible only in the light of what had gone on before in the affairs of both countries. History is more than a chronicle of events. Attitudes, reactions, prejudice and common sense all play a part, while propaganda, of course, uses these different factors for the purposes it has in mind. Yet behind the facts and the propaganda lies the truth and it is what each individual component of a nation takes to be the truth that alone allows a consensus to be made.

In a democracy a consensus may perhaps be gauged. It can almost never be known with any certainty at the time except through a General Election, and in the France of 1940 there could be no possibility of that. This is what makes it so difficult even today to know how the French themselves *really* considered Pétain and de Gaulle. What the French Navy, or at any rate the bulk of its officers, felt about Churchill and to a lesser degree the Royal Navy which executed his orders became very much clearer. They detested both. Mers-el-Kébir, indeed, provided a convenient smoke-screen for much deeper feelings of resentment, jealousy and inferiority stretching far back into the past. It is important to see why this was so.

3

La Royale and after

'France is probably the only country with vast maritime frontiers', Etienne Taillemite observes, 'where the very existence of naval power is frequently questioned even in principle and where all naval matters have been met with a continuing public indifference never dented for long except by Richelieu, Colbert and Georges Leygues.' Since the first two operated in the seventeenth century under Louis XIII and Louis XIV and the latter in the troubled period between the two world wars of the twentieth century, this can scarcely be called a prescription for a sound and enduring naval tradition.

Indeed the eleventh edition of the *Encyclopaedia Britannica* published in 1911 well summarizes what had happened up to then:

On paper the organisation of the French royal navy was very thorough. In reality it worked ill; the severity of the 'inscription maritime' (a very severe law of compulsory service affecting the inhabitants of the coast and of the valleys of rivers as far up as they were capable of floating a lighter) made it odious, and owing to the prevailing financial embarrassment of the crown after 1692 the sailors were ill-paid, ill-fed and defrauded of the pensions promised them. They fled abroad, or went inland and took up other trades. The military and civil branches were always in a state of hostility to one another and their pay also was commonly in arrears. The noble corps (the 'grand corps de la marine' being officered exclusively by men of noble birth some of whom never went to sea) was tenacious of its privileges, and extremely insolent towards the 'officiers bleus' (recruited from the merchant service in war or emergency). By Louis XV (1715–1774) the navy was neglected till the last years of his reign when it was revived by the Duc de Choiseul. Under Louis XVI (1774–1792), when the Revolution broke out, the long accumulated hatred for the noble officers had free play. Louis XVI had indeed relaxed the rule imposing the presentation of proofs of nobility on all naval officers but the change was made only in 1786 and it came too late. The majority of noble officers were massacred by the Jacobins or driven into exile. The revolution subjected the French navy to a series of disorganisations and reorganisations by which all tradition and discipline were destroyed. Old privileges and the office of Grand Admiral were suppressed. The attempt to revive the navy in the face of the superior power of England was hopeless. Neither the Republic nor the Empire was able to create an effective navy. They had no opportunity to form a new body of officers out of the lads they educated.

Things continued in this vein up to, through and immediately beyond World War I in 1914–18. The French fleet was 'ill-adapted, insufficient and ill-assorted' and by the Armistice of 1918 had been virtually wrecked materially and morally, as evidenced by the Black Sea mutinies of 1919–20.

Then for the first time since the Second Empire, France succeeded in forming and following a coherent naval policy which to a certain extent took account of previous errors and of lessons to be learned from World War I. Georges Leygues came on the scene. Leygues had been Minister of the Marine under Clemenceau in 1917 and thereafter continued his naval connection fully understanding and promoting the importance of the maritime factor in war. Like Voltaire 150 years before (but Voltaire had not pressed the point) Leygues saw that it was on the sea that wars are won. Leygues let no one forget that the Allies led by Great Britain had won the late war by neutralizing the action of German submarines which in the spring of 1917 had come near to assuring victory to the Central Powers.

From then on he fought passionately to restore the fleet and to bring the importance and value of the navy to the attention of an indifferent and uncaring public opinion. From November 1925 to his death in September 1933 Leygues became one of the most powerful Ministers of Marine in French history, ranking in effectiveness with Colbert, Sartine, and Castries. This was the navy which François Darlan, a young Captain in his mid-forties, helped to build as Leygues's Chief of Staff and which after the latter's death he continued to promote with passion. Darlan was appointed the sole French Admiral of the Fleet on 6 June 1939 and, a week before the outbreak of the World War II, Commander-in-Chief of the whole French Navy. He was just 58 years of age. Moreover, and this mattered more than anything else, the French Navy proved to be the only one of the three Armed Forces fully prepared, ready and in a fit state for war.

4

Darlan

François Xavier Darlan was not of noble descent. He was born on 7 August 1881 at Nérac some 75 miles south-east of Bordeaux where his father was a lawyer who had just been elected Mayor of the thriving riverside town. Darlan *père* also happened to be a friend of Georges Leygues who became godfather to the infant François. Darlan's mother died when he was 3½ years old and the lonely child was then brought up in the austere family house in the rue Gambetta by a surly country bumpkin of a servant while his father, whose politics were deeply radical, got himself elected first as the local Counseiller Général in 1886 and then in 1890 as Deputy of the Lot et Garonne *Département* in the National Assembly.

Despite his father's foray into politics and from which the young man acquired his penchant for intrigue, the Darlans were basically a long-established naval family, his great grandfather having died at Trafalgar in the *Redoubtable*, from the foretop of which was fired the shot which killed Nelson. Indeed the maritime background reached so far astern that rumour had it at Nérac that Noah's Ark had been captained by a Darlan. The future Admiral of the Fleet's provenance, therefore, was from practical seafaring folk, a far remove from the aristocrats who had officered the French Navy since its inception and, bar the decimation of the Revolution, have continued to do so until today. The pushy little Gascon thus had to contend with the disdain and jealousy of his peers, factors which were to have no small bearing on the events this story tells. Darlan was respected rather than loved and the political manoeuvring which ran like a dark river throughout his career in no way helped this reputation.

I dwell on this aspect because France, since the Revolution, has always been and remains to this day a divided country where feelings run deep. In a sense the civil war which began with the Revolution of 1789 continues in an underground fashion even now in current affairs. The belligerence is no longer open. Guillotines no longer clang and crash. The divisions, however, remain.

French history is full of deep wounds and in World War II the hurt suffered by the French was of a different nature from that suffered by the British on the other side of the Channel. I am not talking about the depth of the wounds which in any case it would be pointless to try to assess, but the difference of experience of the two nations. The French Army was defeated and the country occupied during the first 10 months of the war. Thereafter the dissimilarity in vicissitudes may perhaps be comprehended by saying that the British had the bombs, the French the Gestapo. It is difficult for a people who have never known the knock on the door in the middle of the night to understand those whose continuing nightmare it was.

But how did Darlan come to be where he was at this crucial time? 'I am the only Republican Admiral' he used to tell the politicians in Paris during the 1930s when the government of France bore some resemblance to the game of musical chairs. Those politicians of the Popular Front were, of course, aware that the French Navy remained in great measure royalist in its soul and its traditions. It might be said, therefore, that Darlan rose to the top because there were few other Republican naval officers around and none with the opportunity to keep in with the left-wing politicians of the day such as Léon Blum.

Darlan was a close although often contemptuous student of politics and was at one time described (in the *Revue des Deux Mondes*) as having 'an aptitude for grasping and solving any problem. He has adapted himself to all circumstances, being in turn negotiator, naval expert, diplomat, organiser, administrator. He succeeded in every command, in every mission he undertook.' Another commentator put it less kindly: 'The Darlan of Vichy stands out in the crude light of day as in truth having all the bad qualities of Talleyrand.'

However a *'clientèle'* soon formed itself around this up-and-coming Admiral who had the ear of the government. This clientèle became known in the navy by its nickname 'les A.D.D.' (amis de Darlan). Almost all reached high posts, often without passing through the usual intermediary stages, and it is of interest to bear in mind that Darlan was one of the few officers in French naval history to reach the top without ever having had command of a ship.

Although from September 1939 to May 1940 Darlan made a great show of anti-German feelings, his rancour against the British lay just under the surface, having first been expressed to a Parisian journalist during the Abyssinian war in 1936. 'Yes', he is on record as saying, 'the English are our enemies, our real hereditary enemies. From their lair in the Channel Islands they spy on us incessantly. We cannot move a ship between Cherbourg and Brest without their knowing it. For my part it is quite simple: I had an ancestor killed at Trafalgar. Our family has always hated perfidious Albion.'

Darlan's entry into the destiny of France began on 5 May 1940 when Pétain visited the French Admiralty which Darlan had moved from Paris to Maintenon. This was five days before the Germans invaded Holland and Belgium and the old Marshal was still French Ambassador to Spain. He had, however, been summoned back to Paris for discussions since it was felt, as he afterwards put it, that 'his presence would soon be needed'. A year later Darlan described this meeting to Henri Bérand of the newspaper *Gringoire*.

Up till then I had had very few personal contacts with the Marshal. At the committees on which he sat, I had always been struck by the pertinacity of his judgments and the clarity of his summing-up. A very minor personage myself, overawed by his clear blue eyes, having had no contact with him except on official occasions, I had never been able to talk to him frankly. On May 5th he came to the French Admiralty and we had a long conversation. Then he inspected our command set-up in great detail and asked a certain number of precise questions to which he got equally precise answers.

Everything he saw and heard must have satisfied him for, before leaving, he said to me: 'At last I have seen something in working order. My congratulations, Admiral.' Then he added: 'We must stand shoulder to shoulder. Can I count on you?' 'Naturally, Monsieur le Maréchal, I am completely at your service.'

I admit that at the time I did not realise the full sense of his question. I knew that things were not going well but I had no idea that they were already in such a perilous state.

Then on 12 June (two days before Paris fell) the definitive meeting took place. Again in Darlan's own words:

We were together at Briare, at General Weygand's headquarters where a meeting of the Supreme Council was being held. The Marshal took me in his car to meet Churchill who was arriving by plane from England. He told me how revolted he was at the incapacity of the existing government to take any decision whatsoever. 'We need a sort of consulate', he declared, 'and if I am asked to state my choice for the role of first consul, I shall name you, my friend.'

'That is a very fine present you are offering, Monsieur le Maréchal. I am not at all anxious to have it.'

'Yes, yes, I have thought it over carefully. You are the only one who has made a success of his job, therefore it is you who should undertake the task.'

Four days later Darlan was made a Minister of the

Government, then at Bordeaux. This was the major turning point in his life. Duplicity began, or more accurately perhaps, the double-act of Darlan the sailor and Darlan the politician took to the boards. Darlan was certain, then, that Germany would win the war. On 1 July he expressed to the American Ambassador William Bullitt a deep bitterness towards Great Britain. The Royal Navy had disappointed him as much as the French Army, he said, being run not by one man but by a committee, so you could never find out who was responsible for success or defeat. It was absolutely certain, he went on, that Great Britain would be conquered by Hitler in five weeks, if the British Government had not already surrendered before. The Germans could easily seize Ireland and close the ports of Glasgow, Liverpool, Cardiff and Bristol. England would then die of asphyxia without a German invasion. He did not think that either the government or the British people would have the courage to withstand bombardment by the Luftwaffe. They would surrender after the first few air attacks and this would then be followed by an attack on the United States. In reporting these surprising opinions to Washington, the Ambassador commented that they seemed to give Darlan considerable pleasure and that when he remarked on this fact, the Admiral merely smiled.

Three days later the attack on Mers-el-Kébir took place.

5

Mers-el-Kébir

With hindsight it seems fair to say that the French essentially were defeated before they even entered the war. Things were different in Britain. There were, of course,

Munich men in London and Hitler's astonishing success in overrunning Europe in a matter of weeks had unbalanced the British as it had the French. The circumstances and reactions thereto, however, were distinct. Stripped of its weaponry the British Army had been skewered out of Dunkirk and now needed a pause in which to recover. But although the guns had gone, morale remained high. The Royal Air Force, dramatically outnumbered, nevertheless continued to be aggressively alive and was soon to 'achieve the impossible' in the Battle of Britain. Most significant of all, though, and the factor overshadowing the rest of the scene, was the Royal Navy's command of the sea. With that maritime bulwark in place, no invasion could hope to succeed. Moreover the British Admiralty, whether Darlan thought it a committee or not, knew what had to be done and possessed a depth of experience greater than any other Admiralty in the world. The five Sea Lords and their supporting civilian staff had their feet firmly on the ground. Finally and to cap it all, the British had Churchill staunch at the top instead of an octogenarian 'realist' with cold feet and the cancer of injured pride.

The urgent matter in hand, however, was to judge the timing of the next move Hitler would make. Since invasion was thought to be certain and since its success or otherwise depended upon control of the seas, the possible addition of the French Navy to Hitler's resources became overnight an unacceptable threat. It was not Darlan's word of honour which lay in doubt, it was Hitler's. Now powerless, the French Government had no option but to trust that the Armistice terms would be kept, even though already they were being given almost daily proof that Hitler would do exactly as he pleased.

The British War Cabinet kept a cool collective head about these current realities and, as Churchill put it bluntly to the House of Commons: 'What has happened in France makes no difference to British faith and purpose. We have become the sole champions now in arms to defend the world cause. We shall do our best to be worthy of that high honour ... the full fury and might of the enemy must surely soon be turned on us. Hitler knows he will have to break us in this island or lose the war.'

In July 1940 the British resolve to withstand assault and invasion was no more in doubt than it had been when facing the threat of Napoleon a century and a half before. The problem of the French fleet, however, had still to be solved and time was running out. Resolve requires action. So on 3 July 1940 the dire decision was put into effect. To the great and expressed distress and disapproval of the Royal Navy, which had to do the dirty work, the French fleet at Mers-el-Kébir (Oran) was given four stark options. The first was to sail to a British port in order to continue fighting the war at Britain's side. The second was to immobilize their ships to British satisfaction where they lay. If both alternatives were to be unacceptable, the French might then sail their ships with reduced crews and under British escort to a French West Indian port such as Martinique or turn them over to the United States for safe keeping. If that, too, could not be agreed then the ships were to be sunk by the French themselves in six hours. Finally and only if none of the options was taken, the Royal Navy would then destroy the fleet itself. In the event this was the tragic result, with the consequence that we had now added Vichy France to our foes.

Later, Churchill was to write that General de Gaulle who had not been consulted beforehand was 'magnificent in his demeanour' and that 'the genius of France enabled her people to comprehend the whole significance of Oran and in her agony to draw new hope and strength from this additional bitter pang'. The action was abrupt, brutal and effective. It achieved its purpose which was to convince the British and American people that the British would never give in. The only benefit to France observable at that time was that the Allies continued to survive and might eventually win the war, however unlikely that seemed in the summer of 1940. This indeed was how Churchill saw it himself, reporting the event in his own inimitable way:

When you have a friend and comrade at whose side you have faced tremendous struggles and your friend is smitten down by a stunning blow, it may be necessary to make sure that the weapon that has fallen from his hands shall not be added to the resources of your common enemy. But you need not bear malice because of your friend's cries of delirium and gestures of agony. You must not add to his pain. You must work for his recovery. The association of interests between Britain and France remains. The cause remains. Duty inescapable remains. So long as our pathway to victory is not impeded we are ready to discharge such offices of goodwill towards the French government as may be possible and to foster the trade and help the administration of those parts of the great French Empire which are now cut off from captive France but which maintain their freedom. Subject to the iron demands of the war which we are waging against Hitler and all his works we shall try so to conduct ourselves that every true French heart will beat and glow at the way we carry on the struggle and that not only France but all the oppressed countries in Europe may feel that each British victory is a step towards the liberation of a continent from the foulest thraldom into which it has ever been cast.

Yes, indeed. This was not of much comfort, however, to the men of Vichy about to take the path of collaboration with the Reich, convinced that Hitler would 'wring the British neck like a chicken's' in a matter of weeks and that by co-operating with the occupying force they would secure a better deal for themselves.*

*Time and again while researching this book and the previous one (*The Deadly Stroke*, Collins, 1973) I wrote about the action at Mers-el-Kébir, my French friends have pointed out that the men of Vichy did not consider themselves 'defeatist'. No, no, no they were 'realists' instead. Once again I wonder. Perhaps they were both. In any event the behaviour of Vichy has always been and I think still is incomprehensible to the island mind. After all, we learnt the hard facts about danegeld 1000 years before.

Nothing can expiate the tragedy of Mers-el-Kébir to the French mind or rather to the French naval mind, and there are French Admirals today who detest the British, who will never forgive Churchill in the first place and the Royal Navy in the second for carrying out his orders. 'It was an absolutely bloody business to shoot up those Frenchmen who showed the greatest gallantry', Admiral Somerville, commanding Force H, wrote to his wife and this remark is still trotted out even now when Mers-el-Kébir is discussed. In fact there can be no justification for the deaths of 1297 officers and men and the wounding of a further 351 except for the political necessity to take over or neutralize the French Navy at that time. And that, I think, remains valid, Darlan's and Hitler's promises notwithstanding.

It is always tempting to be wise after the event and during the past 50 years few historians have resisted the snare. The facts, however, remain and among those facts must be numbered the hurt *amour-propre* of the French Commander-in-Chief that a mere Captain and not an Admiral had been sent to put the options to him, one of which – the Martinique alternative – he failed to report to Darlan and the further fact that he would not even receive this negotiating officer on board his flagship till ten agonizing hours had passed. In total defeat there is or there should be no time whatever for wounded pride.

6

Alexandria

Circumstances and events were happily different at the eastern end of the Mediterranean. 'At Alexandria', as Taillemite observes, 'the exemplary entente concluded between Admirals Cunningham and Godfroy shows just how such disasters could be avoided.' It shows no such thing, of course, since circumstances were entirely different and even at Alexandria disaster was only just avoided.

The French Force X, hurriedly assembled at the end of April 1940, had been put under the operational command of the British Commander-in-Chief, Mediterranean Fleet, when it seemed likely that Italy's entrance into the war had become imminent. This ill-assorted force, of which the newest ship was already 10 years old, consisted of the 22,000-ton battleship *Lorraine* launched in 1916, four 10,000-ton cruisers all constructed between 1926 and 1930 and three destroyers of the same vintage. During the whole of its 3½ year life until its dissolution at Dakar in August 1943, Force X remained under the command of the French Vice-Admiral R.E. Godfroy.

According to Admiral Royer Dick, at that time Deputy Chief of Staff and Staff Officer (Plans) to Admiral Sir Andrew Browne Cunningham (known throughout the service as A.B.C.), Commander-in-Chief, Mediterranean, both fleets were at sea exercising or rather doing a sweep 'and working very well together' when news of the impending Armistice was received. Godfroy was described by Dick as an Admiral of the old school, a man of great honour and an aristocrat (his English wife had only recently died), who admired the British without envy or jealousy and who even had his clothes made in Savile Row. A.B.C. liked him very much and found him co-operative while remaining in every respect 'correct'. Perhaps not as elderly and hidebound as were Admirals Gensoul at Mers-el-Kébir and Esteva at Bizerta, Godfroy nevertheless made it clear at every point of stress that he was under the direct orders of the ultimate French authority to whom he had sworn allegiance and that was that. Notwithstanding this loyalty, however, Godfroy and Darlan, in Dick's opinion, 'hated each other's guts'.

The crisis began at sea when a Top Secret Most Immediate signal from the Admiralty was received stating that the French fleet could no longer be relied on. They therefore returned to harbour at once, whereupon Admiral Godfroy came on board the British flagship H.M.S. *Warspite* to say he could no longer co-operate. This was received with sympathy by A.B.C., everyone at that time being in a state of shock, and although from then on the French refused to answer any signals, a telephone line between the two flagships remained connected and Captain Auboyneau, the French liaison officer with the British, stayed on board the British flagship.

Auboyneau, described by Dick as a very charming and capable officer (with for good measure a beautiful wife) later joined de Gaulle and became his naval commander-in-chief. I record these personal facts to show that, unlike the situation at Mers-el-Kébir, French and British officers had already begun to work together as a single unit. Indeed both French and British ships had been paired, rather as after the war towns in England and France were twinned, on the old but still current custom in the Royal Navy that every ship in a fleet should have its 'chummy ship'.

What happened next comes out vividly in the exchange of letters between A.B.C. and Godfroy, the originals of which are in the French public record office in the Château de Vincennes. It began on 25 June 1940:

> British Naval Commander-in-Chief
> Mediterranean Station
> HMS 'Warspite'

My dear Admiral,

1. I feel that a stage has now been reached when it is most important for us both to be in the closest contact as regards our mutual intentions and to treat each other with the most complete frankness in order that we may do what is best for the interests which we have each of us to guard. Further, in achieving this object we will, I know, wish to consider how to cause least hardship and

difficulty to those under our commands. I appreciate that you, as also I myself, will receive instructions from our Admiralties which it may be a breach of loyalty to communicate in their entirety but saving that, I feel that to the uttermost limit we should collaborate since this must work to the good of our countries.

I therefore lay before you without reserve the situation as I see it.

2. There are the following alternatives:

   (a) The French ships in your command go to Beirut. There the decision is reached to continue the fight in conjunction with Syrian Forces or to return to France.

   (b) The ships go direct to French ports where they are demilitarised if the Germans keep their word, if not they come into action against us – a situation which it is unfortunately not in French power at the moment to prevent.

   (c) The ships proceed to sea and are sunk at your direction after taking precautions for the safety of the crews.

   (d) The ships are handed over to us, arrangements being made to send the crews to Beirut, or perhaps to France.

   (e) Volunteers are called for to fight on under your command and in collaboration with me and such ships as can be manned – it might well be all – continue to operate with us.

3. Of these alternatives I must tell you that (b), though I know you realise it, is not permitted to me by the Admiralty and I should have to take steps to prevent the French ships sailing should they desire to do so without my – or your – permission.

   Nor do I feel that (c) is acceptable and I am entirely confident that I can rely on the loyalty of all your officers and men not to take action to sink their

ships inside this harbour with the dire consequences which would result to its usefulness as a
base.

As regards (a) I feel that if the decision to fight
on were reached then the move to Beirut would
probably be advisable for many reasons, and after a
period in which to recover from this terrible shock
and in face of gathering French determination we
might well continue to fight from Alexandria at a
later date.

You will realise I know what a great risk the
Admiralty would feel they were taking if this
action were permitted. Our wish is not to take the
ships from France, of course, but primarily to
make absolutely certain that they do not reach
enemy hands and secondly if it be humanly possible to retain their aid preferably with French
crews to help us in the bitter struggle which must
now develop out here.

Can you suggest a way of providing some
guaran-tee in this respect?

Your word is more than sufficient as regards
your own intention but one must face the danger
of ships' companies possibly getting out of hand.

There remains alternatives (d) and (e) and I feel
these present the crux of the matter and that a
decison on them would greatly clear the air, that
is to say:

(1) Will all the ships in the Near East continue to
fight on?

(2) If not, can you, by calling for volunteers induce
a proportion of ships' companies to do so?

(3) If insufficient officers and men are available are
you prepared to evacuate the ships and leave
them in my hands? (Under the stress of force
majeure if you so wish)

(4) Do you feel that loyalty to the home government permits none of these alternatives?

4. With all the earnestness at my command I trust that this last situation can be avoided since it can only mean that your splendid ships will lie decaying at their moorings with ships' companies demoralising till a stage of grave danger to all concerned is reached. Moreover it would mean a further crippling in our own naval effort since I may not let the ships sail.

You are aware, my dear Admiral, that I am at your disposal at any time should you wish to discuss our difficulties? I will willingly visit you in 'Duquesne' or receive you on board here at any time.

Believe me, Yours very sincerely,
(sd) A.B. Cunningham

By any reckoning this initial letter from the Commander-in-Chief of the Royal Navy's prime fleet must be considered a warm, sympathetic and understanding analysis of a situation unique in naval history. It was answered the next day, naturally in French, by an equally understanding Admiral faced by circumstances at first sight almost impossible to disentangle, uncertain of what the French Admiralty and Government would require of him and also of the real loyalties and subsequent behaviour of the Governors and Military Commanders-in-Chief of French Morocco, Algeria, Tunisia and Syria. 'My dear Admiral', Godfroy wrote on 26 June from the flagship *Duquesne*:

What follows is in response to your letter of yesterday and to the questions it contained and sets out our general situation together with a study of the different solutions which could come about so far as Force X is concerned.

Situation in France

According to information received from the French Admiralty and confirmed by Admiral Esteva (the Commander-in-Chief at Bizerta) who sent one of his staff officers to France to find out what is going on, our unhappy country now finds itself in a desperate situation.

The Army having wanted to resist at all cost on the spot has been almost entirely destroyed unit by unit by the German motorised armour picking off one element after another. Our bombers have been reduced virtually to nothing. Our fighter aircraft also suffering heavy losses have been compelled to remain in France as they have not the range to reach North Africa or even England.

All the productive areas of France have been invaded and their products destroyed by us or captured by the enemy. Bridges, roads, railways all destroyed.

Millions of refugees have made their way to the south and without shelter or food are cluttering up the roads of a region short of natural resources and now in acute danger of famine.

Faced with such a situation the Government considered its first duty to be to rescue these wretched people and to re-establish order in France by remaining there rather than in abandoning its protective role by leaving France to continue the struggle without the means to do so.

Those were the reasons which led it to ask for an Armistice and remain on metropolitan soil. The British Government was kept informed of this situation, has appeared to understand it and to begin with acquiesced in French intentions. But at this moment one has to believe that it is not sufficiently aware of the strategic complications for the British navy which would result from this immobilisation of France including that of the French fleet. Politicians generally lack understanding of naval matters even when they think of them at all. That is how the present political situation has come about.

For us Frenchmen the fact is that a government remains in France, a government supported by a

Parliament established in non-occupied territory and which in consequence cannot be considered as irregular or deposed.

The setting up elsewhere of another government and all support for this other government would clearly be rebellion. I do not think this will happen because it would be difficult to find a leader qualified to head such a movement under present circumstances knowing what is happening in France and the additional ills which would result for the country.

However that may be, we have all been reminded of our duty to obey the orders of the French Admiralty which warns us that any act contravening the terms of the Armistice would give our enemies an excuse to go back on those terms and would also compromise the rescue of what is left of France.

In the state of affairs I have just outlined and which would be less intolerable for us were there not such repercussions on you, does a solution exist which would allow some of us to continue the fight whilst maintaining at least an appearance of regularity?

The only one, perhaps, which could reconcile the different sides of the problem would be a feigned declaration of independence by our great North African territories, a secession originating in themselves and made by themselves so as to avoid the metropolitan government being accused of breaking the agreed Armistice conditions.

In any case such a situation, full of danger as it is, could not come about in the near future and to come back to Force X for the moment, it would be necessary to have time to study the conditions in the waiting period in which we now find ourselves. I shall now deal frankly, as you asked me, with the various possibilities you chose to put to me.

(a) <u>Force X to sail to Beirut</u>   I was thinking of suggesting this solution to you myself. It has the advantage of putting an end to the sad situation in which we now are, here at your side, after what has happened in France. I see a further advantage in being in direct contact with General Mittlehauser [the French Commander-in-Chief in Syria] and through him with other French authorities on the chance that a resistance could be properly organised in which we could take part without flagrant disloyalty to our chiefs in France. The question of the seizing of my ships by the enemy would not arise at Beirut and if it ever were to arise then the ships could be sabotaged before anything could happen.

(b) Force X to return to France I understand the reservations you have about this, although it is always possible to destroy a ship. However this does not seem to be envisaged for the moment by the French Admiralty which, as you know, has directed me to go to Beirut rather than Bizerta.

(c) Destruction of Force X This could not be undertaken except as a last resort. In any case you may rest assured that my ships will not be sunk in the harbour of Alexandria provided, of course, that you yourself do not try to seize them where they are by surprise or by force.

(d) Handing over the ships to you Such action would not be possible except with the tacit consent of the French government and could only be done in some way which would disguise this consent, which is scarcely believable. So far as I am concerned, there is nothing I can do without being condemned for dishonour, a condemnation which would be well deserved.

(e) A call for volunteers If the French government were to authorise in secret the preceding idea, I could certainly find volunteers to continue the fight at your side but it is difficult to guess their number. All reservists must soon be demobilised: as for the rest many want only one thing – to go and help their families now that they are beginning to realise the depths of distress existing in France.

On top of that warfare at sea is no longer possible under our flag.

Here then, Admiral, in all frankness are the results of my thinking. I realise sadly that it will not give you much satisfaction at least not in the immediate future. In judging their value, however, I ask you to think what you would be doing if our roles were reversed.

I feel even more saddened by events when I see clearly – which some do not – the situation in which the British navy has now been put. I will go further and say that even if my mind accepts the terrible fate of France and must think now only of the future, my heart and soul remain tortured by the harm done to you in the present.

Yours very sincerely,
(sd) R.E. Godfroy

7

Before and after the Armistice

The Armistice granted by Germany to France came into force at 35 minutes past midnight on the night of 24–25 June 1940. So far as the British were concerned, the French Navy was what the crisis was all about, but the French themselves did not accord their silent service the same status. To French politicians the navy was regarded as an adjunct of colonial power, ranking with but after the Empire itself, together with the colonial governors and the military commanders-in-chief. Such differences in valuation were to be tragic both for the French Navy and for the tormented country itself. As Churchill put it after the war:

Admiral Darlan had but to sail in any one of his ships to any port outside France to become master of all French interests beyond German control. He would not have come, like General de Gaulle, with only an unconquerable heart and a few kindred spirits. He could have carried with him outside the German reach the fourth navy in the world, whose officers and men were personally devoted to him. Acting thus, Darlan would have become the Chief of the French Resistance with a mighty weapon in his hand. British and American dockyards and arsenals would have been at his disposal for the maintenance of his fleet. The French gold reserve in the United States would have assured him, once recognised, of ample resources. The whole French Empire would have rallied to him. Nothing could have prevented him from being

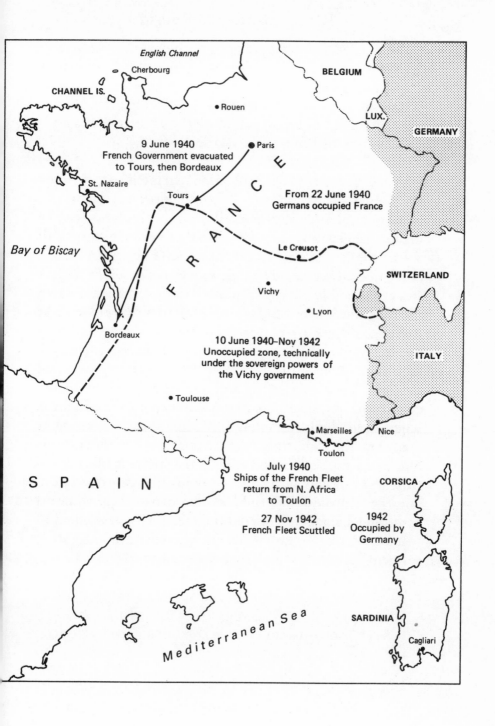

English Channel

CHANNEL IS.

Cherbourg

BELGIUM

Rouen

LUX.

GERMANY

9 June 1940
French Government evacuated
to Tours, then Bordeaux

Paris

St. Nazaire

Tours

From 22 June 1940
Germans occupied France

Bay of Biscay

FRANCE

Le Creusot

SWITZERLAND

Vichy

Lyon

Bordeaux

10 June 1940–Nov 1942
Unoccupied zone, technically
under the sovereign powers of
the Vichy government

ITALY

Toulouse

Marseilles

Nice

Toulon

July 1940
Ships of the French Fleet
return from N. Africa
to Toulon

CORSICA

S   P   A   I   N

27 Nov 1942
French Fleet Scuttled

1942
Occupied by
Germany

SARDINIA

Mediterranean Sea

Cagliari

the Liberator of France. The fame and power which he
so ardently desired were in his grasp. Instead, he went
forward through two years of worrying and ignomin-
ious office to a violent death, a dishonoured grave and
a name long to be execrated by the French navy and
the nation he had hitherto served so well.

I am not so sure today that Darlan's name is execrated by
the French. All nations and their individual historians take
pains to straighten the record if such manipulation can be
made to appear as a latterday 'discovery' or 'rediscovery' of
the truth. Darlan's achievement in building up the French
Navy from its seaweed base demands and deserves respect
and a reasonably uncritical admiration. Unfortunately like
the Maginot line on land (on which Hitler was prancing at
the end of June 1940), Darlan's navy never really had a
chance. After the Armistice the French Navy won no
battles, fired no shots in anger except at its former ally and
to cynical eyes served little purpose except as a piece on the
chessboard of power, emerging briefly into the limelight
when individual units defected to de Gaulle, were later
placed by the Provisional Government under Allied command or were scuttled or sabotaged where they lay. At no
time in the Vichy years did the French Navy exercise the
power it was designed to have. Its only use was to be an
asset on a balance sheet that no one at Vichy bothered to
read. It was a heartbreaking misuse of a proud fighting
service.

8

The run-up to Operation CATAPULT at Alexandria

Operation CATAPULT – the seizure or the taking under British control of the French Navy outside metropolitan ports – was ordered by the War Cabinet during the week following the Armistice. This was no light decision. Although foreigners at large considered the confidence with which the British faced the immediate future at that time to be based on a combination of bluff and rhetoric, in fact as Churchill was at pains to make clear: 'Those of us who were responsible at the summit in London understood the physical structure of our Island strength and were sure of the spirit of the nation.' The self-assurance of the British, therefore, was based upon 'a sober consciousness and calculation of practical facts'.

One of those facts, which had now acquired a sudden urgency, was that the addition of the French Navy to those of Germany and Italy with 'the menace of Japan measureless upon the horizon', confronted the United Kingdom with mortal danger. At one remove it would also affect the security of the United States. This risk had been repeatedly pointed out as the crisis developed throughout that anguished summer of 1940 for one simple reason – the British understood sea power; the continental nations did not.

So, having offered national unity with France and having had that offer brusquely rejected, having been promised that the French fleet would never be allowed

to fall into enemy hands and then having to face the fact
that the Armistice terms and the way they were interpreted made the opposite only too possible, 'the War Cabinet
never hesitated . . . and resolved that all necessary measures should be taken . . . the life of the State and the
salvation of our cause were at stake. It was Greek tragedy.
But no act was ever more necessary for the life of Britain
and for all that depended upon it. I thought of Danton in
1793 – "the coalesced Kings threaten us and we hurl at
their feet as a gage of battle the head of a king". The whole
event was in this order of ideas.' In July 1940, however,
the 'gage of battle' was to be the slaughter at Mers-el-
Kébir.

Operation CATAPULT was still a week in the future
and unknown to either of the 'dear Admirals' at
Alexandria when on the 27 June A.B.C. again wrote to
Godfroy:

My dear Admiral,

1. May I thank you for your very full and frank
    review of the situation and tell you how thor-
    oughly I understand the mental distress in which
    you find yourself and to which you refer. The
    situation is one where the conflict of loyalties is
    such that any man in your position must find his
    situation very hard indeed.

2. As I see it certain things emerge from your letter
    of 26th June:
    First   You tell me in effect that in view of
             your instructions which you must
             obey, your forces can take no further
             part in the war until some circum-
             stances arise – and I feel you have some
             hope that they may do so – which will
             permit of your receiving orders more in
             accordance with your wishes.

Secondly I would like to make one point clear. You say 'the British Government at first acquiesced in the intentions of the French Government'. This is, of course, perfectly true for at that time it had been agreed that all French warships should go to British ports. What has caused the unfortunate exchange of accusations – as painful to you as to me – has been the fact that French ships have remained in French ports with the consequent worry to us that at any time the Germans will find some pretext, such that the conditions of the Armistice have been broken, to seize the ships and will use them against us.

Thirdly I should like to make it clear that it has never been in any way my idea to seize your ships by force nor is it my intention now (I am assuming, of course, that the ships remain amenable to your discipline and control. If they did not then any action would be a matter of our mutual collaboration).

Fourthly I agree with you that it is probably highly desirable that the reservists should be removed. I have telegraphed most urgently to that effect and hope to be able to send them to Beirut in 'Athos II' at the first possible moment. I shall ask you, however, to make arrangements to ensure that 'Athos II' is not detained in Beirut but returns at once to Alexandria.

Fifthly I am deeply moved by your truly helpful offer to discharge your fuel, but for my part I prefer to rely on your word – I feel there can be no better guarantee. The

45

only reason that would cause me to accept your suggestion is if you yourself feel it would strengthen your position in any way. Otherwise I would leave it to you that if for any reason you had cause to suppose that you no longer had control of any one of your ships, you would inform me at once and order her to discharge her oil.

3. I have now received from the Admiralty confirmation of the fact that they consider that the Germans have held your codes since 20th June. This was the day of Admiral Darlan's order 'Whatever orders are received never abandon a ship to the enemy intact'. And though this order is re-iterated now it may be merely a cover for German inspired instructions. This point is of cardinal importance.

4. In conclusion, therefore, I regard the situation to be now:

Reservists will be sent to Beirut as soon as permission is received.

The ships under your command will remain at Alexandria and I may assume I have your undertaking that none of them will raise steam to go to sea without a direct order from you after consultation with me.

The situation will be reviewed between us at frequent intervals since it is evident that rapid changes in events may need a review of our mutual arrangements.

5. You will notice that I have not reverted to the idea of sending the ships to Beirut. This is because I could only conscientiously do so if I knew they would be going there intending to continue the war on our side and if I furthermore could feel that Syria herself intended to continue the fight. Un-

fortunately this latter possibility also remains in some doubt and for that reason I fear this solution must remain in abeyance for the moment.

6. Once again, my dear Admiral, please accept all my sympathy. I understand only too well your predicament and I trust that you equally will appreciate my position and the standpoint I have necessarily to take up in this matter but I trust neither of us will allow this problem to touch the cordiality of our relations one with the other. I am always at your disposal should you wish to come and see me at any time.

P.S. I have just been informed by the Vice Admiral, Malta that the submarine NARVAL has arrived at Malta but that she requires repairs which will take a considerable time.

The next day Godfroy replied in English:

My dear Admiral,

1. I thank you for your letter of yesterday (27 June). I venture to answer in English, hoping it will save your time. If some words are too incorrect to be understood or some phrases not sufficiently clear you will, I hope, ask me what I want.

2. I agree with you on all the main points you have made known to me in your letter.

   First   I must see at first how things will turn in North Africa (if you can obtain reliable intelligence about the exact situation there, I should be much obliged to you to let me know it).

   I do not suppose that after the Armistice General Noguès will fight if not attacked but I think they will stand on their positions refusing to leave the

47

Tunisian position. On the other hand I believe that Admiral Gensoul will stay at Oran taking no new offensive against Italy but not willing to accept disarmament in France under enemy control. We shall see the effect of that attitude; if Italians and Germans do not accept it and try to attack us in North Africa we shall have, in that case, good reasons to fight again in the Mediterranean sea and even elsewhere.

Secondly and Thirdly I agree with your opinion on these points.

Fourthly These reservists are a little troublesome, because they know the word 'demobilisation' is in the Armistice terms. Some of them might probably be volunteers to stay.

If they leave we shall remain with our peace time crews. It will be sufficient, if necessary, for short operations in the Med sea.

Other sailors are in a rather good situation of mind. Many of them have very high spirits. On board the 'Athos II' their spirit is very good too.

So, if they go to Beirut, to make the come back to Alexandria will be easy.

Fifthly You have my words we shall not leave our moorings. And I shall have tomorrow the words of my Captains not to try to proceed to sea without my ordering it.

3. Orders received from Admiral Darlan are authentificated by a special convention which is not written in any code. Any signal not having that sign is of no value to me.

4. My conclusion is yours.

5. We shall stay here and wait.

6. I cannot say how I am grateful to you for all the comprehension I feel you have for my difficult situation. Military servitude is sometimes hard to bear but it exists and the struggle of conscience it creates is a terrible ordeal.

   I do not feel inclined to go and see you in the present situation but I like to say I am, as well, your devoted

                                                    R.E. Godfroy

Thus at Alexandria the exchange of letters between the 'dear Admirals' in the immediate aftermath of the Armistice showed an almost complete accord between the British and the French. Unfortunately a few days later Operation CATAPULT was to blow into smithereens that accommodation and mutual trust.

9

The *Narval* epic

The French submarine *Narval* mentioned in the postscript to Admiral Cunningham's letter was the first of only two out of 77 submarines to rally voluntarily to General de Gaulle, and *Narval* alone left a French base to do so. The other submarines which later joined the F.N.F.L. (Forces Navales Françaises Libres) – *Minerve, Junon, Orion, Ondine* and the minelayer *Rubis* (which earlier had been attached to a British flotilla) were then seized in Operation CATAPULT with other French warships working from British ports (such as the giant submarine *Surcouf*) whose crews subsequently elected to be repatriated to France. The *Narval*, therefore, is unique and her story epitomizes the tragedy of the French Navy at the time of the Armistice. When in mid-December 1940 *Narval* was accidentally blown up in a French minefield off the Tunisian coast, A.B.C. commented sadly: 'There goes all that is left of an alliance.' Although this might not be strictly true so far as the overall picture of de Gaulle and the F.N.F.L. was concerned, in the Mediterranean *Narval* nevertheless became the sole emblem of any French determination to continue the war.

Aptly named, perhaps, since *'Narval'* is the French for sea unicorn, the whale with the one straight horn, the 1000-ton submarine was attached to the French 11th Submarine Flotilla at Bizerta in June 1940 and had been working out of Sousse in the south of Tunisia patrolling Libyan waters, Libya then being an Italian colony. Both the Captain, 36-year-old Lieutenant François Drogou, and his First Lieutenant, 32-year-old J.M. Sevestre, were men of independent spirit and intensely individual as submariners of all navies are apt to be since otherwise they could not carry out the exacting, lonely and responsible duties required of a motorized metal cigar on war patrol.

From the journals, letters and reports these officers made and from the official reactions of their superiors at Sousse and Bizerta, the general state of despair at what was happening in mainland France can easily be visualized. So far as Drogou and Sevestre were concerned this lingering malaise was made worse by the scorn they privately felt for their own senior officers cowering supinely behind their telephones waiting to be told what to do next. These fires of contempt were further fuelled by officers of a detachment of the Foreign Legion garrisoned at Sousse whose opinions Drogou summarized as follows:

All is lost in France. However *we* can fight on in North Africa provided the Government gives us freedom of action. The Resident General in Tunisia, M. Peyrouton, seems to have a fighting spirit. At Sousse we know the Colonel in charge is prepared to lay down his arms if given the order. On the other hand his officers have no intention of following him but will continue to fight right on to the end. They and some of their men plan to seize a merchant vessel in the harbour and force it to take them to Egypt. They asked if 'Narval' would escort them.

Thus it began. However before anything could happen *Narval* was ordered out on a three-day patrol from 18 June. While at sea the submarine deciphered a long and extraordinary signal from Admiral Darlan, addressed to all serving officers. This ordered them to fight on fiercely till the end, so long as a properly constituted French Government, independent of the enemy, had not countermanded this order. They were further instructed to obey no other government. Finally whatever orders were received no warship was at any time to be abandoned to the enemy intact.

Had Admiral Darlan continued along this path he could have made himself Head of the Resistance, Drogou commented. But the signal in its entirety shattered the *Narval* officers. 'The impression we got,' Drogou wrote, 'was that our country had had it: everything had gone. The Germans were the masters now. Yet at least honour could be saved. This message contained very definite instructions and a formal command: "Whatever orders may be received in the future, no warship is to be abandoned intact to the enemy". No one could doubt what that meant. Darlan was writing his Last Will and Testament.'

However the message had also indicated that 'should Admiral Darlan not be able to exercise his powers freely, naval forces would be put under the orders first of Admiral de Laborde (at Toulon) and then of Admiral Esteva (at Bizerta).

The return of the *Narval* to Sousse on 22 June was doleful; the crew had not even been able to let off steam by having a shot at the Italians. In the swept channel *Narval* crossed

with her sister submarine *Réquin* on the way out to patrol
and *Narval* then took her place at the Phosphate Jetty
alongside the *Marsouin,* the Flotilla leader, on board which
ship Drogou proceeded at 1400 hours. Having reported on
his mission to Commander Lorthioir, Drogou asked for
news of France. Lorthioir replied:

'The Armistice with Germany is about to be signed
but we don't know the conditions. We don't even
know where the German troops are. Bordeaux is
threatened: Brest and Cherbourg already occupied.
Armistice negotiations are also under way with Italy.'
   'What are the orders, sir?'
   'I've had none, nothing from Bizerta nor from the
Fleet.'
   'What? Haven't you received the cypher from
Admiral Darlan?'
   'No.'
   'I'll get it at once.'

On reading the signal Lorthioir made no comment. Then
as the day wore on, the lack of news became agonizing. At
that moment the idea of defection came into Drogou's
mind. In the evening, he remembered, when they were on
deck after dinner discussing the situation in France, he and
his officers were all agreed on the following point: 'Every
one of us here in North Africa has the duty to go on
fighting. This is absolutely necessary both for the honour
of France and in our own interests.' He also remembered
that when an Army officer asked what the fleet would do if
France capitulated, he answered: 'I don't know if every one
will go on fighting, but no ship will fall into German or
Italian hands.'
   It was on that evening too that Lieutenant Sevestre and
an Army officer called Robert went on board the *Jeanne
Schiaffino,* a merchant ship moored in the port, to make an
agreement with her Captain to embark personnel and
stores and then to sail.

The Narval *epic*

The next day, 23 June, brought nothing new. Everyone waited in pain and distress to know the Armistice conditions. Would the fleet be handed over to the Germans? This was what the Allies had demanded and obtained from Germany in 1918. To kill time Sevestre wrote up his journal. He said he was ashamed to be French. In such a situation an Englishman or a German who sat doing nothing would be considered the worst kind of traitor. As he wrote he heard other members of the crew discussing the situation in little groups, each jealous of one another and all of them blaming their superiors for the mess they were in. He realized he would have to take the Petty Officers in hand, almost all of whom were against rallying to de Gaulle. They felt unsure of their Captain and also that Drogou was unsure of himself. So then Sevestre realized he would have to build up the spirit of resistance in his Commanding Officer as well. Petty Officers would always follow a firm lead and then there would be no problems with the rest of the crew who were disciplined men.

Yet all the while as the fateful moment came near both the Captain and his First Lieutenant felt a heavy pain gripping the heart. How could they lead their men to defect when they themselves owed obedience to their own superior officers, Commander Lorthioir at Sousse, Rear Admiral Ven at Bizerta and Admiral Darlan somewhere in France?

Darlan! That was it. Had not Darlan himself said in his last *free* message that no one should obey future orders which were contrary to honour? But where did honour lie? Once again the temptation arose just to give it all up, to become like the others, mute, non-resisting, all beaten men seeking mercy from the triumphant Germans. 'To stop fighting is to cease to be alive', Drogou told himself, 'the whole drift of our society has to be fought, the sad idea that we are no more than cattle getting our muzzles in the trough.'

That night *Narval* kept Duty Radio Watch and received

a long cypher message (No. 5128) from the French Admiralty which struck them like a cold douche:

> Ever since the legal government of France has, for pressing reasons, begun Armistice negotiations with Germany and Italy, a violent campaign has been put out on the radio and also by foreign agents to create confusion and spread disunity among the French. The British government appears to be the instigator of this campaign which, were it to succeed, would result in the French colonies and the Fleet being put in the hands of the British Government for the defence of its self-interests alone.
>
> The French General de Gaulle who is urging rebellion from London has just been dismissed. In this grave and perilous time we are going through each of us must think only of what is best for France.
>
> So far as the Fleet is concerned, it will remain French or will perish. But if we cease to fight, the Fleet will not be at the disposition of any other power whosoever that power may be.

Then followed a long diatribe against Churchill and Great Britain 'in large measure responsible for our present situation'. This signal, although coded in the current French Admiralty code, not only put the *Narval* officers into trauma, it also convinced them that the whole message was German inspired since it so obviously read as nothing more than a Goebbels propaganda bulletin aimed at splitting the French from their English allies.

It therefore followed that French codes and cyphers had fallen into German hands (we now know this was so, but communication by landline between Toulon in the unoccupied zone and North Africa was still private to the French). If that were so then the only conclusion to be drawn was that the French Government must be acting under duress. The worst fears expressed in Admiral Darlan's 'testament' must therefore now have been realized.

The Admiral of the Fleet was no longer in a position of command.

These fairly simple deductions seemed unfortunately to be corroborated by the fact that this German-inspired signal was neither confirmed nor denied by other cyphered or plain language messages. Indeed the submarines at Sousse waited in vain for any indication from their immediate superiors as to the line to be taken. All were left to wait in the dark.

Matters got worse throughout that ominous day of 24 June. During the forenoon the *Narval* officers met their Foreign Legion friends who had been listening to the B.B.C. Together they went on board the *Marsouin* to get a reaction from their Flotilla Commander, Lorthioir. Drogou and Sevestre pointed out that the French Admiralty messages they were now receiving were clearly German in origin. Did Lorthioir not agree? 'Well no,' Lorthioir answered weakly, 'I think they may well be from the Bordeaux government.'

None of them knew whom to believe nor was any lead given by the High Command at Bizerta. The general opinion, however, was that the government, even with Pétain at its head, would be powerless in the face of a Germany dictating the orders. In other words France was in bondage.

It was during that day, therefore, that Drogou made secret preparations to go to sea while there was still a chance to escape. He ordered Sevestre to reposition the submarine with its bows towards the harbour mouth while he himself was ashore lunching with his army friends. He also came to an agreement with one of the Harbour Masters that the boom at the harbour mouth would be quietly opened to let the *Narval* out whenever Drogou gave the word.

It became known during the day that Monsieur Peyrouton, the Resident General, would broadcast that evening and although some of them thought he would opt to continue the fight, together with the Governors of Algeria and Morocco, neither Drogou nor Sevestre had much confidence that that would happen.

At 2100 hours Drogou went to the office of his Harbour Master friend, Lieutenant Rouxéville, to listen to the Peyrouton broadcast. Drogou wrote in his journal:

> The Resident General had scarcely spoke ten words before I realised that it was all over. His tone of voice, the terms of the Armistice – every single thing indicated craven collapse and an end to our hopes. France had been broken from top to bottom and the man I had thought could and would begin a resurrection had instead integrated himself into the national disaster. My decision, therefore, was quickly made. I asked Rouxéville to open the boom, at the same time apologising for the trouble this would provoke. 'Don't worry', he told me, 'I couldn't care less. I'd do exactly the same if I were in your shoes.'

Drogou then returned on board his submarine to find everyone as dispirited by the Peyrouton broadcast as he was himself. 'We sail in an hour', he told his crew, an announcement which to Drogou's surprise was accepted without being questioned. But then all were in a state of shock and it was better to be at sea than on shore. Shortly before slipping out of harbour a carload of their Foreign Legion friends drew up alongside and one of them, Captain Robert, asked if he could come too. Drogou agreed and as they slipped their moorings told Rouxéville to let them get clear of the harbour and then inform Commander Lorthioir that *Narval* was *en route* to a British port to continue the fight.

The nearest British port to Sousse was Malta, some 250 miles to the east. Reaching Malta was to be fraught with danger not only because *Narval* might be mistaken for an Italian submarine (the Franco-British recognition codes having been abandoned or changed) but also because some of the ship's company were having second thoughts and

Drogou and Sevestre could no longer be sure of their loyalty. Indeed, as Drogou put it in his report, they were navigating as if on a razor's edge with a possibly mutinous crew, having left one navy which would henceforth disown them for another, the English, who had not been warned of their arrival and with the Italians, now the Armistice had been signed, considering them as outlaws. A further risk had also to be borne in mind. A submarine approaching Malta with out-of-date recognition codes might well be sunk without warning and no one need ever know.

They averaged 10 knots using their diesels at night on the surface and continuing submerged on their electrics at about 30 metres depth as soon as it was light. In fairly heavy seas they sighted Gozo, Malta's sister island to the west, at about 0530 hours on 26 June and when they came within visual signalling distance tried to get in touch by semaphore (this was before radar came into general use). No one answered. Then only three miles off shore they began light-signalling with an Aldis lamp. Still no one replied.

Now Drogou began to be really worried. In addition to the force 5 sea which was breaking over the conning tower, he knew that the approach to Grand Harbour, Valletta would be well protected by mines, the swept channels through which had no doubt been altered since the Armistice. He had hoped to meet a patrol vessel of some sort which would lead him in, but the horizon remained alarmingly bare.

Then suddenly at about 0800 a British destroyer H.M.S. *Diamond* hove up on them from astern at high speed. As soon as the destroyer had sighted what the British took to be an Italian submarine, Action Stations had been sounded, guns cleared away and depth charges made ready. In fact although *Diamond* demanded that *Narval* identify herself by signal projector on the bridge, the Captain and the Officer of the Watch were almost certain that they had caught an Italian submarine since they knew that no

British submarine would be in the area. This impression was confirmed when *Narval* signalled ASR, a reply not in the current code book. *Diamond* had already just sunk two Italian submarines in the approaches to Malta, this would make the hat trick.

They were on the point of opening fire when the First Lieutenant came on the bridge and from previous experience exercising with French submarines recognized the non-Italian profile of *Narval*. He asked whether the old Franco-British code book, which had been superseded two days before, had yet been destroyed. Quite by luck it had not and ASR was in it. 'Make BES and our own identification', the Captain ordered. To this *Narval* replied XRJ and thus established herself as French. Asked *en clair* if she had any orders, *Narval* replied: 'French submarine "Narval" making for Valletta to join the Royal Navy.'

A huge shout of joy rang out from the destroyer's bridge 'which could have been heard in Sicily'. A French submarine captain had had the guts to say 'Non!' to capitulation and to bring his boat to Malta. The British were no longer alone.

10

The *Rubis* patrol

On 3 July 1940 there were seven French submarines in United Kingdom ports. These included one, *La Créole*, only three-quarters completed which had been launched at Le Havre on 8 June and had then been towed round to Swansea, there to remain unfinished until after the war. Of the other six just one, the invaluable minelayer *Rubis*, opted for de Gaulle. In large measure this was because

Rubis happened to be the only French submarine which had been integrated into a British submarine flotilla (the 9th, based on Dundee) before the fall of France.

The decision on the *Rubis* as to whether or not to continue the fight became just as agonizing as it had been for the captain of the *Narval*, the only difference being that the circumstances at Dundee and in London generated pressures of a dissimilar kind. Whereas Drogou and Sevestre in the *Narval* had had to plan and execute their escape in desperate and despondent secrecy, Commandant Cabanier (later to become an Admiral and Chief of Staff) lived and worked as part of a spirited British team, his 'voice of conscience' being Vice-Admiral Odend'hal, the Head of the French Naval Mission in London.

The story of the *Rubis* at that critical time has all the ingredients of a thriller. Their adventures began in early June 1940. During the previous two months a round dozen French submarines had been working in the North Sea with the Royal Navy blockading the German coast and, in the case of *Rubis*, sowing mines in the fjords of Norway, only recently invaded by the Germans. Initially based on Harwich, the French submarine group with its depot ship *Jules Verne* fell back on Rosyth in the Firth of Forth after the overrunning of Holland and then, with the exception of *Rubis*, returned to Brest on 9 June.

Rubis was a small minelaying submarine, one of six in service in the French Navy (the other five all being in the Mediterranean) and she was invaluable to the Allied command at that time since the Royal Navy had no such small-sized boats capable of laying mines in the path of the capital ships of the German Navy then lurking in the Norwegian Fjords. Throughout her service (and she survived the war) *Rubis* led a charmed life, being justly described by Jean-Jacques Antier as 'L'enfant chéri des sous-mariniers britanniques'. By the end of the war she had carried out 22 patrols, laying 683 mines and accounting for the sinking of at least 14 merchant ships and eight German warships.

A week after Dunkirk and five days before the German Army entered Paris, *Rubis* carried out a patrol off Bergen, laying 32 mines. Vice-Admiral Max Horton, the British submarine chief at that time, then directed *Rubis* to Dundee, a base somewhat less exposed to Luftwaffe attack than Harwich. Although the French Admiralty had ordered all the North Sea submarines to return to Brest, Vice-Admiral Odend'hal in London decreed that *Rubis* should carry out an already planned minelaying operation which would neatly use up her remaining stock of mines. The mission was so risky that Horton told Commandant Cabanier he should think about it alone for 24 hours (who knows what would have happened if Cabanier had asked to be relieved of his duty?).

By then the disastrous news from France had begun to come through by the hour. So Cabanier was summoned to London by Admiral Odend'hal and asked if he knew that armistice negotiations were under way. When Cabanier said he did, Odend'hal then drew his attention to French Admiralty message 5025 addressed to all ships: 'The President of the Council reminds every fighting man that no armistice is yet in force and the duty of all is to continue to fight to the best of their ability. This order applies especially to the navy.' Odend'hal then went on to say that he had agreed with 'our British friends' that *Rubis* should carry out this last minelaying operation: 'So you should sail and if in the course of the patrol, an armistice is agreed I shall let you know and you should then return at once to Dundee where further orders will be given you.'

Odend'hal is further on the record as adding 'avec un air bizarre' that whatever orders may have been given *Rubis must* cease all war activity on signature of the Armistice. With this ambiguous remark in his ears, Cabanier returned to Dundee. 'I was very depressed', he wrote, 'this was the most disheartening experience I had had since the start of the war. I was convinced that everything was breaking down, that those who had built up the grandeur of France no longer existed, that no leader was at the helm and that from now on I had no one to trust but myself.'

The next day, 20 June, *Rubis* had been ordered to sail at dawn. Just as they were casting off the departure was cancelled and Cabanier was sent for by Admiral Horton in London. 'Your Naval Attaché refuses to let you sail', Horton told him, 'the Armistice is on the point of being signed at Rethondes. I've talked to the [British] Vice Chief of the Naval Staff who considers it idiotic to leave your last set of mines unused and has promised to bring pressure to bear on Admiral Odend'hal to let you carry out this last patrol.' Cabanier then returned to Dundee and half an hour afterwards received a signal from Odend'hal: 'Sail immediately as ordered by Admiral Horton with whom I agree.'

So at 1530 hours on 20 June 1940 *Rubis* set off east for the Norwegian coast. The timing of events now became crucial. Although the Armistice was signed on 22 June at 1800, the actual cessation of hostilities was to be delayed until 0035 on 25 June to allow for the Franco-Italian Armistice to be signed as well and to come into effect. *Rubis*, proceeding submerged into Trondheim fjord, knew nothing of this nor of Odend'hal's decision to obey Darlan's instructions to the letter and recall all French vessels on the northern front. This meant that if caught by the Germans after 0035 on 25 June, *Rubis* would be considered a pirate. What worried Odend'hal more was that he had in front of him a copy of the Most Secret sailing orders given to *Rubis* which directed the submarine to enter Grip Holm at 0100 on 26 June, reconnoitre Solvaersboen at 0200 and start laying the mines on the northern and western approaches to Trondheim at 0300.

So Odend'hal began pestering the British Admiralty to cancel the patrol and recall *Rubis*. Although assured by the Admiralty that the necessary signals had been sent, Odend'hal could not secure a copy (nor are they in the Public Record Office) and considered himself to have been tricked. Whether or not this was so (and the British Admiralty did have other matters it was engaged on at the time) it is also unlikely that *Rubis* could technically have received any messages deeply submerged in a northern Norwegian fjord. So, a day later, having duly laid all her mines and slipped safely out of the fjord, *Rubis* set off back to Dundee, getting in on 1 July to receive warm congratulatory signals from the Admiral (Submarines) and from the Commander-in-Chief of the Home Fleet (the latter in impeccable French).

They also learned to their great dismay that the Armistice had indeed been signed and that de Gaulle was strongly urging all Frenchmen then in the British Isles to back him in what he called 'Resistance' and the French naval and government representatives in London, Odend'hal included, called 'Dissidence' or in English 'Rebellion'. What were they to do?

Faced with this desperate dilemma, Cabanier and his officers decided not to exercise their authority on either side but to let the men make up their own minds. This they did, giving their officers the unusual experience of hearing what the lower deck really thought about their great bemedalled leaders in France. The next day when the vote was taken 42 out of 44 decided to join the F.N.F.L.

So the day before that fateful 3 July 1940 when Operation CATAPULT was put into effect only two French submarines, the *Narval* at Malta and the *Rubis* at Dundee, had opted for the tall phlegmatic General de Gaulle whom Churchill was already calling 'the Constable of France'.

I I

Paralysis

In these satellite days, when the power of exchanging information almost instantly has shrunk the entire world into a village, it has to be remembered that things were very different in the pre-radar, pre-television, pre-electronic days of 1940. Plastics, semi-conductors, micro-chips and tape recorders had yet to come on the scene. Radio transmission and reception depended on the fragile thermionic valve, so easy to break or burn out. No transatlantic telephone existed and even the lines to France often gave users the impression that they would have done better with two tin cans and a piece of stretched string.

Indeed had communications been even marginally more reliable than they were, Operation CATAPULT might never have been necessary or at any rate it might have been executed in a different way. But how do you beat the clock when every secret communication between the leaders of two great countries on either side of the channel had to be made either face to face or in writing 'By Hand of Officer' letter or else by signal in Morse code, the message being laboriously encyphered into numbers at one end and decyphered at the other provided both parties had the right code books and the figures had been correctly transmitted?

As Churchill observed: 'The manner of the fall of France was decided on June 16 1940 by a dozen chances, each measured by a hair's breadth.' That was the day, two days after the Germans entered Paris, when the Bordeaux government was offered union with Great Britain. Had communication with Bordeaux not been defective at that crucial time, Churchill would have been there himself the next day 'accompanied by the most powerful delegation that has ever left our shores, armed with plenary powers in the name of the British nation.' Had this meeting taken place, the whole course of history might well have changed. 'Certainly', Churchill goes on, 'we should have confronted Pétain, Weygand, Chautemps and the rest with our blunt proposition – No release from the obligation of March 28 unless the French Fleet is sailed to British ports. On the other hand we offer an indissoluble Anglo-French union. Go to Africa and let us fight it out together.'

Most important of all Darlan and Churchill would have been together on 17 June, the day Darlan changed his mind about ordering the French Fleet to sail to British, American and French colonial ports. That was the moment of destiny. That was the day when Darlan in addition to being Head of the Navy also became Minister of Marine. That morning, after the fall of Reynaud's cabinet, he had declared to General Georges: 'I am determined to give the order to the Fleet to sail.' But the order was never given. The next day when Georges met him in the afternoon and asked him what had happened, Darlan replied with disarming simplicity: 'I am now Minister of Marine.' As such he had acquired a different point of view. Now what mattered to Darlan the politician was that the Armistice for which the new Pétain government was asking would never be granted were the fleet to be put into Allied hands. Nothing could then be saved from the wreckage of defeat. The whole of metropolitan France would be occupied and in all likelihood French North Africa as well. So the fleet remained in paralysis wherever it happened to be. It was ordered to do nothing except to scuttle or sabotage itself should it be in danger of falling into enemy hands. Thus the man who had so brilliantly built up the body and soul of the French Navy, broke its spirit almost without a thought except, perhaps, for himself. Overnight their steadfast ally across the Channel became once more the hereditary enemy.

Little or any of this was known or appreciated, although speculations could be made and implications drawn, by the officers and men of the French Navy in their individual ships and establishments all over the world. They waited loyally for a lead, as always ready to obey, but no orders came. France had been defeated, ruined and occupied but the navy, of which he was so rightly proud, was to be put into some sort of time cocoon by its Admiral of the Fleet newly become the Minister of Marine. The French Navy in those crucial post-Armistice days was simply left to carry on its daily routine without aim or purpose and, in a sense, as if nothing had happened.

The Marshal and the scared politicians of Vichy might claim that theoretically French honour and pride had been salvaged but what about the underlying feelings of shame, disgust and despair? No guidance was given there, no remedy suggested for the wounds of the spirit which had been so stunningly inflicted. Apathy was to reign and no consolation, no lead from on high was to be handed down. Just carry on more or less as before until Hitler and his allies Stalin and Mussolini got Europe sorted out in the way the Nazis saw best. Such was the condition of the French mind at Alexandria, Mers-el-Kébir and in the ports of the United Kingdom when Operation CATAPULT was executed on Wednesday, 3 July 1940 and a new outrage was done to the demoralized and inconsolable French Navy.

12

The take-over in British ports

A thought should also be spared for the officers and men of the Royal Navy at the pointed end of this stark political requirement. Abruptly told to do something for which there had been no training since the sailing-ship days of boarding and seizing, they were ordered to take possession of their ally's ships by stealth and, of course, with the minimum use of force. In other words they were called on to act as nautical bailiffs, but with diplomacy and tact, and to do this to their late colleagues and friends. By any tally it was a mean and dirty job which they carried out with as much fellow-feeling as could be mustered at dawn after a dark night and, except for the *Surcouf*, without loss of blood.

At Portsmouth the French submarines *Ondine* and *Orion* had been moved to an inner basin the previous day for work to be carried out on their batteries, during which time the crews were billeted ashore. It was therefore not too difficult for the British boarding party to overpower the two sentries left on board each boat and invest these submarines. The two Captains – Vichot of *Orion* and Bourgine of *Ondine* – were not informed of this *coup* until they awoke and they were then summoned in a fine state of shock to Fort Blockhouse, the British Submarine Headquarters. There they were read the following ultimatum:

The Franco-German Armistice terms require the French Fleet to be disarmed under German-Italian control. The British Government is aware that the Germans have already broken their word. Under these circumstances therefore we much regret – but you will realise that we have been so ordered – to require you to choose either to continue to fight loyally and whole-heartedly on the side of Great Britain and its Empire or to return to France. Those who opt to continue fighting with us will have all the rights of British citizenship and will be paid on the same scale as our own Navy. Those who wish to return to France must be ready to assemble at Southampton this Wednesday afternoon.

Unnerved by this devastating ultimatum, the two Commanding Officers asked if they could consult with their senior officer Rear Admiral Gaudin de Villaine who flew his flag in the pre-World War I battleship *Courbet* and was in charge of all the French warships which had taken refuge in Portsmouth. They were told this could not be allowed. Not even a telephone call would be permitted. They were all prisoners and would be held as such until each officer and man had given his answer, and they had one hour in which to sort this out.

That hour, during which there was an air raid compelling them all to go down to the shelter, saw further complications in the fact that *Orion's* Captain Vichot, the senior of the two, while giving no order or advice to his ship's company, made it clear that he himself would be returning to France, whereas the Captain and Coxswain of *Ondine* were rallying to de Gaulle. The anguish of the decision each officer and man had to make in what amounted to a matter of minutes can be imagined. When the vote was taken Vichot was to be further humiliated in that the rest of his officers opted for de Gaulle and only 13 of his ship's company at that time wished to go back to France. The percentage in the other submarine was similar, although all who were staying realized only too well that they might never see their families again. All this took place on the morning of 3 July 1940. By the evening of that same day the British Force H had largely destroyed the French Atlantic Fleet at Mers-el-Kébir. After that grievous event, the scene was to change yet again.

So far as the *Rubis* at Dundee was concerned matters were conducted on a more gentlemanly basis. No force was used, no treachery implied. A British Captain, Roper, commanding the 9th Submarine Flotilla, went personally and alone on board the French submarine and waited patiently until the Commanding Officer had been awoken and had had time to dress. Cabanier, in turn, astonished to find the senior British officer under whose command he had been placed, alone on the deck of his submarine at dawn, asked what was going on. With slight hesitation Captain Roper told him that the Admiralty had confiscated all French ships in British ports and the crews were to be interned. Before Cabanier could vent his surprise, Roper went on:

'The "Rubis" is in a different category. You've fought extremely well. We've just heard that a German minesweeper has been blown up in the last minefield you laid.'

'So what do you want?'

'As you can see I am here alone. No armed boarding party. You and your officers are free on parole: only your ship's company must remain in the base. However I would like you and your officers to come to my office.'

Once there Roper showed them the Admiralty signal ordering the action and then gave Cabanier a personal letter from Vice-Admiral Horton, the Admiral (Submarines). This read:

It is with much regret and sorrow that I have to restrict you and your men's freedom since you are among the bravest of those who have done such good work in the North Sea. I am sure you will understand that this is the result of a general order to which no exception can be made in the present confused situation. I say this because I and those of my officers who have served in the 'Rubis' have complete confidence in you and your ship's company. I hope these restrictions will not be for long. I assure you of my wholehearted sympathy in this unfair blow which Fate has struck you and your country in these last few days. Please come and see me as soon as possible.

Cabanier then asked Captain Roper what was to happen next. Roper told him that in his capacity as Captain (S) 9 he was going to sea on trials in an hour's time in a Dutch submarine which had also got away. He wanted *Rubis* to proceed into the inner harbour, to be taken there by her own crew. During that time Cabanier could then scuttle his boat if he felt that to be his duty, Roper only asking that he did not do so alongside the jetty, as that would make trouble for everyone, but out in the stream where the wreck would not be in anyone's way. With tears in his eyes Cabanier shook hands on that.

Operation CATAPULT became something of a boomerang in the matter of the 'giant' submarine *Surcouf* which had been ordered to Plymouth from Brest on 20 June and in which the only casualties of the whole operation (apart from the slaughter at Mers-el-Kébir) took place. *Surcouf* was no ordinary submarine. Built in 1934 she was at that time the largest submarine in the world. She drew 2880 tons and in addition to a normal armament of torpedoes, carried two six-inch guns and in a watertight casing on deck a small seaplane. Theoretically *Surcouf* was a powerful, versatile and unique submarine cruiser. In practice she was unwieldy, unreliable and a danger to herself, in that her bulk made her a vast target, especially in the clear waters of the Mediterranean where a submarine could be spotted by aircraft at depths down to 100 metres. *Surcouf* in any case could only dive to 80 metres and because of her size took three minutes to submerge even to a depth of 18 metres. In addition to the above she was unstable underwater, rolled like a cork on the surface and was underpowered. If *Surcouf* could not be given the classic definition of a camel as a horse designed by a committee, she was in the opinion of one British submarine captain 'simply bloody useless'. However there she was at Plymouth under the command of an Anglophobe captain who had wanted to take her to Casablanca but owing to the fact that she had had to leave Brest while still under repair and could not use her diesels, had been forced to hazard the channel crossing on the surface using her inadequate electric propulsion.

Since no British officer had ever visited (or rather been inside) *Surcouf*, one of the problems a boarding party faced was how to find their way around. Luckily the Commander-in-Chief at Plymouth, Vice-Admiral Sir Martin Dunbar-Naismith V.C. had been a submarine officer in World War I and, as a courtesy, had been invited to inspect *Surcouf* shortly after her arrival where he was received with full military honours. The next day the British submarine liaison officer, Lieutenant Commander Griffiths, asked to visit *Surcouf* accompanied by Lieutenant Commander Sprague, captain of the submarine *Thames* lying close at hand. At first the captain of *Surcouf* refused but since he had previously been on board *Thames* himself and this visit was put to him as a sort of friendly 'return match', he eventually thawed and the two British officers were received on board and shown around. Had that visit not been made it is doubtful if *Surcouf* could have been successfully boarded by stealth. However during the early hours of 3 July that is what happened. Griffiths, Sprague and a Midshipman, together with a boarding party of 35, duly seized the submarine. In the course of this action both Sprague and Griffiths were killed together with a French engine room artificer. Three more were wounded. Terrible though these casualties seemed at the time they were nevertheless the only ones in the take-over of some 130 French ships of all sorts and sizes in British ports, a take-over which included two battleships, two light cruisers, eight destroyers and five submarines.

13

Reaction to Mers-el-Kébir

Reaction to the butchery of Mers-el-Kébir took a number of forms. At Alexandria a compromise was arranged, summarized in the following exchanges between Cunningham and Godfroy. This dialogue began at 0700 hours on 3 July (Force H did not open fire on the French fleet at Mers-el-Kébir until 1800 that evening) at which early and most unusual hour Godfroy and his Chief of Staff had been requested to repair on board the British flagship. They were piped over the side with full honours, the Royal Marine guard and band being paraded. Then a few minutes later, sitting in armchairs in the Commander-in-Chief's after cabin, the French officers were handed the British bomb-shell:

His Majesty's Government have instructed me to inform you as follows: They agreed to the French Government approaching the German Government only on condition that *before* an Armistice was concluded, the French fleet should be sent to British ports to prevent it falling into the hands of the enemy. The Council of Ministers declared on the 18th June that before capitulation on land the French fleet would join up with the British navy or sink itself.

Whilst the present Government may consider that the terms of their Armistice with Germany and Italy are reconcilable with these undertakings, His Majesty's Government find it impossible from our previous experiences to believe that Germany and Italy will not at any moment which suits them seize French warships and use them against Great Britain and her allies. The Italian Armistice prescribes that French ships should return to metropolitan ports and under the Armistice France is required to yield up units for coast defence and minesweeping.

It is impossible for us, your comrades up to now, to allow your fine ships to fall into the power of the German or Italian enemy. We are determined to fight on till the end and, if we win, as we think we shall, we shall never forget that France was our ally, that our interests are the same as hers and that our common enemy is Germany. Should we conquer we solemnly

declare that we shall restore the greatness and territories of France. For this purpose we must make sure that
the best ships of the French navy are not used against
us by the common foe.

Then followed the conditions or rather the four options
which formed the heart of the matter and which have been
set out before.

Godfroy replied that he could do nothing without
consulting his government. How, he asked, could their
ships fight except under the French flag? The officers and
men would be deserters. Furthermore if he used any of his
ships for the war, he felt sure that the Germans and Italians
would demand an equivalent number of ships of the same
class to be handed over to them.

After Cunningham had pointed out that he could communicate these terms to the French squadron over Godfroy's head but preferred not to take this step, they went on
to discuss the options in detail and Godfroy returned to his
own flagship an hour and a half later with the ultimatum,
tactfully dressed up as *force majeure*, that he must make
up his mind by the end of the morning.

The reply, when it came promptly at noon, was a bitter
disappointment to Cunningham. Godfroy felt his military
duty would not allow him to continue fighting with the
British. He went on to say he felt inclined to accept the
second proposal (disarmament) if he could communicate
with the French Admiralty who alone could give him
permission. Were this to be forbidden he was reduced to the
third solution, the sinking of his ships at sea, as the only one
compatible with his sense of naval honour. In a separate
letter he asked for 48 hours' grace in which to make
arrangements for the safety and transport of his crews.

Whilst accepting Godfroy's painful decision and setting a
deadline of noon on Friday, 5 July, Cunningham then wrote
a further personal 'My dear Admiral' letter:

I have been casting round in my mind for some solution

to this terrible impasse. I understand that you are primarily concerned with the fact that it is incompatible with your duty to remove the crews from your ships. Does not a solution lie in a compromise suggestion?

If you can make a gesture, one which indeed you have already made, which will allow our Government to realise that your ships will not proceed to sea, perhaps even now we may prevent a disaster as painful to me as to you. Would you be prepared:

(1) To give orders to remove the oil fuel from your ships
(2) Take the warheads off your torpedoes?

Meanwhile the question of the retention or otherwise of the crews would be a matter for discussion.

You will appreciate that I write this appeal to you personally and privately and for the moment it cannot affect the measures which you will be putting in hand in accordance with your formal decision. I should greatly appreciate an early reply.

To this Godfroy agreed without demur and by 1730 hours the French ships were already discharging their fuel. A peaceful albeit temporary solution had been achieved. A.B.C. allowed himself a sigh of relief.

The British Admiralty, however, thought otherwise. At 2015 the Commander-in-Chief received the following signal: 'Admiralty note that oil fuel is being discharged by French ships. Reduction of crews especially by ratings should however begin at once by landing or transfer to merchant ships before dark tonight. Do not, repeat NOT, fail.'

Apart from the fact that it was already after sunset when this signal was received 'it showed no comprehension whatever', A.B.C.'s own words, 'of the explosive atmosphere at Alexandria or the difficult conditions in which we were working.' It put the Commander-in-Chief into a rage and he decided to ignore it completely, writing afterwards: 'This is a perfect example of a signal which should never have been made.'

The receipt of this *billet doux* from the Admiralty was followed almost immediately by a formal note in French from Godfroy. There was no 'My dear Admiral' now:

> I have just learnt that an ultimatum has been addressed to our Atlantic Fleet by the British Admiralty. On the other hand my Admiralty has ordered me to sail, though I have demanded to be assured that the order is authentic. I have replied that sailing is impossible but that the situation is definitely changing.
>
> So that I may not incur reproach for having discharged oil fuel after receiving an order to sail, I have stopped the discharge of oil pending events. But that changes nothing. I give you my word as to my intentions which remain unchanged from those which I expressed to you in writing this morning.

A.B.C. then sent his Chief of Staff, Rear Admiral Willis with Royer Dick (his Staff Officer [Plans]) to reason with Godfroy on board the *Duquesne*. They found him obdurate. Godfroy now refused to discharge any more fuel. He refused to remove any of his men. He refused to go to sea to sink his ships and said that if he were allowed out of harbour he would run for it, fully realizing that this would lead to a battle. Nothing would move him, although he appeared resigned to remaining at Alexandria with his crews on board. He stated bluntly that any demand backed by force would result in his scuttling his ships in the harbour, only relenting to add that he would do so in a way as convenient as possible to the British.

Both sides were back where they were at the start of the day.

14

Resolution at Alexandria

The drama at Alexandria raced to its climax the following day. A.B.C. wrote: 'in the small hours of July 4th we retired to bed, much fatigued and worried.' This must have been something of an understatement. It had not been a quiet night across the harbour either. On board his flagship, the 10,000-ton cruiser *Duquesne*, Godfroy records:

> In the middle of the night and of my sleep, my Chief of Staff woke me up with a new signal from our Admiralty which he had just decyphered himself. This signal ordered me categorically and immediately to attack the British fleet but it was worded in such an unusual way, ending in the words 'An eye for an eye' that I had grave doubts as to who had written and sent the signal. My reaction and that of Captain Tisserand was 'So *they've* gone mad as well'. I gave him back the signal which I said I did not understand and went back to sleep, having given orders that at dawn all our ships were to be at 'Action Stations' ready for immediate battle. We would thus be prepared for any other measures which might be necessary, dependent also on those taken by the British fleet.

There was indeed a factor that no one knew about either in London or on the spot at Mers-el-Kébir and Alexandria which could have altered the chain of events. This particular was that on that same 3 July Darlan and the advance echelons of the French Admiralty were *en route* by road

from Nérac south-east of Bordeaux to Vichy in the centre
of France. This necessitated a journey of a good 300 miles
over roads cluttered up with the human and material
débris from the collapse of France and, of course, at that
time there were no autoroutes in France. Darlan simply
could not be reached and it fell to his Chief of Staff,
Admiral le Luc, to deal with those ill-starred events. But
this only came to light at a later date.

Events moved considerably faster than we anticipated A.B.C. wrote: What happened on board the
ships of the French squadron during the night I do not
know, but it was evident that Vice-Admiral Godfroy
had received a full account of the action against the
French ships at Mers-el-Kébir. Just before 0700 on July
4th I was awakened by being given another letter from
him in which he repudiated each and every undertaking he had given, reserved to himself complete liberty
of action and left me in no doubt that he proposed to
try to get to sea, if necessary by fighting his way out of
harbour.

I went on deck at once and sure enough the French
ships were raising steam. By the appearance of their
armaments they were cleared for action. The crisis
had come. There now seemed to be no chance of
evading what I wished at all costs to avoid, a battle in
Alexandria harbour.

We, of course, were not behind hand in our preparations. Where necessary our battleships were kedged
round to bring their broadsides to bear. Our destroyers
and submarines were warned off to torpedo the French
ships at once if they moved from their berths or
opened fire.

One chance only remained. I knew it would take the
French ships six to eight hours to raise steam and be
ready to move, so this short space of time was
vouchsafed to us to take what measures we could to
induce Vice-Admiral Godfroy to see reason. We de-

cided to appeal to his officers and ships' companies over his head and suborn them from their allegiance to him. It was a most distasteful task; but the only possible thing to do.

Commander Dick's fluent French was again brought into play and a message was composed addressed to all the French officers and men. In it we set out the hopelessness of their situation; our sincere desire not to fight with or kill any of them if they tried to get away and the generous terms the British Government offered which we assured them could be accepted without loss of dignity or honour. This was flashed several times to every ship and though we received no acknowledgement we knew very well that their signalmen could and would take it in, and that its purport would be discussed. The same message was written on large blackboards which were taken round the French squadron in boats so that all the ships' companies could read it.

Every French ship had a British opposite number to look after her [the 'chummy ship' principle referred to before] and the Captains of those of our ships lying next to the French were directed to go on board the vessels for which they were responsible and to reason with their Captains. This measure, combined with the messages, had an excellent effect. It very soon became apparent that not all the officers agreed with Godfroy in his obduracy. Indeed the Captain of the French cruiser lying near the 'Neptune' received Captain Rory O'Connor with the greatest cordiality, saying as he went on board: 'When I saw the tompions being removed from your guns, I immediately ordered the tompions to be placed in mine.' Captain Philip Mack's powers of persuasion won round the French destroyers without much difficulty, while Captain H.T. Baillie-Grohman of the 'Ramillies' boarded the battleship 'Lorraine' and Captain I.B.B. Tower of the 'Malaya' and others, more of the French ships.

During the morning as we watched, it was interesting to see the leaven gradually working among the French sailors. In most of their ships big meetings were held on the forecastle, in one case on the quarterdeck, and we could usually see ratings haranguing their shipmates. We also noticed the French captains visiting Vice-Admiral Godfroy in the 'Duquesne'. The French liaison officer Commander, now Vice Admiral, Auboyneau, worked tirelessly to bring about a peaceful settlement. One of our staff officers had managed to get through to him by telephone.

The morning passed in suspense. Then, after luncheon, we saw all the French captains go on board Godfroy's flagship. About an hour later he signalled his desire to come on board to see me. During his visit he conducted himself with great dignity and the upshot of our meeting was that he yielded to overwhelming force. We concluded an immediate agreement on the following terms:

(a) All oil fuel to be discharged from the French ships forthwith.

(b) Ships to be placed immediately in a condition in which they cannot fight.

(c) Discharge of ships' companies to be a matter for further discussion but it was agreed they should be reduced.

It was all over. Not a shot fired, not a drop of blood spilt. How different matters might have been the day before at Mers-el-Kébir had Admiral Somerville himself gone on board the *Dunkerque* to reason with Admiral Gensoul. But such hindsight only adds to the grief.

'Never in my life', Admiral Cunningham continued, 'have I experienced such a whole hearted feeling of thankful relief as on the conclusion of this agreement, and the same was felt by every officer and man in our Fleet.'

A few hours later the First Sea Lord signalled from

London: 'After what must have been a most trying and anxious time (again something of an understatement) your negotiations have achieved complete success. We offer you our most sincere congratulations. The Prime Minister also wishes his congratulations to be sent to you.'

The war in the Eastern Mediterranean could now recommence and in signalling to the Admiralty the terms agreed, A.B.C. commented: 'With the completion of the defuelling and de-arming measures, I shall feel quite free to take the Fleet to sea to continue operations against the enemy.' This enemy now of course also included the Vichy Government of France.

15

Aftermath

So the war began. To start with, of course, neither side, so far as the generality was concerned, realized or chose to think too much about the facts. All were in a state of shock. The collapse of France had been so complete and so unexpected, the implications could wait. Now also there was the added blight of Mers-el-Kébir. Both sides were sickened by it all, but mercifully for the British they had other more urgent things to do. They had to survive. Like the prospect of being hanged, the virtual certainty of invasion wonderfully concentrated the British mind. On the other hand the humiliated French had nothing but defeat and despair and the incipient civil war between those who accepted their fate and the few, the very few at that time, who were determined one way or another to carry on the fight.

On 3 July 1940 the F.N.F.L. numbered a dozen officers and less than 400 men. When de Gaulle broadcast from London on 13 July 1940 that 'He was in a position to announce that already he had under his command an appreciable military force capable of fighting on land, on sea or in the air' he actually had 101 Army officers, 125 N.C.O.s and 1768 other ranks. On 21 July, when he announced proudly that French airmen were again flying over Germany, the exact number was three, all of course with the R.A.F.

Among the crews of French warships dispossessed of their ships on 3 July and interned in the first instance at Aintree; then at Barmouth and in the Isle of Man, a bitter division took place between those with differing conceptions of honour and duty. Although theoretically free to choose, Petty Officers and seamen were buffeted on the one hand by appeals from the one retired Admiral, Muselier, who had rallied to de Gaulle and whose reputation was by no means whiter than white and on the other by the authority and often direct orders of the great majority of their officers who had declared their loyalty to Marshal Pétain at Vichy.

Indiscipline reigned in the enforced idleness. Ferocious arguments and occasional drunken fisticuffs took place and at least one officer committed suicide. The situation was in no way improved by the sinking in the Channel *en route* to Brest of the merchant ship *Meknès* on 24 July by a German E boat whilst attempting to repatriate 1100 French naval officers and men of whom 400 drowned, nor by the numbing failure of de Gaulle and the British supporting force at Dakar at the end of September. When finally the *Djéné* sailed from Liverpool on 21 November 1940 with the remaining 1700 French naval officers and men who had opted to return to France, they had spent 144 days detained by the British they had now come to hate and by whom they were in turn despised. Of the 147 complement of the *Surcouf* only 15 joined the F.N.F.L. and they were accused of being bribed to do so. All in all the story of the post-CATAPULT French in the United Kingdom reads like a murky account of derelict men mooning about behind the scenes while the Battle of Britain raged in the skies and the U-boat Battle of the Atlantic opened up.

Indeed one of the saddest tokens of those early days of the Anglo-Vichy war was a letter Cabanier, Captain of the *Rubis*, wrote to Martin, Captain of the *Surcouf* under whose command Cabanier had served earlier on as Electrical Officer of the great submarine.

How bitter it is to see only one of the boats of your division here at Dundee when there is work to be done by all of us. We have all had our good times together and now I at least have the consolation of being among those who are really doing the job for which we have all been trained for years. All my crew have followed me and I must say that in the midst of great weariness, this has been a source of comfort to me. I have here real men, men of great heart who have always shown me the greatest understanding even in the blackest hours.

The letter went unanswered. Commandant Martin's own attitude, indeed, is summed up in a report he made to the Préfet Maritime at Toulon on his return there in December 1940. 'Churchill's policy', he wrote, 'makes one fear a demagogic disaster. Thinking Englishmen fear for the future being carried away as they are by democracy, international financiers and Jews. It is undeniable that the French corrective to this is envied.' By that time, of course, the French corrective had got under way when Hitler and Pétain shook hands at Montoire on 24 October 1940 and real collaboration began.

16

Divided France

The undeclared but unpredictably eruptive war which now commenced between Vichy France and Great Britian should be kept in perspective. It should also be said that it did not much exercise the High Commands in either capital. Except for the 'set piece' operations of Dakar, Syria and Madagascar, hostilities in the main took the form of a sea blockade of France by the British and the evasion of it by the French. On a secondary level the initial duel between de Gaulle and Pétain, the one supported by the Allies, the other by the Axis, developed from the shadow boxing of the early days into the bitter period of the Resistance ('l'impitoyable guerre civile' as Henri Amouroux accurately calls it) and finally after the Normandy landings and the establishment of de Gaulle in Paris in August 1944 into the grim settlement of accounts as between *Résistants* and *Collaborateurs* which the French are only just beginning to forget after nearly half a century.

During the three months following the fall of France the two main protagonists, Great Britain, her Empire and the Allies on the one hand and the Axis of Germany and Italy on the other, crouched back on their haunches like two tom-cats, the one licking its wounds and the other its chops, readying themselves for the next encounter. So far as *matériel* was concerned there followed a recuperative pause except in the air and in the build-up of landing barges in North Sea and Channel ports. In the war of words, however, the razing of the French Navy at Mers-el-Kébir and the bombing of the new battleship *Richelieu* at Dakar on 8 July gave the quintessential Dr Goebbels (I use the adjective on purpose because in that era the German Minister of Propaganda had a clear lead in the game) a chance which he took with both hands.

What, however, was happening in France itself? On 22 June 1940 in that same railway carriage in which the Germans had signed the Armistice of 11 November 1918, the regime later to be known as Vichy first saw the light of day. At the same time the framework of collaboration between defeated France and triumphant Germany was set up. The terms of the Armistice were severe. Although theoretically the French State maintained its control over the whole country, in fact France was divided into seven distinct zones roughly two-thirds of which were to be occupied by German troops. The French themselves were disarmed; materials of war were to be delivered up to the Germans who would also control all French aerodromes. In addition to this, the cost of the occupation was to be borne by the French themselves. They had lost the war and now they were going to pay for the privilege.

In the occupied zone French authority was to be subject to overall German military control and as hostages for this two million French soldiers continued to be held in Germany as prisoners-of-war. However stiff these conditions might seem to be (shameful, moreover, in that one secret clause required the free zone French to hand over to the Reich all German political refugees therein), France still disposed of an independent government, its empire and its fleet. De Gaulle might consider himself the sword, but Pétain was certainly the shield, apologists for Vichy were to claim after the Liberation. It was true that the first German armistice terms had been even harsher, envisaging the occupation of the whole of France together with the handing over of the fleet and of military bases in the colonies. In the event Hitler granted a more liberal arrangement because it gave Germany many advantages.

In the first place the Wehrmacht economized in manpower since French administration was made to pay for itself and the occupation. Moreover the German overlords had control of the French police who proved to be even more efficient than their German *confrères* when it came to hunting down dissidents, Jews and later on Communists. The French *milices* in fact were to use methods of interrogation in no way inferior to those of the infamous Gestapo.

Such then was the general state of affairs when the Third Republic was abolished and Pétain was elected overwhelmingly as Chief of State on 11 July 1940, in effect becoming the French dictator with more power in his hands than any of the ancient kings of France. In the next immediate circle of authority stood Darlan, Weygand and Laval: 'a group of men', according to the U.S. Ambassador William Bullitt, 'determined to make a clean sweep of everything which France has represented for the last two generations.'

17

Dakar – the beginning

The next big clash between the two nations came at Dakar in Senegal on 23–25 September 1940. The operation was codenamed MENACE and is recorded as the first Allied combined operation of the war. It was also a complete and embarrassing failure. To this outcome there were varied reactions, all of them critical. 'The Dakar expedition is one of those military operations where all concerned did their duty but which gave no opportunity either for brilliance in leadership or for heroic adventure', wrote General Spears who with de Gaulle and Desmond Morton had devised the outline plan. 'It would be difficult to find in the whole history of war a more deplorable fiasco than this', was the verdict of Admiral Sir Herbert Richmond, while the N.C.O.s and men of the 2nd Battalion Royal Marines summed it up in a brief verse they sang after MENACE had been abandoned with no landings made – 'We went to Dakar with General de Gawle: We sailed round in circles and did bugger all.' So what happened to make the events Churchill described as 'a series of accidents' into what the press in unison called 'a first class blunder' or 'the bungling of an expedition' which, had it succeeded, might well have changed the course of the war to the advantage of the Allies?

During July 1940 Anglo-Vichy French relations had degenerated from bad to worse. Open war – or rather its declaration – had just but only just been averted; diplomatic relations, however, were broken off on 5 July by Vichy and a growing Anglophobia engorged itself on the tidbits British propaganda served up against the Pétain regime via the B.B.C. to which all Europe clandestinely listened, on the dropping by the R.A.F. of leaflets in Morocco, on further efforts by British agents to provoke French North and West Africa into declaring their independence of Vichy, on British support for de Gaulle and on the extension of the British blockade of metropolitan France to French North Africa. Such was the political situation when Churchill 'undertook in an exceptional degree the initiation and advocacy of the Dakar expedition'. In this operation, unlike CATAPULT, de Gaulle was 'included in' from the start.

In London de Gaulle had already begun to play the prima donna in an opera with so far not much of a plot and only a small cast of supporting players. Sentenced to death by a Court Martial in Toulon a few days after the Armistice, de Gaulle in London had to face the fact that by the end of July no part of France or her Empire had declared for the Croix de Lorraine. However, his passionate love of France, his determination to restore her independence, if need be single-handed, his culture, his powerful brain and his vast

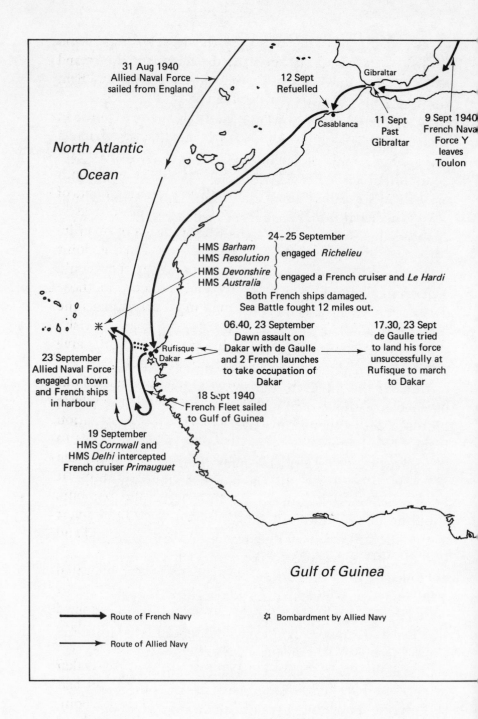

31 Aug 1940
Allied Naval Force
sailed from England

12 Sept
Refuelled

Gibraltar

Casablanca

11 Sept
Past
Gibraltar

9 Sept 1940
French Naval
Force Y
leaves
Toulon

North Atlantic

Ocean

HMS *Barham*
HMS *Resolution*

HMS *Devonshire*
HMS *Australia*

24–25 September
engaged *Richelieu*

engaged a French cruiser and *Le Hardi*

Both French ships damaged.
Sea Battle fought 12 miles out.

06.40, 23 September
Dawn assault on
Dakar with de Gaulle
and 2 French launches
to take occupation of
Dakar

17.30, 23 Sept
de Gaulle tried
to land his force
unsuccessfully at
Rufisque to march
to Dakar

23 September
Allied Naval Force
engaged on town
and French ships
in harbour

Rufisque

Dakar

18 Sept 1940
French Fleet sailed
to Gulf of Guinea

19 September
HMS *Cornwall* and
HMS *Delhi* intercepted
French cruiser *Primauguet*

Gulf of Guinea

▶ Route of French Navy   ✿ Bombardment by Allied Navy

→ Route of Allied Navy

untiring diligence caused those with whom he worked and in whose flesh he became so often a thorn, to admire and respect if not to love his utter dedication, dignity and firm belief in himself as a latter-day Joan of Arc.

In July and August 1940 both Churchill and de Gaulle in their respective spheres of influence and activity shared a common although not a joint necessity. This was to regain the initiative and to do so without delay. In a sense both men had their backs against the wall and were prisoners of their own great qualities. Churchill has been described by Arthur Marder as 'a giant tied with the bonds of insufficient resources which the Service Chiefs and the Joint Planners were determined to conserve until they could take the offensive against really vital targets'. In those early days he was very much a man in a hurry and, as the aphorism goes, 'a man in a hurry is a man at risk'. Churchill was 'carried away by his magnificent offensive spirit beyond the bounds of ordinary common sense'.

Indeed the Dakar operation might well have turned out differently had Churchill heeded the independent requests of the Force Commanders to postpone the whole operation by a month or at the very least two weeks in order to acquire and digest more reliable intelligence about the realities in Senegal. But with invasion threatening at home, the British bulldog became desperate for some military success, it did not matter where, that might divert Hitler from invading, enhance British prestige abroad and raise morale at home.

On 25 July Churchill asked the recently appointed Director of Combined Operations, Admiral of the Fleet Sir Roger Keyes, for 'three or four proposals for medium-sized action i.e. between five and ten thousand men to take place in September and October'. It was then, and before Keyes could come up with any proposals at all, that the Dakar operation, possibly originating with de Gaulle and certainly worked out jointly with Spears (the General appointed as liaison officer to de Gaulle and the Free French) and Morton (one of Churchill's private secretaries) came to the top of the pile. Operation SCIPIO which preceded MENACE had already been mooted and turned down earlier in the month, as a follow-on to CATAPULT. The first plan, however, foundered on French pride. 'It cannot be emphasised sufficiently,' Spears had then reported, 'that neither de Gaulle nor Muselier will march unless they have some French ships flying the French flag . . . de Gaulle would be unable to man more than a very limited number of French ships' and that was not enough. Now however the idea had changed and a plan was outlined for an indirect attack on Dakar.

18

The early plans

The object of the expedition was simple. This was to 'hoist the Free French flag in French territory in West Africa, occupy Dakar and consolidate the French colonies in West and Equatorial Africa under Free French aegis'. To achieve this the British would supply the necessary arms, equipment and shipping, the ships to be manned to the extent possible by French crews, the expedition to be escorted by the Royal Navy but with some units commanded and manned by Free French officers and men. Were this to succeed, an operation would then be mounted to rally French North Africa to the Croix de Lorraine. All this was heady stuff.

The first plan was concocted by de Gaulle, Spears and Morton, the latter two having the ear of the Prime Minister but without responsibility and therefore being regarded sourly by the Chiefs of Staff and the Joint Planning Sub-Committee (who *were* accountable) as 'mischievous influences at the centre and a pain in the neck for them, as perhaps all unofficial advisers are bound to be when they indulge in special pleading without full knowledge of or responsibility for the conduct of the war as a whole', as Arthur Marder puts it, adding that there was no love lost between Spears and Morton.

De Gaulle favoured Konakry in French Guinea, a state some way south of Senegal, as the expedition's port of arrival. Although some 500 miles away, there were road and rail links with Dakar and it was de Gaulle's intention that 'a resolute column would proceed towards the objective rallying, as it went, the territories through which it passed and the elements which it encountered . . . One might hope that in this way the forces of Free France, growing by contagion, would reach Dakar by land.' One might hope indeed, but this noble endeavour was never to be put to the test since no landings were made, and the contagion such as it was worked in favour of Vichy.

Churchill seized upon this outline plan and, as he was wont to do when he scented opposition, kept the project as much in his own hands as he could. He told the War Cabinet that this was 'entirely a political decision and he did not want a lot of military objections put up by the Chiefs of Staff'. Naturally the Chiefs of Staff were disgruntled, the more so since they were faced with a decision to implement a plan which their own planning staff had not previously examined. The seeds of disaster were being sown. 'There was a very grumpy discussion', the Naval Assistant Secretary to the War Cabinet wrote, 'and clearly the Chiefs felt that there was far too much optimism about the reception de Gaulle would get at Dakar. I think I summed up the general feeling when I passed a chit to Ismay [Military Secretary to the War Cabinet] at one point "Why not let the first flight be our Marines – dressed as Frenchmen if necessary but ready to fight like Royal Marines". Ismay grimaced his agreement but of course said nothing.'

Nevertheless on 5 August 1940 the War Cabinet approved

the operation in principle. Then the troubles began. That same day the First Sea Lord and the Vice-Chief of the Naval Staff conferred with de Gaulle, Spears and Morton and quickly concluded that de Gaulle's conception of the operation diverged seriously from that of the British Chiefs of Staff. De Gaulle stipulated that the expedition should be guaranteed against the arrival of Vichy reinforcements in the French colony in which he had landed or which he was invading from a neighbouring British colony. He also thought that Vichy warships might interfere at sea and this would require a Royal Naval escort of the Free French ships to the anchorage, this escort possibly having to sink the Vichy ships. Although he agreed that such a situation should not be allowed to develop, it inevitably involved greater and more lasting commitments than the British had foreseen and this would essentially detract from its Free French character.

The Chiefs of Staff reacted to this naval opinion by telling the Prime Minister that they had visualized the operation as basically Free French in character, British assistance being strictly limited and as unostentatious as possible 'nor had we visualised commitments anything like so great or so enduring as those which General de Gaulle's suggestion involves'.

So the plan after much argument was modified. Now the target was to be a peaceful take-over of Dakar itself. Generally speaking and throughout the war Churchill gave his Chiefs of Staff a hard time, since he was not only Prime Minister but also Minister of Defence and therefore their immediate and ultimate superior. Their loyalty however remained unswerving throughout. De Gaulle, too, allowed himself to be seduced by Churchill's eloquence and reasoning, once it was agreed that a frontal attack on Dakar was not envisaged.

De Gaulle made it clear that he would have no part in a fight between Frenchmen: a *'coup de main'* through a mixture of persuasion and intimidation would do the job. No one seemed to recall that this mixture had not exactly succeeded at Mers-el-Kébir. In any event de Gaulle realized that the British would probably go ahead on their own with or without his consent and therefore it would best serve the interests of the Free French to agree as gracefully as possible. This he did and the next day, as if shaking hands on the deal, Churchill signed an agreement with de Gaulle setting out British obligations to the Free French movement, which included the Churchillian promise of 'the integral restoration of the independence and grandeur of France' when victory was achieved.

The object of the revised plan which was approved by the Chiefs of Staff (against the sustained opposition of the Joint Planners) on 9 August and by the War Cabinet on 13 August was to install de Gaulle in Dakar where he would hoist the Free French flag and rally the French West African colonies to his standard. There were two ways of bringing this about. The first – an unopposed entry into the port of Dakar – could not be contemplated as a serious proposition unless the port and fortress were known to be under the control of friends of General de Gaulle and the absence of suitable beaches precluded an unopposed landing elsewhere in the vicinity. The second required a dawn attack by means of simultaneous landings on six beaches on the north, west and south shores of the Cape Verde peninsula with a seventh landing on Gorée Island. Success would depend on the use of highly trained British forces, namely five battalions of Royal Marines, two independent companies and one field company. It would also rely on tactical surprise, the low morale of the French *in situ* and the dispersing of their defence efforts. No Free French troops were to be used in the main attack. De Gaulle, some hours astern, would not disembark until local resistance had been overpowered or his safe landing could be guaranteed. In other words British troops had first to do the tough work and gain military control of the city.

'Note,' says Marder, 'that the events described above were all crammed into about a week. It had been a case of hurry, hurry, hurry from the start, with the Prime Minister pushing hard for the launching of an immensely tricky and hazardous combined operation thousands of miles from home. He had his way by issuing what was virtually a ukase for the operation on 8 August. This seems to me to be a copy-book model of how to court disaster in the circumstances of 1940. Indeed "Menace" is an object lesson on how a combined operation should *not* be conducted by politicians and High Command in Whitehall.'

19

Vichy under pressure

Meanwhile what was going on in the enemy camp which now included Vichy France? On 11 July 1940 Hitler had conferred with General Keitel and Admiral Raeder on the matter of invading the United Kingdom. The next day General Jodl produced a summary of his ideas for a landing which then formed the basis for further studies. The extraordinary fact, not known by the Allies until after the war, was that until then Hitler had had no plans formulated after the defeat of France for the invasion of the British Isles but was relying on a verbal peace offensive by himself to achieve British capitulation. This of course was firmly and scornfully rejected by Churchill who made it clear beyond all doubt that he would never negotiate with Hitler. Accordingly by 16 July the German outline plan codenamed SEALION had been drafted and the threat to the United Kingdom stepped up.

In so far as Vichy France was concerned, disturbing backstairs anxieties had already begun to smoulder. On 15 July, less than a month after the Armistice had been signed, Hitler demanded the use of eight aerodromes by the Luftwaffe around Casablanca in French Morocco. This was rejected by Vichy on 19 July without, to the surprise of the French, arousing the wrath of the German dictator. On 31 July Hitler, Keitel, von Brauchitsch and Jodl fixed on 15 September as the date for the invasion of England but Hitler expressed doubts on the practicalities of the operation and ordered the German General Staff to start planning an attack on Soviet Russia, at that time their ally. This too was not known by the Allies until very much later.

On 13 August Admiral Raeder expressed grave doubts about operation SEALION and Hitler with some reluctance agreed to order its execution only as a last resort. Instead he approved in principle an attack on Gibraltar and on 25 August unilaterally decreed that the Atlantic coast of French Morocco was to be taken under German control as and when he so decided. So much for the Armistice terms! Meanwhile Goering's four-year plan for the 'methodical exploitation of the occupied territories of Western Europe for the benefit of the German war economy' was put into force, the basis of which, it seemed to Vichy, was a determination to bleed France white with a demand for the expenses of occupation of 20 million reichmarks *per day* or 400 million francs at the then rate of exchange. To add to this burden, a back debt of 3600 million francs for previous expenses was also claimed. Memories of the French occupation of the Ruhr after World War I were already being revenged, and defeated France was now additionally in the process of being enslaved and semi-starved.

While Vichy French reactions to these impositions and miseries is not really the concern of this book, it must be observed that the men of Vichy whether civilians or members of the armed forces did not speak at that time with one voice. Laval, Darlan and Weygand, for example, held very differing views on all matters affecting the life of occupied and unoccupied France and the relationship of the latter with the outside world. Only in one thing were all agreed and that was in their loyalty to Marshal Pétain, their Head of State (except, of course, for Laval whose professions of loyalty were pure hypocrisy). However just as there were highly placed Germans who detested Hitler, so also there were Vichy Frenchmen who did not regard Great Britain as their enemy. At this time, for instance, the German General Georg Thomas, one of the Chiefs of Staff of the Wehrmacht and as such in charge of the exploitation of France, had since 1937 been among the brave group of officers which secretly opposed Hitler and which in 1939 had discussed eliminating the Fuehrer. After the failure of the bomb attack on Hitler of 20 July 1944 General Thomas was sent to Dachau, his life only just being saved by the Americans in the spring of 1945.

In the autumn of 1940 Thomas did what he could to ameliorate the harshness of the conditions imposed by Goering on France, being scornfully labelled 'père des français' by the German Field Marshal for this lack of brutality. Thomas's French opposite number after 17 August 1940 was General Fornel de la Laurencie who had distinguished himself in the fighting before Dunkirk and who had a declared respect and admiration for the British soldier. To begin with, Laval thought he had this General 'dans la main; il me montre tous ses papiers' and was then rash enough to confide to him that he, Laval, had a personal hatred of England, that he would like to associate de la Laurencie in the Anglophobe politics of Brinon, Head of the Vichy Mission in Paris and that the Germans would be in London by 10 October. When de la Laurencie politely disagreed, Laval became instantly 'un adversaire irréconciliable' and from then on did everything possible to discredit him in the eyes of the Marshal and to get him removed.

The activities of Laval, Brinon and their associates helped to give the Vichy Government the morality of a thieves' kitchen. No one could be trusted. This fact became very apparent to Darlan who soon proved himself to be far less naive in his relationships than de la Laurencie, Weygand or indeed the Marshal himself. But there were limits to what this pre-collaboration fraternizing could achieve. Sacha Guitry might succeed in persuading de la Laurencie to let him re-open the Paris theatres so that life for the rich with access to the black market became much as it had been before and German soldiers on leave could amuse themselves in the dazzling French capital. The German Military Command in Paris, however, remained studiously correct and aloof so that when Laval approached Marshal von Brauchitsch on 28 August without authority from or even the knowledge of Pétain to propose that France should combine with Germany in the war against England, offering what remained of the French Air Force to join in the bombing of London, he was rejected with contempt. Nevertheless Laval, thick-skinned as ever, continued in and out of office to scheme and manoeuvre for the removal from the government and 'the higher directing spheres' of anyone in the French administration whom he judged Germanophobe.

Such then was the political situation when, on the same day that Laval made his bid to von Brauchitsch in Paris, an unknown Colonel, de Larminat, seized power in French Equatorial Africa and with a handful of followers declared that Chad, Cameroon and French Congo had come over to the side of General de Gaulle.

20

Miscalculations and developments

The rallying of what the French called 'les trois glorieuses' of French Equatorial Africa – Chad, Cameroon and the Congo – to the 'ex-Général félon de Gaulle' (so described by the Paris paper *Le Matin*) became the only positive and encouraging event in the whole dismal story of Dakar. A fortnight later de Gaulle established himself at Duala in the Cameroons, thus acquiring for the Allies control of Central Africa and the vital trans-continental air route from Takoradi in Ghana to the Middle East.

For himself and the Free French movement de Gaulle got what he most needed at that moment – some 17,500 fighting men together with their equipment plus command of the greater part of French Equatorial Africa. Now he had for the first time a firm base on which to build 'la France combattante' and valid backing for his claim that once again there would be honour and glory for his great country. Duala had been taken by Leclerc and de Bois-lambert and some 20 men landing at night from three native canoes. It showed what could be achieved by determined leadership once there was the will to continue the fight. Four years later Leclerc, by then a General, accepted the surrender of the German garrison of Paris and on the following day, 26 August 1944, de Gaulle walked in triumph down the Champs Elysées to the Place de la Concorde and on to a service of thanksgiving in Notre Dame. He had reached the end of that particular road and France had been restored. But these achievements seemed in 1940 to be beyond the horizon of possibility as things then were.

Those initial successes in French Equatorial Africa between 26 and 28 August 1940 produced an unfortunate side effect just at that very moment on 27 August when the British War Cabinet gave its general approval for Operation MENACE to go ahead. These equatorial gains allowed de Gaulle grossly to overestimate the backing he thought he would receive in French West Africa where very different conditions prevailed. In this he was understandably influenced by messages of support his London headquarters received from individual Frenchmen in Dakar and other towns in Senegal. Furthermore his agents there assured him that 70 per cent of the Dakar garrison supported his cause, 20 per cent were neutral and only 10 per cent were for Vichy. No one mentioned the effect on both armed forces and civilians of the slaughter at Mers-el-Kébir. In addition the subsequent torpedo bomber attack on the *Richelieu* did not exactly make new friends for the British in French naval circles at Dakar where in fact the burning core of Anglophobia had begun to glow.

For the British Military Commander to assess the situation he expected to find at Dakar as 'Senior officers and the Navy [particularly *Richelieu*] unfriendly: majority of junior officers, garrison troops and population in sympathy with General de Gaulle' was so wide of the mark as to constitute wishful thinking. Much closer to the true position was the estimate of an officer of the French submarine *Ajax* at Dakar who classified the French population there on the eve of the Allied attack as '20 per cent favourable to de Gaulle, comprising mainly those with a vested interest, merchants or producers of peanuts who wanted at any cost to sell their produce; 50 per cent indifferent desiring above all to be left at peace; 30 per cent mostly the naval and military elements who wanted to resist à outrance.'

Blame for this miscalculation of Vichy and Free French interests is not to be borne by de Gaulle alone. Churchill, the War Cabinet and the Chiefs of Staff were equally at fault in allowing a critical operation to be planned and executed on what can at best be described as derisory intelligence, both political and topographical, evaluated much as one skims cream off a jug of milk and dependent in almost every case on what the particular source providing the information wanted to happen, in other words on opinion rather than fact. Spears summed it up by saying: 'A further mistake was to base a serious military operation on unverified and unverifiable political assumptions.'

With the exception of Gabon which was not persuaded into the Gaullist camp until 8 November 1940 and then only by Larminat's use of force with Frenchmen firing on Frenchmen, the defection of the whole of French Equatorial Africa provoked another unpredictable chain of events which was to have a deleterious effect on Operation MENACE. It also ended the career of a senior British Admiral who found himself the scapegoat for a grave Whitehall lapse. The way this event occurred was as follows.

When Vichy learnt on 27 August that Chad had declared for de Gaulle, Darlan leapt into action to counter what he immediately and rightly suspected Hitler's reaction would be. Darlan realized that the German High Command would soon appreciate the serious military and economic consequences if French West Africa, and in particular the naval base at Dakar, were to follow French Equatorial Africa in opting for de Gaulle. He knew that Hitler would judge the ability and determination of the Vichy Government by its success or otherwise in defending the rest of the French Empire against the dissidence in Equatorial Africa. He therefore decided to reinforce the naval power at Dakar and Libreville with the utmost despatch by sending from Toulon a squadron of three modern cruisers and three super-destroyers or light cruisers by British classification.

Under the Armistice terms this necessitated German and Italian permission to move warships from one port to another. Such authority was requested on 30 August three days after the squadron had been formally constituted as Force Y under the command of Rear Admiral Jean Bourragué. On Admiral Raeder's recommendation Hitler consented at once subject only to Italian agreement. This was more reluctantly given two days later, qualified by requiring that the ships would fight back if attacked and would be scuttled if the Royal Navy attempted to take them in prize.

Accordingly Force Y set sail west from Toulon at 1600 hours on 9 September, aiming to pass Gibraltar as dawn broke on 11 September. This timing was deliberately calculated to avoid any night errors in congested waters and the squadron then set off at its full speed of 25 knots so that surveillance, except from the air, automatically became chancy and demanding. Indeed in those pre-radar days it can easily be understood that unless the Royal Navy had units of greater or at least similar speed and power in the right place at the right time, interception would be almost impossible. In the event the French squadron executed their dash through the Straits of Gibraltar with brilliant success.

21

The Admiral North affair

The effect on the British Flag Officer Commanding North Atlantic Station at Gibraltar of this apparently innocent movement of French warships was to lose him his job, ruin his career and turn him into an embittered man for the rest of his life. In the vernacular Admiral Sir Dudley North was given 'the old heave-ho' for mistakes made at a crucial time by the Foreign Office and the Admiralty and not by himself or by anyone at Gibraltar. Moreover the resulting chain of misfortune contributed in no small degree to the eventual failure of Operation MENACE. This happened in the following way.

Although the destination of Force Y became an open secret in Toulon at the beginning of September, no Allied agent managed to latch on to it so that no advance intelligence was passed to London before the squadron sailed on the 9 September. However at 2045 hours on that same evening Admiral North at Gibraltar received a signal from the British Consul-General at Tangier saying that information had just been received from a highly reliable Grade A source (in fact from a certain Captain Luizet, a French Intelligence Officer who had recently joined the Free French) that a French squadron, destination unknown, might try to pass through the Straits of Gibraltar within the next 72 hours. North took no action on this except for assuring himself that the message had been repeated to London and would therefore be received and dealt with by the Admiralty from whom he would receive in due course whatever orders they saw fit to give.

But at that time the Battle of Britain raged in the skies of south-east England, London lay under almost continuous bombardment and owing to recurrent stoppages of work caused by these air raids, the decyphering of signals became seriously delayed. Furthermore this particular message had not been marked IMPORTANT or IMMEDIATE so took its turn with the huge pile of messages from Ambassadors all over the world. Although received in the Foreign Office at 0750 hours on 10 September, it did not reach the Admiralty until *14 September* by which time Force Y was nearing Dakar at high speed.

This initial accident was then to be compounded by one much worse. At 1800 on the 10th the British Naval Attaché in Madrid, Captain Hillgarth, was contacted by the Vichy French Naval Attaché to Spain with whom he was on terms of cool friendship, although the pair of them maintained a studiously correct outward relationship with one another. Hillgarth was then 'officially' informed that the French Admiralty wanted the British Admiralty to know that three cruisers of the Georges Leygues class and three destroyers had left Toulon and intended to pass the Straits of Gibraltar on the morning of 11 September. Churchill acknowledges in his memoirs that this was normal Vichy procedure at that time and 'was a measure of prudence taken by them only at the latest moment'.

The British Naval Attaché at once sent an IMMEDIATE signal to the Admiralty repeating it to North at Gibraltar. This was received in the Admiralty at 2350 on 10 September. After its being decyphered the Duty Captain passed it to the Director of Operations Division (Foreign) who for some unknown reason took no immediate action. This was astonishing in view of the fact that he was fully in the picture about the Dakar operation whereas the Admiral at Gibraltar was not. Instead he let it go through in the ordinary way with the First Sea Lord's telegrams in the morning. For this mistake, as Churchill remarks in the parlance of the day, 'he received the expression of Their Lordships' displeasure'. A reprimand is one thing but it is also on such tiny acts of carelessness that the fate of great operations depend and the delay was made worse by the fact that Captain Hillgarth in Madrid had been kept as much in the dark as the Flag Officer Commanding North Atlantic Station concerning the vital operation about to take place on their doorstep. Had either Hillgarth or North been briefed about MENACE both would have marked their signals MOST IMMEDIATE (a priority used only when the enemy is in sight) and perhaps also 'Personal for First Sea Lord'. The danger of too much security about operations seems in our naval history to have to be constantly relearned.

The French squadron, however, did not pass through the straits unobserved. At 0515 hours on 11 September a British destroyer H.M.S. *Hotspur* sighted Force Y travelling at high speed 50 miles east of Gibraltar and reported this to Admiral North. Moreover Admiral Somerville commanding Force H at Gibraltar had by then also received the Naval Attaché Madrid's signal and at 0700 brought the battlecruiser *Renown* to one hour's notice for steam. *Renown* was the only capital ship with the speed and armament capable of stopping the French. Thus the possibility of parleying with or shadowing the French squadron existed, but in default of any orders or guidance from the Admiralty which naturally was assumed by all on the spot to have full knowledge of this French movement, the equal importance of avoiding unnecessary incidents (Mers-el-Kébir being still very fresh in the memory) made both North and Somerville conclude that the French must have received permission to make these movements unhindered so that their procedure was 'friendly'. Once the French ships had identified themselves to the Port War

Signal Station as requested, North recognized that some of them had previously served at Gibraltar under his command and decided to make them a friendly gesture by signalling 'Bon voyage'. 'The continued silence from the Admiralty', North wrote, 'confirmed us in our opinion that we were acting in accordance with Admiralty wishes. I had kept the Governor of Gibraltar (General Sir Clive Liddell) informed by telephone as to what was happening and he agreed with me that everything pointed to it being a pleasant sign that the French Navy was now coming to its senses.' Bon voyage indeed!

When at last the War Cabinet came to grips with what had happened, they demanded action by the men on the spot which was manifestly impossible to take and in any case too late. 'They must be mad', Somerville remarked to his Flag Lieutenant on receiving a signal at 1546 on the 11th (long after the French squadron had reached the Atlantic) which read:

A. If French Force is proceeding southward inform them there is no objection to their going to Casablanca but that they cannot be permitted to go to Dakar which is under German influence.

B. If Force appears to be proceeding to Bay ports inform them this cannot be permitted as these ports are in German hands.

C. In A and B minimum force is to be used to enforce compliance.

Unable to get an adequate destroyer screen for *Renown* until nearly 1600, since half the destroyers were on patrol hunting Italian submarines, Somerville duly sailed as ordered. A few minutes later he was informed by aircraft from Gibraltar, shadowing the French ships, that they had already entered the heavily defended port of Casablanca at 1610.

22

Dakar – the expedition sails

The ships did not stay there long. The French naval establishment in Morocco, commanded by Admiral d'Harcourt at Casablanca, had made careful preparations to refuel Force Y with all despatch and this was completed by 2200 hours that same night. Admiral d'Harcourt then advised Rear Admiral Bourragué commanding Force Y to leave Casablanca as soon as he could, since otherwise he might well be trapped there by superior British forces which possibly included an aircraft carrier.

Borragué accepted this advice and by 0400 the following morning (12 September) the six ships of Force Y had left Casablanca and were steaming south at full speed. However a further snag then arose for Bourragué in this cat-and-mouse game. The top speed of the Georges Leygues cruisers was 27 knots whereas the older contre-torpilleurs could not make more than 21 knots. To stay together, therefore, the squadron could only proceed at the speed of its slowest ship, thus risking being overtaken by the British. Accordingly on the afternoon of the 12 September Bourragué wisely ordered the destroyers to turn back to Casablanca, while he and the cruisers pressed on to Dakar at 27 knots. The main French quarry thus stayed ahead of the British hunter and the three cruisers were duly moored safe and sound inside the port of Dakar by noon on 14 September. The defences of Dakar had thus been significantly increased at a crucial time.

Meanwhile the main armada of the MENACE operation had sailed from the United Kingdom a fortnight before on

31 August, the naval component being under the command
of Vice-Admiral J.H.D. Cunningham (no relation of A.B.C.)
and the military under the command of Major General
N.M.S. Irwin. Both were men of forceful character. Of
Cunningham it was said that few liked him but everyone
respected and trusted him as an eminently sound, practical,
level-headed officer of the highest professional compet-
ence; of Irwin that he was fit, confident with an immense
reserve of energy and was never discommoded by either
personal danger or hardship. Both commanders found
themselves 'in complete agreement and accord when called
on to make combined decisions'. Both were 'solid' officers
of great experience who indeed needed all the qualities they
possessed for what they were to undergo in MENACE,
neither subsequently being blamed in any major respect for
the disaster the operation turned out to be.

The accord between the two British commanders and
their staffs who had to blend into their final plan the ideas of
Churchill, the Chiefs of Staff, the Vice-Chiefs of Staff, the
Joint Planners, the Inter-Services Planning Staff and the
Force Commanders did not extend to de Gaulle and his Free
French staff. All who had to do with de Gaulle discovered
him to be aloof, unsmiling, difficult and tetchy, but what
the British found especially incomprehensible was his
scarcely concealed contempt for the junior officers working
with him. In this connection it is only fair to observe that
Frenchmen in general seem to like and approve of the
detachment and haughtiness their senior officers display in
their dealings with their subordinates. The French have or
seem to have a very different idea of team spirit,* except
perhaps in very small units such as a submarine. The
concept of village cricket with the Lord of the Manor
playing under the captaincy of the local innkeeper is totally
alien to the French, as indeed is the Anglo-Saxon habit of
turning everything possible into a joke or a game or both.

Even so, a viable plan for MENACE *had* been made, agreed
upon and approved by the War Cabinet and the expedition

*Naturally, barring sports such as rugby.

had duly sailed. However no sooner were they at sea than it became apparent to the two Force Commanders that the facts they had been given on landing conditions, defences and attitude of the French at Dakar were all gravely at fault. This realization came about as follows.

Until the fall of France there had been two British liaison officers, Commander Rushbrooke RN and an Army Captain, Poulter, at Dakar which had been in use by both the Royal Navy and the Royal Air Force for nearly a year. As soon as the Armistice had been signed, however, and at Darlan's instigation both officers had been ordered to leave by the end of June and they had then gone to Freetown in Sierra Leone. The Chiefs of Staff and the Inter-Service Planning Staff decided on 10 August to fly both of them home post-haste since they alone would have the most up-to-date local knowledge available. But post-haste in Whitehall and in Freetown meant two different things and the pair did not arrive until close on midnight on 28 August. The hurried cross-examination they were given the next day was unsatisfactory and disturbing in that it countered most of the assumptions on which the plan had been based. Since, therefore, there was insufficient time in the remaining two days before the expedition sailed for their vital knowledge to be embodied in the orders, they were directed to embark in H.M.S. *Devonshire* with the Force Commanders and their staffs and go at any rate as far as Freetown whither the expedition was to stage before the assault on Dakar itself took place.

What these two officers had to say *en route* effectively destroyed any confidence the Force Commanders had in the plan they had been given in London. In the first place they were unable to improve on the wholly inadequate intelligence on the landing conditions on the beaches – such as precise surf levels – the only guidance available being on the lines of 'It may be rough or it may not be'. On the defences of Dakar, however, both officers were firmly agreed that they were very much stronger than the planners had believed. As Marder observes: 'The approximate date of the information about Dakar handed to the Commanders before sailing may be judged from the statement in it that the construction of certain buildings was projected for *1919*.' Rushbrooke and Poulter said the coast artillery was roughly twice as strong as that set out in the plan and for good measure produced a copy of the French West African Defence scheme which Poulter had sent to the War Office in June where it had since remained unseen and unused by the planners. This revealed that instead of seven companies of Senegalese infantry amounting to some 1400 men, there was now in addition a regiment of three battalions under French officers, totalling a further 7000 men.

The most disturbing matter, however, on which both officers stood firm was that Dakar would never rally to de Gaulle who, indeed, would not be welcomed by any important section of the community. De Gaulle was regarded as a Jeremiah and Poulter even went so far as to say to the Joint Commanders: 'Not one man, woman or child is pro-de-Gaulle.' The Governor-General, the Dakar garrison and the French Navy in the port were all loyal to Vichy and would put up a determined and effective resistance to any landings that were made.

Had the sailing of the expedition been delayed even for a couple of weeks to allow this up-to-date intelligence to be digested, the whole operation might well have been cancelled. Now, however, it was all too late.

23

Breaches of security

To lamentable misinformation must be added breaches of security which would have been hilarious had they not also been tragic. As General Irwin wrote in his operation report: 'I was most disagreeably impressed with the number of officers I met in the War Office who seemed to know about the operation. I dare say this is inevitable . . .' It was not, of course, and one of the few dividends paid by MENACE was a drastic tightening-up of security in the planning of future combined operations and the putting about of decoy plans.

The British were certainly at fault in what has been described as 'the careless competition of the three services ministries in the collection of information' – an instance of this being the young officer who walked into a city map-making firm and asked openly and directly for a plan of Dakar. British misdemeanours, however, were as nothing compared with the almost unbelievable folly of de Gaulle and the Free French, three examples of which were, first that General de Gaulle himself when purchasing a considerable quantity of tropical equipment at Simpson's in Piccadilly remarked in public that his destination was West Africa; secondly, that at a dinner in the Adelphi Hotel, Liverpool, the French officers toasted 'Dakar'; thirdly, that prior to the sailing Free French soldiers in tropical uniforms raised their glasses in Liverpool bars and restaurants in toasts 'à Dakar'.

This virtual advertisement of a secret operation climaxed at Euston when de Gaulle, his staff and the Spears Mission left for Liverpool at 10 a.m. on 30 August 'in a blaze of glory or should I say publicity?' wrote Spears. 'I have never seen so many people from V.I.P.s, civil and military, to wives and girl-friends gathered together to see off the heads of an ultra secret expedition.' Then just as the train was about to pull out, a porter rushed up trundling a large case on a barrow which fell off as the result of a collision, burst open and allowed handfuls of blue, white and red leaflets headed 'Aux Habitants de Dakar' to blow about the platform until they could be hastily gathered together and put back in the case.

Although these and a large number of other security indiscretions allowed the Vichy Government to be told on 8 September by courtesy of the Spanish Ambassadors in

London and Vichy that de Gaulle had left England for Freetown and would attempt an African landing with British ships, the ultimate destination of Dakar was not suspected by the Vichy French, extraordinary as that may seem, until the eve of the attack. This remarkable deception was achieved by the fact that all convoys for the Mediterranean round the Cape called at Freetown anyway and also because the Inter-Service Security Board carefully let it be leaked that a Free French expedition was being sent to Egypt. This idea was confirmed by the marking-out of camp sites in the Suez Canal zone for the supposed arrival of this French contingent from England and by the report to Vichy by two well-known agents that de Gaulle was about to sail round the Cape to Egypt. The confusion over MENACE, therefore, was not entirely one-sided.

24

Dakar – doubts and decisions

When the expedition sailed from the United Kingdom the unanimous opinion of the naval and military staffs was that unless received with open arms they were in for a defeat, ships' guns being no match for well-placed shore batteries. The pessimism of the Force Commanders which now included Vice-Admiral Sir James Somerville, Commanding Force H, with very fresh memories of what he had had to do at Mers-el-Kébir, was shared by the entire Board of Admiralty who regarded MENACE as an unacceptable and relatively useless diversion of their meagre resources at a time when the bombs were raining down on London and the country itself lay under the pressing threat of invasion. The Board of Admiralty did not resign as in more normal times it might well have done, but loyally did its best to make a success for political and strategical gain of what the Naval Assistant to the Vice-Chiefs of the Naval Staff described as

an ill-omened operation, sponsored on us by the P.M. in spite of bitter opposition from the Service Chiefs. It is part of the price we pay for having Winston as P.M. . . . I hate this operation. We don't want to dissipate our energy fighting the French, when every blow we can strike should be delivered against the Germans or Italians (at that moment poised to invade Egypt from Libya). There was indeed an overall feeling of regret that if there had to be an 'enemy' it would be the French and not the principal and established foe, the Germans.

The expedition took 17 days to arrive at Freetown, the British Force Commanders and their staffs being embarked in the flagship, with the 8-inch gun cruiser *Devonshire*, and de Gaulle and his staff together with the Spears Mission travelling in a 16,000-ton Dutch liner *Westernland*. This separation of the leaders into different ships added to their troubles. Wireless silence was of course rigorously imposed on all ships at sea in wartime for obvious reasons, so communication could only be made by signalling lamp. Nothing therefore could be discussed except in the briefest terms. The troops were virtually cut off from their Commander as were the British from the French. These were needless complications but when after 10 days at sea the British suggested that better control of the operation might be achieved if de Gaulle joined the Combined Headquarters ship, he curtly refused claiming that the chances of a French success would be greatly diminished if directed from a British ship and that he ('moi la France') would not wish to direct a purely French operation from a British ship since even if successful it would result later on in unfavourable repercussions, whereas if unsuccessful, to have been in a British ship during the shelling of French forces would not only be very distasteful but would have impossible repercussions on the eventual operation. So that was that.

The next crisis to hit the luckless force a day before they reached Freetown was the sudden cancellation of the entire MENACE operation as planned. This bombshell burst as the result of a War Cabinet meeting at noon on 16 September which considered that the situation had been dangerously altered by the arrival at Dakar on the 14th of the three French cruisers of Force Y, no doubt carrying reinforcements. At 1400 hours that day, therefore, the War Cabinet decreed in a telegram to the Force Commanders that instead de Gaulle should land his force at Duala and use it to consolidate his position in the Cameroons, Equatorial Africa and the Chad colony, extending his influence to Libreville, while the British force remained for the present in Freetown. This new plan was to be executed forthwith 'unless de Gaulle has any strong objections'. To Churchill's surprise not only de Gaulle but the British Commanders *did* have the strongest objections. They pointed out that the presence of the French cruisers did not materially alter the previous naval situation and that these ships were so berthed in Dakar, with awnings spread, as to be virtually impotent and also to present excellent bombing targets. Nor had the military situation altered, the only point in doubt being whether the cruisers' arrival had raised morale at Dakar.

Churchill's reaction to this was to give the Joint Commanders on the spot full liberty to examine the situation themselves and to consult with de Gaulle. They were also assured that the War Cabinet would give careful consideration to their advice. Churchill's own view was that 'if there was any danger of having to use considerable force, it was better not to proceed with the operation but there could be no harm in hearing what the officers in charge of the operation had to say in regard to the situation.'

To this the Joint Commanders replied that the slight

Dakar – doubts and decisions

increase of naval forces available to the Vichy administration of Dakar did not warrant the abandonment of the operation. The political issues were more difficult to assess. However Spears on behalf of de Gaulle struck a far firmer note and it was the following telegram he sent to Churchill which probably just weighed down the scales in favour of going ahead as originally planned:

> If changes in policy are often puzzling in London they are heartbreaking here. It is impossible to understand why naval action under most unfavourable circumstances British alone against French, was boldly faced on Friday, 13 September whereas on Monday, 16 September the prospect of tackling these same ships now lying helpless in harbour under awnings is considered impracticable.
>
> De Gaulle's presence here must inevitably be known and it is quite clear that if he fails to seize the opportunity so obviously within his grasp, of rallying West Africa and agrees to vegetate at Duala, his power to rally any other part of the French Empire is gone for ever. If the Fleet departs leaving de Gaulle here, the accusation of having abandoned him to his fate will swing French opinion totally against us in France as well as in Africa.

This was powerful pleading, the unknown factor still being the real attitude and will to resist at Dakar itself. As the bombs continued to set London alight, the First Sea Lord summarized naval opinion on this distant operation as follows: we should not get embroiled in a war with the Vichy Government (this was a trifle ingenuous since undeclared hostilities had been waged by both sides since Mers-el-Kébir) nor was it possible to provide an adequate force for the blockade of Dakar which would be entailed by de Gaulle's alternative operation of landing at Konakry and attacking Dakar from the rear by land. Otherwise the First Sea Lord saw no reason why MENACE should not go

III

forward. He did not assess the morale of the Vichy forces as being much improved by the arrival of the three cruisers. Their fighting strength was not great, although they might well stiffen the will to resist of the pro-Vichy forces at Dakar. That was the vital consideration especially in the manning and resolution of the coastal batteries. The new factor in the situation was the eagerness for action of the commanders on the spot.

This, to Churchill, was 'a refreshing twist in the situation. It was very rare at this stage in the war for commanders on the spot to press for audacious courses. Usually the pressure to run risks came from home . . . I was therefore agreeably surprised at the evident zeal to put this complicated and semi-political operation to the test. If the men on the spot thought it was time to do and dare, we should certainly give them a free hand.'

Accordingly at 1320 hours on 18 September the War Cabinet sent the Force Commanders the backing they sought: 'We cannot judge relative advantages of alternative schemes from here. We give you full authority to go ahead and do what you think is best in order to give effect to the original purpose of the expedition. Keep us informed.' MENACE was definitely 'on', scheduled for the 22nd but postponed till the 23rd at de Gaulle's request in order to give his agent de Boislambert time to get into Dakar where he would try to influence opinion in advance of the operation.

25

Sea encounters

Meanwhile on that same day, 18 September 1940, and following direct orders from Darlan, Force Y sailed from Dakar 'pour opérer à grande vitesse' in the Gulf of Guinea. In fact Boisson, the Governor General of French West Africa, had only the previous day appointed Rear Admiral Bourragué as overall Commander-in-Chief of all the local navy, army and air forces for the express purpose of re-establishing full Vichy control in Gabon where a state of siege had been proclaimed to try to counter Gaullist intrigues and manoeuvres to occupy Libreville.

Darlan's hunch had been right in organizing Force Y and sailing it from Toulon to Dakar at the end of August. Eleven days later and three days before Force Y reached Dakar 'the Nazi knife was at the Vichy throat'. At Wiesbaden where the Armistice Commission sat in permanent session, the President, General von Stülpnagel, sent his French opposite number, General Huntziger, a letter saying that the government of the Reich expected the French Government to take all the necessary measures without delay and with the utmost energy to repress the dissident movement in French Equatorial Africa and should another uprising take place to strangle it at birth. Then came the rub: 'If the French government had need of greater forces to re-establish the situation in Africa, it must at once inform Germany [and of course Italy].' The letter ended with a heavy threat: (1) if Vichy did not succeed in re-establishing order, Germany and Italy reserved the right to act as they thought fit; (2) a joint German–

Italian control commission was planned for the French Atlantic coast of Morocco, French West and French Equatorial Africa.

This opened up alarming perspectives. To justify his obedience to the government, Governor General Boisson had formally and publicly stated that as French West and Equatorial Africa had not been part of the Armistice agreement, there would therefore be no Germans or Italians in these territories. Indeed he made it clear that any German presence in Dakar would play straight into Churchill's and de Gaulle's hands. General Barrau was even more explicit. His troops, already sensitive to Gaullist propaganda, were violently anti-German. What might they not do to Germans arriving uninvited in Dakar?

The departure of the cruisers of Force Y from Dakar had been observed by aerial reconnaissance and the British at once gave chase. On board this intercepting force was a French commander, Thierry d'Argenlieu, who had retired before the war in order to become a monk and had then rejoined, being among de Gaulle's first adherents. He now carried a message from the Free French leader inviting Admiral Bourragué either to rally immediately to 'la France libre' or to return without delay to Casablanca (not repeat not to Dakar). Spears had rightly judged that so humiliating an order stood a better chance of being obeyed were it to be given in the first place by a Frenchman, the point not being missed that the order would have to be obeyed since it emanated from the deck of a British cruiser.

Towards noon on 19 September, H.M.S. *Cornwall*, a 10,000-ton County Class cruiser and H.M.S. *Delhi*, an older and lighter cruiser, intercepted the French cruiser *Primaguet* and the tanker *Tarn*. Captain Ford Hammill of the *Cornwall*, who had been British Naval Attaché in Paris for three years, pulled across *Primaguet*'s bows and signalled her to stop, which she did. The *Delhi* then closed the French ships and delivered de Gaulle's message together with official instructions as to what they must do together with a personal letter from Hammill to the French Captain

Goybet stressing his friendly feelings towards France and the French and reminding Goybet of his experiences in Paris 'where I had got into the habit of considering myself as a brother of the French navy' and also of the pleasant memories of the summer of 1939 when *Primaguet* and *Cornwall* had entertained each other at Shanghai. Finally the British Captain implored Goybet to turn round with *Tarn* and sail to Casablanca 'without forcing me to do what I would deplore all my life'.

This excellent piece of psychology, allied to the fact that *Primaguet*'s 6-inch guns were no match for the combined 8-inch guns of *Cornwall* and the 6-inch guns of *Delhi*, resulted some five anxious hours later in French acceptance of the British demands. Admiral Bourragué ordered *Primaguet* back to Casablanca, while he in his flagship *Georges Leygues* having escaped British surveillance in torrential rain which reduced visibility to a few yards, returned to Dakar and called off the operation. The third cruiser *Gloire* developed engine trouble which reduced her speed to 4 knots and agreed to proceed to Casablanca under British escort. The next day, when still 190 miles south west of Dakar, the British accepted her captain's word of honour that she would continue to Casablanca and not try for Dakar. Eventually four days later the *Gloire* limped into Casablanca by which time the action at Dakar was over.

These contacts were characterized by an exchange of polite messages rather than shells. Admiral Bourragué's wisdom and skill in avoiding what might have been a mini Mers-el-Kébir drew congratulations from the Governor General Boisson there on the spot and the fury of Darlan in Vichy, who relieved him of his command on 20 September and in a rare old fit of pique renewed the Vichy order to fire on all British ships encountered within 20 miles of French shores. This Darlan did without even waiting for Bourragué's report and it took him six months to relent, whereupon 'the kindly and courteous Bourragué who had left Dakar with unanimous regrets of the officers and men of

Force Y' was promoted to Vice-Admiral and appointed to the naval staff.

Thus ended the high seas preliminaries to the invasion of Dakar.

26

Dakar – the first attacks

The attack on Dakar began at dawn on Monday, 23 September 1940. From H hour nothing went right either for de Gaulle or for the British. To begin with the weather. Instead of benefiting from the normal bright sunlight and clear weather on the West African coast at that time of the year, the assault force approached in thick fog. Then at 0530 hours de Gaulle's two little Luciole aircraft which had been taken on board H.M.S. *Ark Royal*, decked out in French colours with the crews wearing French uniforms, landed at Ouakam airfield. Both pilots confidently expected to be welcomed with open arms. Instead they were promptly arrested. Since one of these Gaullist aviators had on him a list of the leading Free French supporters (which included the Mayor of Dakar) that cat was out of the bag and the round-up began.

Then at 0640 two launches wearing the Tricolour and a white flag with Commander d'Argenlieu on board slowly approached Mole No. 2. On the jetty d'Argenlieu recognized an officer he knew on the naval staff. He called across saying he had come as spokesman for General de Gaulle and was charged with delivering personal letters to the Governor General Boisson, the Army Commander General Barrau and the Naval Commander-in-Chief Admiral Landriau. The officer to whom he spoke, Lieutenant

Commander Lorfèvre, instantly sought instructions from higher authority and was told to put d'Argenlieu under arrest. As soon as this was apparent the Gaullists turned tail and fled, shouting to a launch which was trying to block them in 'Don't fire! Don't fire!' However the Dakar launch did open fire putting some 250 machine gun bullets into the Free French boats and seriously wounding both d'Argenlieu and his assistant.

By this time the Governor General had received a radio message from de Gaulle saying that he had come with his troops to reinforce the defence of Dakar and to revictual the town, being supported by powerful British forces. Boisson's reaction was to establish a command post with General Barrau and Admiral Landriau, alert the *Richelieu* which at once went to Action Stations, and arrest the Mayor, Monsieur Goux, together with other adherents of de Gaulle. As Churchill wrote later:

All hearts were hardened, and the British fleet approached through the mist to within five thousand yards.
At 10 a.m. a harbour battery opened fire on one of our
wing destroyers. The fire was returned and the engagement soon became general. The destroyers 'Inglefield'
and 'Foresight' were slightly damaged and the 'Cumb-
erland' was struck in the engine-room and had to quit.
One French submarine ['Persée'] was bombed by an
aircraft at periscope depth [and sunk] and one French
destroyer ['L'Audacieux'] set on fire.

At about 1130 hours, with the fog as thick as ever, the firing died away and all the British and Free French ships retired.

Confusion now began to reign on board de Gaulle's Headquarters Ship the *Westernland*. De Gaulle had signal-led the Governor General, earnestly requesting him to stop opposing the entry of Free French ships into the port and the disembarkment of troops under his orders, only to have the retort hotly flung back at him that 'any landing would be fully opposed by force. You have taken on yourself the shedding of French blood, so you can keep that responsibility because blood has now been shed.'

All day long the fog continued. However at 1730 in the late afternoon de Gaulle made an attempt at landing his troops at Rufisque with the intention of then marching on Dakar by land. This too failed and the marines were withdrawn with casualties on both sides. Out at sea a second French submarine, the *Ajax*, was sunk.

What should now be done? Mindful of Churchill's signal that 'having begun we must go on to the end. Stop at nothing' de Gaulle had been visibly shaken by opposition he had not expected to find. According to Boisson's report to Vichy 'the 23rd September was dominated by the marked indecision of the assailant, visibly disorientated by the unexpected resistance'. This was further confirmed by General Barrau who said in his own report: 'The reactions of the military chiefs here at Dakar was such that M. Boisson would not have been obeyed had he adopted any other attitude and taken any different decision (i.e. to resist) than those he took at the time.'

One very disagreeable fact loomed out of the fog, a fact de Gaulle had little desire to face. The Free French with himself as leader were in no way wanted at Dakar. Allied Intelligence had been gravely at fault. Wishful thinking had been taken as reality, but the wish was not held by anyone in a responsible position in French West Africa. Indeed the Dakar authorities had made it only too clear that force would be met by force, the real surprise being the strength of the offensive spirit exhibited by the Vichy French.

The British found this very difficult to understand but in reality, of course, the French civil war had already begun. 'If feeling amongst the Free French on board H.M.S. "Ark Royal" was typical, we need not have been so squeamish of setting Frenchmen against Frenchmen', Rear Admiral Sir William Jameson later wrote, 'Furious at their reception on the first day, they were longing for action. "If only fifteen

hundred men of the Foreign Legion had been put on shore",
they said, "To the Gallows with Admiral Landriau" cried
one. Another, patting a 500 lb bomb which was being
wheeled to one of the Skuas, exclaimed "Aha! voilà un joli
petit déjeuner pour l'Amiral." '

Just before midnight on that first day of the operation the
British Force Commanders sent an ultimatum to the
Governor General at Dakar. Broadcast in French and
English, it ran:

> General de Gaulle informs us, the Commanders of the
> British Naval and Military Forces, that you have
> prevented him from landing his troops for the revict-
> ualling of Dakar. Your attitude gives us every reason
> to believe that Dakar may at any moment be handed
> over by you to the common enemy. In view of the
> importance of this town and this base in connection
> with the development of the war, and also in view of
> the fact that the seizing of Dakar by the enemy would
> cause the population to be oppressed, the Allies regard
> it as their duty to take such immediate steps as are
> necessary to prevent this eventuality. Desiring that
> Frenchmen should not fight against Frenchmen in a
> pitched battle, General de Gaulle has withdrawn his
> forces. Our forces are approaching. It is for you now to
> speak: you will not be allowed to hand over the French
> and native people who wish to remain free to the
> slavery to which Germany and Italy would subject
> them. Yours is the entire responsibility for what may
> happen.
>
> We have the honour to inform you that, if by 0600
> the 24th September [i.e. the next morning] you have
> not given your decision to General de Gaulle, the very
> powerful forces at our disposal will open fire. Once
> fire has begun it will continue until the fortifications
> of Dakar are entirely destroyed and the place occupied
> by troops who will be ready to fulfil their duty. Only a
> proclamation that our conditions are accepted could

interrupt the carrying out of this programme. Our troops would not land if you decided to join your compatriots in the liberation of your country and not to remain tied to the enemy who holds France at his mercy. There is no compromise possible.

This ultimatum, the Vichy General Barrau wrote, constituted 'a veritable outrage' to the French officers in estimating them to be capable of handing over to the Germans the port and town of Dakar. 'Whether or not this was Cunningham's intention, the clear result was to provoke the indignation of all of us. Almost the whole of the military chiefs around Boisson considered that the message merited no answer. It was on my own intervention that the Governor General sent his rejection of the British proposals.'

This impression of yet another outrage to French pride is sustained to this day by French historians. 'But where were the Germans?' they ask, and certainly the wording of the ultimatum was somewhat extravagant and violent and could well have been improved. It is also certainly true that contrary to the opinion of Allied Intelligence at that time, there were no Germans in Dakar. So the men on the spot felt justifiably aggrieved. They were right by the letter of the law or, if you prefer it, by the official Vichy interpretation of the Armistice terms. But we know now (and Vichy knew then) that the Germans were on the way and that Hitler had every intention of taking over Morocco and French West Africa just as soon as expedience, with Laval's assistance, allowed him so to do. For that matter, too, the sacred Armistice terms had not envisaged Alsace, Lorraine and the Pas de Calais being taken over by the Germans but they had been, to Vichy protests it is true but these were about as effective as a whistle in a 10-acre field. Vichy could obstruct and delay but was otherwise impotent and this must have been apparent to the Governors-General of the French Empire and the High Command of the Services. It was more comfortable, however, not to face up to these hard facts but to solace the soul with conventional and blinkered loyalty to the elected Head of State.

'Outrage' at Dakar? Perhaps. Certainly to the navy with Mers-el-Kébir in mind these were monstrous demands from the hereditary enemy. Moreover how could they know, the defenders of Dakar, that their revered Head of State would be shaking hands with Hitler in a matter of weeks? How could they know what was being done in their name in far away Vichy? In point of fact it simply did not suit Darlan at that time to do a deal with the Germans in return, say, for the release of French prisoners-of-war or for more food for starving France, but that kind of collaboration was exactly what Laval had already offered and nine months later what Darlan himself was to agree over Syria and the bases the Germans were so anxious to obtain. Maybe at Dakar – although of course Governor General Boisson, General Barrau and Admiral Landriau would never let the idea enter their minds – *les perfides anglais* were not so wide of the mark. And whatever they thought personally about de Gaulle, he was as French as they were and considered himself just as loyal to the real interests of France as they did. Therefore to equate the British who were assisting de Gaulle with the Germans and Italians as 'the enemy' must surely have caused the French logical mind to pause and reflect. If that were ever so, and now no one will ever know, the pause was momentary and the immediate response to the British ultimatum came in a signal from Boisson at 0400 hours on 24 September sent via the *Richelieu* and saying not just 'Merde!' as his staff had proposed but, in rather more noble terms, 'France has entrusted Dakar to me. I shall defend Dakar to the bitter end'.

'France?', the wrathful Legionnaires and Gaullists asked themselves as they waited off shore, 'What France?'

27

The second day

In essence the whole of this needless war between Vichy France and the Allies was caused by the misjudgment and wounded pride of the politicians and the generals who had let France down in that summer of 1940. If politics is the science and art of government, as the dictionary defines it, then the politicians of Vichy have a lot to answer for when the accounts are made up. A certain amount of cynicism, hypocrisy and corruption is, of course, inevitable in politics of any kind and the conventions differ in individual countries to suit the character of the people governed. At that time the leadership given by the men of Vichy was devious and uncertain, relying upon a sort of Maginot line of high-sounding words. The total impotence of the Vichy regime, following upon the collapse of the country in June (and this was only three months later), endeavoured to hide itself behind a pomposity of attitude, a facade with nothing to prop it up from behind.

'France follows with emotion and confidence your resistance to the partisan treachery and the British aggression', Pétain signalled to Boisson during the forenoon of the second day, 'under your high authority Dakar is giving an example of courage and fidelity. The entire mother country is proud of your attitude and of the resolution of the forces under your command. I congratulate you and assure you of my entire confidence.'

One has only to remember that two-thirds of the France referred to above was occupied by the Germans and not under Pétain's control to appreciate how nonsensical were phrases such as 'the entire mother country is proud of your attitude'.

This mist of verbiage was matched physically by a second day of hot and hazy conditions at sea. Visibility on 24 September, although slightly better than on the previous day, was still very poor and made range-finding almost impossible. Naval gunnery control by radar still lay in the future and the horizon or the target had still to be identified by eye as it had been since man first went to sea. The French shore batteries opened fire on the British fleet as it closed the coast, the battleships *Barham* and *Resolution* engaging the *Richelieu* at 13,600 yards. The cruisers *Devonshire* and *Australia* engaged a French cruiser and the destroyer *Le Hardi* which was damaged. This action in the forenoon proved to be inconclusive and was broken off in mid-morning.

Little more was achieved when the bombardment opened up again in the afternoon. 'The enemy will to resist appeared unimpaired', Cunningham noted in his report, and the fire from the shore batteries was accurate and damaging. The *Barham* was hit four times, three by heavy shells, but sustained no serious damage. Altogether at the end of the day when nearly 400 rounds of 15-inch ammunition had been expended, the British had very little to show.

In the late afternoon and having withdrawn out of range, *Barham* closed the *Westernland* and invited de Gaulle on board the flagship for a conference on the Admiral's bridge. The British mood was grim but there were no recriminations. De Gaulle was by general accord 'magnificent in his dignity in adversity'. He blamed only himself for so gravely underestimating the strength of the defences and the morale of the defenders. General Irwin wrote that 'de Gaulle's bearing was remarkable for its brave acceptance of a great disappointment and immediate readiness to offer constructive proposals. Both Vice Admiral Cunningham and I felt the greatest admiration for a man with such quiet courage and with so cool and clear a brain.' Cunningham in turn wrote in his report that de Gaulle's attitude 'when he was naturally suffering from the terrible disappointment which his reception undoubtedly gave him was that of a great man'.

The upshot of this conference was that the British Force Commanders felt that given the attitude of the place and of the squadron supporting it 'bombardment would solve nothing. Both commanders considered that a British landing would now be a desperate enterprise under existing conditions with the Vichy warships free to come out'. With this assessment de Gaulle agreed. From the military point of view any landing attempted would be 'a mere adventure'. Nevertheless de Gaulle said he was prepared to give his full support regardless of the consequences should a landing still be decided upon. However he would much prefer not to put his troops ashore even after a successful landing by the British.

On the other hand 'just to slink away and have nothing but a commercial blockade as before' would be 'too much of a knock'. He suggested to save face that the Vichy authorities at Dakar be informed that the bombardment had been stopped at his, de Gaulle's, request to prevent the further shedding of French blood, and that he and his force should proceed to Bathurst where the troops could be exercised, the new situation considered and further intelligence gathered preceding a possible advance on Dakar by land.

Later that evening the British Force Commanders again had second thoughts. They decided that provided the weather improved the next day they would make one further effort to neutralize the ships and forts of Dakar and would then land if that were practicable. During the night a long and somewhat querulous signal was received from Churchill which called for a detailed account of what had so far happened and ended 'Pray act as you think best but ... matter must be pushed to conclusion without delay'. So on the third day it was.

28

The Dakar finale

No one complained of the weather on the morning of 25 September. Maximum visibility, clear skies and bright sunlight gave both sides the perfect conditions they had lacked throughout the previous two days. By 0900 hours the British battleships had taken up their bombarding positions and the action began at a range of over 12 miles. Dakar, however, was no sitting duck as Mers-el-Kébir had been and the French defences by this time were fully prepared and alert. The moment the British opened fire, the French retort was instant and accurate. Stiff fighter opposition from Ouakam airfield made aerial reconnaissance almost impossible. A skilfully laid smoke-screen gravely hindered range-finding and the sole remaining French submarine, the *Bévéziers*, lurked in position undetected and awaiting her chance. This came as the two battleships *Barham* and *Resolution* turned at speed to take up their firing positions.

At a range of less than two miles the *Bévéziers* fired four torpedoes in a fan pattern at the battleships. These torpedoes with their yellow warheads could easily be seen as they streaked towards their target. By skilful manoeuvring *Barham* avoided them, but *Resolution* was struck amidships on the port side while turning under full helm. This hit seriously damaged her port boiler room which resulted in flooding, loss of power and a list to port of 12½ degrees. Screened by her two destroyers *Resolution* then withdrew from the action, steaming south at reduced speed. A few minutes later *Barham* scored a hit with a 15-

inch shell on the *Richelieu*, but her armour plating was such
that this caused little damage. *Barham* then turned southward to cover *Resolution* and some 30 minutes after opening fire the action was broken off with nothing whatever
achieved.

These final events on 25 September decided the Force
Commanders to abandon the operation. They had been
made painfully aware that the Dakar defences were virtually impregnable. The British cruiser fire had had no success
on the Gorée and Cape Manuel batteries. The French air
patrols had been effective and there could now be little
chance of investing Dakar with the inadequate landing
force available. Undaunted to the end, de Gaulle tried one
last appeal broadcast at 1100 hours: 'The men of Vichy are
leading Dakar on the path of destruction. Before this destruction starts General de Gaulle beseeches once more with
all his heart the Frenchmen of Dakar to impose their will
and to unite with him without further delay in order to drive
out the bad chiefs and take up again the good fight for the
liberation of France.' In the circumstances such an appeal
was disdainfully ignored.

By now both British and the Free French realized it was all
disastrously at an end. At 1152 Cunningham signalled the
Admiralty:

> After three attempts in widely different gunnery condi-
> tions result obviously negative and defences including
> cruisers and destroyers operating under cover of bat-
> tery remain intact. This together with evidence of fire
> control by listening device probably moored mine
> make entry of transport even by night impracticable to
> effect landing of troops. Regret must now recommend
> adopting de Gaulle's proposal. Meanwhile continuing
> withdrawal of whole Force to southward.

This signal reached the War Cabinet during its morning
session, and authority to abandon the operation was given.
As Churchill later summed it up:

In three days' bombardment no British ships were sunk, but the battleship 'Resolution' was disabled for several months and two destroyers sustained damage which required considerable repairs in home dockyards. Two Vichy submarines were sunk, the crew of one being saved, two destroyers were burnt out and beached and the battleship 'Richelieu' was hit by a 15-inch shell and damaged by two near misses of 250 lb bombs. There was of course no means at Dakar of repairing this formidable vessel, which had already been rendered temporarily immobile in July, and it could now be definitely dismissed as a hostile factor from our calculations.

Considering the scale of the operation, casualties were surprisingly light. On the Allied side 3 Free French had been killed with 5 wounded, plus some 36 British killed or wounded. The Vichy defenders lost 92 Europeans (82 navy, 2 army, and 8 civilians) and 74 natives with a further 340 Europeans and natives wounded.

The ill-starred operation was over and the post-mortems began. The Vichy French at Dakar deserved and were given full credit for their gallant, determined and effective defence. The Free French and the British were justifiably castigated by their allies and especially by Australia and the United States. To Dr Goebbels the *débâcle* was yet another unexpected gift which he exploited as a further blow to the prestige of Great Britain at a time when the whole world was wondering whether the country could really stand alone against the German onslaught. So far as neutral Spain was concerned, the English Ambassador in Madrid, in the course of reassuring the Spanish Government that the Dakar operation had not been intended as a prelude to a similar coup in Morocco, received in return the wry comment that it did seem to show once again the British incapacity for carrying through any military plan.

Thank you, Franco, for that.

29

Repercussions

The repercussions which followed Dakar must be set in the context of what was happening elsewhere in Europe and the world. To the British and the Free French Dakar had certainly been a naval and military fiasco, but it did happen to coincide with the German failure to gain control of the skies over south-east England and the consequent abandonment by Hitler of Operation SEALION, the invasion of the United Kingdom. Already on 19 September, four days before the Dakar operation, Hitler had ordered not only the stopping of any further build-up of invasion craft in the Channel and North Sea ports but also the dispersal of those already assembled in order to reduce their losses from R.A.F. bombing, 80 barges having already been sunk plus the destruction of an ammunition train.

Naturally this decision was not known until later, but it needs to be remembered that while Hitler continued to be aware that final victory required the defeat of England, during the autumn of 1940 the Fuehrer's main preoccupation lay with eastern Europe and the Soviet Union. As the German General Staff knew to its irritation and distress, Hitler could only with disinclination be induced to interest himself in the sea and if you drew a line from Brest to the Urals, matters requiring attention to the south of that line were considered by the Fuehrer to be of secondary importance.

France, of course, was willy-nilly implicated in this general German strategy, but an examination of the Reich records after the war and in particular the Chancellor's day-to-day diary of events shows that until Dakar Hitler had been adequately satisfied with the neutralizing through the Armistice of the French fleet and the French Empire. He had also given his full agreement to the subjection of the French economy to specialized German control. Overseas adventures, however, could wait. According to Hitler real German colonization would take place in eastern Europe and above all in Russia. One effect of Dakar was to make him think again.

To begin with the doubts which Hitler and his staff had entertained after Mers-el-Kébir about the ability and will of the Pétain government to repay with force any British aggression had now been banished. Vichy's order to defend French territory against aggressors whoever they might be was clearly no longer just an empty phrase. Dakar had been successfully and valiantly defended as were later to be Gabon, Syria, Madagascar and finally Algeria and Morocco, in all of which operations, except Madagascar, Frenchmen were to fire on Frenchmen. But for the situation which now obtained a new German political and strategic initiative was required, a strategy in which Mussolini's Italy and Franco's Spain were necessarily concerned. The events at Dakar merely added urgency to this requirement. They also rescued Vichy from a dilemma into which it had got itself largely through the uncontrolled hanky-panky of Laval.

Early in September, while the MENACE armada had already put to sea but 12 days before the operation itself was effected, Hitler had been pressurized (in so far as this was possible) by the Kriegsmarine and by the Luftwaffe to secure for both services suitable bases in West Africa from which the Battle of the Atlantic could then be fought. It will be remembered that earlier such a request had been passed to the Vichy government which had turned it down. On 11 September, however, General von Stülpnagel who headed the Armistice Commission at Wiesbaden asked the French General Huntziger, to agree to the sending of a German economic mission to Dakar and also to the establishment of a Control Commission further north in French Morocco. On 20 September Vichy (in effect Laval) gave its consent to these proposals. By 25 September, therefore, three German 'economists', plus of course a more than adequate 'secretariat', had entrenched themselves in Casablanca. One of these 'economists', Wehrmacht Colonel Erdmann, made no bones about the real point of the exercise and had already begun to throw his weight about.

That same day saw the climax to the highly successful defence of Dakar and the shamefaced withdrawal of the assaulting British and Free French forces. Vichy accordingly and immediately revoked its consent to the presence of any German in Dakar and General Noguès, the Governor General in Morocco, then had the unpalatable task of turning back some very determined German officers. This he only just succeeded in doing. But it was a very near thing. On 24 September, the second day of the Allied attack on Dakar, the Vichy Government had assured the United States that contrary to what Churchill was asserting, French West Africa was not under German control. This denial was then repeated on 26 September after the MENACE operation had been abandoned. The German economic mission, however, refused to leave Casablanca and made grumbling Teutonic noises against going back to the Fatherland even when ordered to do so by Berlin. The realities of this situation and the prognostication of what might then take place remained in consequence hard to substantiate and even more tricky to assess.

30

The French quadrille

In the immediate aftermath of Dakar what has been aptly described as a 'quadrille' began to be danced round and about poor stricken France, the 'dancers' being Great Britain, Germany, Italy and Spain. Such pressure as could be made without endangering the pressurizers was then applied to Hitler by the German High Command in order to develop negotiations with Laval. At that time Laval was still Vice-President of the Council at Vichy. The object Laval and his German friends had in view was to mount a joint Franco-German repossession of the French colonies in Equatorial Africa which had seceded to de Gaulle. Later the parties concerned were to build up a more considerable Franco-German alliance against England. In these endeavours the Kriegsmarine, which had hitherto regarded the French Navy with scepticism, now actively supported a German–French co-operation against the British in the Mediterranean and in the African theatres of war. Weygand with his strong anti-German views had at the same time been replaced as Minister of Defence by General Huntziger, fresh from his labours on the Armistice Commission. Huntziger, although in no way a 'Lavalist', had encouraged the sending of a German commission to Dakar and in one way or another favoured co-operation with the Germans in the long-term interests of France since Hitler was undoubtedly going to win the war.

Darlan whose Anglophobia was never far off the boil had been stimulated by the Allied *débâcle* at Dakar to send three more submarines from Morocco to Dakar and to order the reprisal bombing of Gibraltar. He also pressed the Germans for more freedom of action for the fleet at Toulon. 'The development of this situation', the Wehrmacht General Halder wrote on 27 September 1940, 'could lead France into becoming our ally and would also resolve some difficult political problems. Opposition to these proposals comes from the Minister of Foreign Affairs. Apparently von Ribbentrop is heavily engaged in Rome in an *anti*-French sense.'

Hitler also, to the surprise and despair of the Kriegsmarine, remained unconvinced and rejected all these various propositions. At a meeting with Mussolini on the Brenner Pass on 4 October Hitler had expressed his deep and long-standing distrust of France

> which will never be our friend. We can do what we like, at the first possible moment the idea of revenge will once more arise. The same thing will apply in the French attitude to Italy. The French are not Romans but Gauls. To hold that the Italians and the French are both 'Latin' is a mistake. It is the English and the French who will get together again. However, the best solution for the present moment is a European coalition and that is why we must now negotiate with the French government.

Thus in deciding to talk to Pétain, Hitler was clear in his own mind that having given up the idea of invading the British Isles, it would be necessary to continue the war with a different strategy, using plans which one way or another would implicate France.

On 27 September the Axis of Germany and Italy had been strengthened in the Far East by the adherence of Japan; on 7 October German troops began to take over Romania, forestalling their then ally, the U.S.S.R., in so far as they could. Finally on 12 October Hitler told his Generals that he had abandoned the idea of invading England in 1940 and two days later conferred with Keitel,

Jodl and Raeder as to what the new strategy should be. In the meantime the Fuehrer had had the questionable benefit of Laval's determination to bring France into active alliance with Germany as expressed to him, together with some wishful thinking presented as facts, by Otto Abetz, the German Ambassador on the staff of the Military High Command in Paris.

Hitler saw Abetz in person on 12 October, but he had already seen Abetz's report to Ribbentrop of 8 October in which he claimed:

After Dakar the French government had renewed its proposal to enter openly into war against England at the side of Italy and Germany at any rate in the French African colonies. [This of course was 'pure Laval'.] In exchange France expected to obtain better conditions of peace from the Axis powers, an improvement in the food situation and in the provision of essential supplies to metropolitan France and then by means of military victories against England to improve the morale of the French people and especially the young thus distracting them from conditions on the home front.

In all this toadying Abetz took care to cover himself by also pointing out that 'people said' or 'information has been received' that French opinion in Oran and Dakar added to the deep resentment of the Vichy Government against England amounted to a co-ordinated drive to obtain from Germany a massive rearmament of the navy, the air force and the colonial army which the French Government could then use *against* the Reich should a change in the military situation on the Continent arise.

To support this double-edged thesis Abetz referred to the intimate (but imaginary) friendship between Admiral Darlan and Admiral Muselier (condemned to death by Vichy) and to that between Weygand and de Gaulle (also condemned to death by Vichy). All this of course was the wildest guesswork and in addition dangerously inaccurate. However it illustrated once again the way in which those at the top were fed information which underlings imagined they would like to know. 'It would be an excellent idea,' Abetz ended up by saying, 'for a meeting to be arranged between Marshal Pétain and the Fuehrer which, in fact, the Marshal asked me to put forward a few days ago . . .'

It did not occur to Abetz that Hitler scarcely needed 'his agent in Paris' to suggest a meeting with Pétain.

31

Hitler, Laval and Pétain

Although Hitler considered the British attitude in the autumn of 1940 to be 'dictated by desperation and also a complete failure to understand realities' and despite the fact that Germany was unquestionably the absolute master of all the European countries its armed forces had conquered, the Fuehrer did not enjoy plain sailing with either Franco or Mussolini. Both dictators, while firmly on the German side, were hard realists in so far as their own interests were concerned and any favours which Hitler might require were only to be had at a stiff price. Thus it was that when plans for the invasion of England were abandoned and Hitler opted for the capture of Gibraltar, he found the terms demanded by Franco for his co-operation to be unacceptably high.

Before Spain would consider declaring war on the Allies, Hitler was informed, Gibraltar, French Morocco and the western part of Algeria (which included Oran) should be given to Spain together with certain expansions of the Spanish African colonies. In addition military and economic assistance would be essential since Spain had only enough grain for eight months. Were these cold-blooded demands to be met, Hitler realized that two things were likely to happen: the British would seize the Canary Islands, using them as a base against the U-boat campaign in the Atlantic, and either the Vichy Government would remove to North Africa with the fleet from Toulon or the French Empire overseas would adhere to de Gaulle.

Hitler now decided to talk to Franco personally which he did on the frontier between France and Spain at Hendaye on 23 October. The talks lasted nine hours and got nowhere. Now in addition to his previous demands Franco wanted French Catalonia *north* of the Pyrenees (i.e. part of France itself). 'Rather than go through that again', Hitler remarked later to Mussolini in one of his rare moments as a human being, 'I would prefer to have three or four of my teeth out.'

Hitler had made this royal progress in his special armoured train with its polished steel and copper fittings and its anti-aircraft gun platform, curiously named 'Amerika'. On the way down he had stopped at Montoire just north of Tours where during the evening of 22 October he had briefly received Laval. The Vichy Vice-President had been brought there at the secret behest of Abetz under the impression that he was to talk to Ribbentrop. On being told he was to meet Hitler himself, Laval was of course both astonished and delighted (his actual exclamation being 'Oh! Merde!'). According to Hitler's interpreter Paul Schmidt, Laval, an opportunist to his nicotine-stained finger-nails began by treating the Fuehrer to a dissertation on how he had done his best since 1931 to effect a *rapprochement* between France and Germany. Hitler abruptly cut him short (the whole parley took only a matter of minutes) and outlined what he expected to happen at the interview he was prepared to accord Marshal Pétain on his way back from Hendaye.

Laval returned to Vichy the next day 'in a state of great exaltation, a smile on his lips, accompanied by Achenbach (one of Abetz's staff) in green uniform' and told Pétain that 'he had had a *long* meeting with the Fuehrer and had reviewed a *large* number of matters'. 'Hitler', he went on, 'fully understands the situation in France. Provided we give him some concessions and guarantees, we shall be back on our feet quicker than anyone imagines. You know what I'm talking about – prisoners of war, demarcation lines, the armistice etc etc.'

At the Council of Ministers in the late afternoon of 23 October Laval swore that he had neither negotiated nor promised anything to Hitler but that France was at a turning point: 'Each one of us must accept our responsibilities. So far as I am concerned, my choice has already been made and I shall defend it passionately when the Council of Ministers discusses it.' Pétain, however, promised to warn Hitler that he would take no decision before the Vichy Government had debated what answers should be given to the German Government. When later that night Pétain was courteously asked by his Chef de Cabinet if he had thought out what might transpire at this meeting with Hitler, the old man tapped his pocket in a knowing manner and said he had his plan all ready. 'Besides', he added, 'there are precedents. Have you never heard of Tilsit?' Tilsit was where Napoleon enforced treaties on the kings of both Russia and Prussia. Tilsit could scarcely be paralleled with Montoire, even in the febrile atmosphere of Vichy.

The bemused ministers realized that this imminent meeting between Pétain and Hitler would be conducted on a scenario devised by Laval, their only consolation being that Pétain continued to state to all and sundry that he would never declare war on Great Britain which is what Laval so dearly sought.

32

Montoire and the Rougier visit

When Pétain shook hands with Hitler on the platform at Montoire on the evening of 24 October 1940, France and indeed the world stood aghast. The meeting was photographed and filmed and Dr Goebbels took good care that the entire globe should be made aware of this historic encounter, together with the conclusions which German propaganda wished to be drawn. As so often happens in the most tragic circumstances, there were also misunderstandings which verged on the comic: 'I am happy to shake the hand of a Frenchman', Hitler said, 'who is not responsible for this war.' Since this was not translated, Pétain was under the impression that the Fuehrer was asking if he had had a good journey and replied in French: 'Bien, bien je vous remercie.' Things scarcely improved once the conference proper began in the saloon car of Hitler's armoured train. Since neither Pétain nor Laval understood German and had not brought an interpreter with them, the two Frenchmen were entirely dependent on Paul Schmidt, Hitler's interpreter, to tell them what Hitler and von Ribbentrop were saying.

When later on at Tours, where Pétain and Laval were to pass the night at the Préfecture, Pétain was asked if Hitler had a good voice, he replied: 'I'll tell you something in confidence, I never heard him.' 'You never heard him?' his questioner asked in astonishment. 'No', Pétain said, 'that fellow who shouts away on the radio spoke almost in an undertone and as I'm a little hard of hearing, you understand . . . but the *interpreter* had a very clear and distinct voice.'

'Little more than shameful civilities resulted' is the summary Churchill gave to this meeting in his *History of the Second World War* and it is certainly true that no concrete decisions were taken. Hitler declared that he had already won the war and that England was beaten. Somewhat illogically he then asked what France would do if England were to attack her again as she had done at Dakar. Pétain replied frostily that France had already suffered too much morally and materially to involve herself in a new conflict. Hitler then blustered that if France did not wish to defend herself and still sided with the English, she would lose her colonial empire at the end of the war and would have conditions imposed on her as strict as those which would be forced on England.

Then Laval 'got into the act' by talking about the French wish to collaborate with Germany in every domain except the military (he had conveniently forgotten his offer of 28 August to Field Marshal von Brauchitsch of the French Air Force to help in the bombing of Britain) and so it went on. Two days later when all this was reported to the Council of Ministers at Vichy, it was clear that the era of collaboration had willy-nilly begun. 'Collaboration' was an explosive word, carrying with it immense repercussions.

'To the stupefaction already provoked in France and in the world by the famous photograph of Pétain and Hitler shaking hands on the Montoire station platform were now added the indignation and anger of others at hearing Marshal Pétain himself talk of "collaboration between France and Germany".' Yves Bouthillier, the Vichy Finance Minister, was right when he commented that the government had made a great mistake: 'In the modern world,' he went on, 'the choice of words is one of the capital tasks of politics.'

Bouthillier was one of the small group of men whom Pétain called his 'Faithful'. Others were Peyrouton (Minister of the Interior), Alibert (Garde des Sceaux and equivalent to the British Lord Chancellor), Huntziger (Minister of War) and, of course, Darlan (Minister of Marine). Laval (the

Vice-President at this time) was very much *not* of this cabal and in less than two months Pétain was to trick him into resigning, to the fury of Abetz and the Germans in Paris, after which Darlan was to become 'the Crown Prince'.

The manoeuvres and praxis of Vichy at this time can only be understood by visualizing what the French called 'la guerre des clans' which raged turbulently around the bland, deaf, half-alive half-dead presence of the 84-year-old Pétain in the Hotel du Parc. But although none of 'les fidèles' went so far as Laval in wanting to declare war on England in wholehearted alliance with the victorious Germans, all had been stunned by the handshake at Montoire and now came to appreciate to a greater or lesser degree that the realities of the present situation in France demanded at least 'co-operation' with the occupying force. The Marshal had told them that whereas he had made no deal (how could he, he asked, when Hitler had done all the talking?), he had accepted the principle of collaboration, that is to say 'un pacte de cohabitation' between the occupied and occupying forces. His hope, he went on, was that his meeting with the Master of the Reich and the assurance he had been given of loyal respect for the Armistice convention would henceforth make more effective the efforts of the military ministers to rearm France, of the civil ministers to improve living conditions and of himself to obtain the return of the prisoners-of-war. It was a rambling statement, partly composed of wishful thinking and worthy of Lear. The one fact apparent to all, however, was that 'collaboration' was now to be the panacea or at least an amelioration of the wretchedness of metropolitan France.

Was it though? So far as Laval, the Germans and to a lesser extent Darlan were concerned, Montoire became a cardinal date in French political history. No one other than Pétain, however, was aware of the fact that at the very moment the French Head of State was shaking the Fuehrer's hand, a certain Professor Rougier of the University of

Besançon was in London meeting the British Foreign Secretary and later Churchill himself under conditions of the utmost secrecy and without the knowledge of General de Gaulle nor of anyone at Vichy other than Pétain himself.

Rougier had arrived in London via Geneva thanks to the protection of Weygand, then the Resident General in French North Africa, and he carried a personal card of accreditation from Pétain. He came as a confidential messenger but considered himself to be something more. When he left for Lisbon, Tangier and Algiers a fortnight later he carried with him what he called a 'Protocol' but which Churchill regarded as only the headings of a provisional gentleman's agreement, the terms of which were allegedly corrected in the British Prime Minister's own hand, which might then serve as a basis for a 'Modus vivendi' provided and only provided that Marshal Pétain gave it his assent.

The essence of what was proposed was a reciprocal agreement on the French colonies. Vichy would not try to regain what the 'dissidents' already held and de Gaulle would not make further attacks on French possessions remaining 'loyal'. However Churchill warned the Professor that if a colony elected spontaneously to join de Gaulle, he would stand by the General. As one of the principal reasons for Rougier's visit was to get the British blockade lifted or at least softened, Churchill said that if Vichy resisted the 'threats and cajoleries [sic] of the Germans' and also organized a zone of resistance in French North Africa, then the blockade would be lightened and B.B.C. attacks on Pétain would cease.

These London discussions were interrupted by two telegrams from Sir Samuel Hoare in Madrid, the first of which said that with the agreement of Darlan and Laval Toulon was being turned over to the Germans at noon the next day and in the second the Ambassador suggested that the King should make a direct appeal to Pétain and to Weygand. These telegrams were swiftly followed by the bombshell news of the Hitler–Pétain meeting at Montoire, together with rumours that a peace treaty between France and Germany would be signed. All this, of course, acutely embarrassed Rougier and Churchill's first angry reaction was to threaten to bomb Vichy and to tell all France that he would search out and destroy their government of traitors wherever it went.

Churchill, however, soon recovered his poise saying that the rumours, in any case soon to be proved false, should not be taken seriously and the Rougier–Churchill discussions were to go on as before. Military help was promised to Weygand if he would 'raise the standard of rebellion' and Rougier then went on his way to tackle Weygand personally in Algiers.

The Rougier visit put both Churchill and Pétain into an impossible situation and the document allegedly amended by Churchill (but this was denied by his staff) was never signed nor was the matter taken further. Professor Rougier gave it personally to Pétain on 11 November 1940 when he returned to Vichy from Algiers. Pétain locked it away in his private safe where it remained until 11 March 1944. On that day Pétain took it out and burnt it in the fireplace of his room. Only one other Frenchman ever saw this tantalizing document and that was Pierre-Etienne Flandin who took Laval's place as Minister of Foreign Affairs in December 1940. When Flandin accepted this post, Pétain opened his safe and asked him to read the only two documents it contained. One was Pétain's own account of what had taken place at the meeting with Hitler at Montoire. The other was the Rougier 'Protocol'. Thus Flandin alone was aware of the two props which shored up the Marshal's policy or at least his thinking about it and, as Flandin told the High Court after the Liberation when at last the Rougier mission became public knowledge, the engagements undertaken towards the English were more substantial and precise than those formulated at Montoire.

33

Misery at Vichy

The next major clash between the forces of Vichy France and those of Britain and her allies took place in Syria in the summer of 1941. Between Dakar in late September 1940 and the opening of the Syrian campaign on 8 June 1941, there were no fleet engagements, no set battles and indeed little activity or contact other than what might be called 'police' checks and controls by the British arising from the blockade of France and the need to regard Toulon as essentially an enemy port.

Darlan vented his rage over Dakar by ordering the bombing of Gibraltar. Although several hundred bombs were dropped in two successive raids in which about 100 aircraft took part, very little damage was done, most of the bombs falling in the sea, and Churchill's conclusion that 'the French aviators did not seem to have their hearts in the business' is probably correct. The other reprisal ordered by Darlan was that any British warship found within 20 miles of the French coastline was to be attacked. This of course included submarines in the Mediterranean and was later extended to 'any British warships anywhere which appeared to be "sûrement menaçant"' – a somewhat puzzling instruction to have to interpret since even the smallest and most antique warship must at least pose some sort of threat. Moreover a prudent qualification was added. Should the British warship seem to be obviously superior in force, then it was not to be attacked.

Although it is always easy to be wise after the event and leaving aside for the moment individual qualities and defects, there is no doubt that the men of Vichy had got themselves into one hell of a mess. They were hamstrung by the Armistice terms which theoretically left the French Empire and the navy under Vichy authority but which in practice put real control in German and Italian hands. An instance of this was the management of maritime traffic in the Mediterranean. This was controlled initially by the Italians, then after April 1941 by the Germans as the incompetence and inadequacies of the junior Axis partner became increasingly apparent.

Then supplies to the French armed forces, especially oil fuel for the navy, were strictly rationed and communications rigorously monitored where not entirely suppressed. Even Ministers in the government were only allowed to cross the frontier between occupied and unoccupied zones with German permission. Letters, phone calls and visits between the two sectors of France were all *verboten*. Enslavement was complete, while lip service was still outwardly paid to the idea of a sovereign French state under Marshal Pétain.

Most humiliating of all, however, was the fact that the clever devious French who prided themselves on their ability to nobble a legal or black market way round any rule, regulation or obstruction consistently found themselves outmanoeuvred, thwarted or caught by the dunder-headed *Herrenvolk*. This was because the French had forgotten one cardinal fact – the savage occupation regime they themselves had imposed on Germany after the World War I. It was through that occupation that the despised, starving and bankrupt Boche taught himself the hard way to work every possible trick that could be devised whereby the slaves of a country could circumvent their occupying masters. So now when the roles were reversed, it was scarcely surprising that the Germans seemed always to be a jump ahead. Almost instinctively they knew the wiles, the ruses and evasions the French would essay before the French had worked things out themselves. This did no good whatever to French *amour propre*, nor did it make the daily individual struggle to survive any the easier. According to Taillemite, when it came to the higher direction of affairs

> the Vichy Government made serious and fundamental errors of judgment. To found policy on a victory by Hitler's Germany constituted an illusion resting on a regrettable historic mistake, inexcusable on the part of admirals who should have known better and meditated on the clear lessons to be learnt from the great conflicts of the past. Hitler's ignorance of naval strategy, his indifference to command of the seas the importance of which he seems never to have understood, could only lead him, as it led Kaiser Wilhelm II, to final defeat since, happily for the Allies, Hitler never listened to his Admirals' advice nor fully employed Admiral Dönitz's talents. Moreover, if in France the politicians and the majority of the generals, including Marshal Pétain, had nearly always shown themselves to be totally unaware of the maritime aspect of wars, is it not strange that the numerous sailors thronging the corridors of Vichy only succeeded when it was too late in insisting on a more realistic appreciation of the scene? The stupefying ignorance of Admiral Darlan in certain matters, his complete misunderstanding of Nazi psychology and of the industrial and military capacity of the United States obscured his judgment for too long. It was only at the beginning of 1942, under the influence of Admiral Battet, that he acquired a clear conception of the way the conflict would evolve.

In the latter part of 1940 and during the first half of 1941, two men made the running at Vichy under the somnolent aegis of the old Marshal – Laval and Darlan. Laval fled to Germany and Spain after the Liberation in 1944 but was brought back, condemned to death as a collaborator and executed in 1945. Had Darlan brought over to the Allied side what was left of the French fleet after the scuttling at Toulon and had he later persuaded Pétain to remove to Algiers, he would no doubt have purged his previous collaborative intrigues, de Gaulle would have been shelved and François Xavier Darlan would or might have been given an honoured place in the French pantheon. Between June 1940 and November 1942, however, his collaboration with the Axis enemy, although less open than that of Laval, was nevertheless equally pernicious, ruinous and fatal to the true interests of France and of her tormented metropolitan population.

34

The coveted fleet

On 8 November 1940 Colonels de Larminat, Leclerc and Koenig attacked and 'liberated' Libreville in Gabon, the one remaining area of French Equatorial Africa still under Vichy jurisdiction. This operation was assisted by the Royal Navy in that reinforcements from Dakar were prevented from arriving. Once again as at Dakar the civil population was divided in its loyalties. For the second time Frenchmen fired on Frenchmen. The new Vichy Governor General Têtu recalled reservists to the colours but was disobeyed. The F.N.F.L. sloop *Savorgnan-de-Brazza* put the loyalist *Bougainville* out of action with regrettable casualties. The Vichy submarine *Poncelet*, having fired a torpedo at H.M.S. *Milford* a 1,100-ton escort vessel, was depth-charged and then had to be abandoned by her crew and sunk. Governor Masson of Port Gentil, south of Libreville, who had rallied to de Gaulle in the summer and then later rallied back to Vichy, committed suicide. On 15

and 16 November de Gaulle established himself at Libreville and Port Gentil (as a result being described by von
Ribbentrop, Hitler's Foreign Minister, to Molotov, his
equivalent in Soviet Russia, as 'the quixotic conqueror of
Africa') and the whole of French Equatorial Africa became
the first part of the French Empire to recover its self-
respect.

Meanwhile the harassment of Vichy by the Germans to
allow them facilities at Dakar to establish Control Commissions in North and West Africa and to secure the active
co-operation of the French Navy continued unabated.
Among the many rumours generated in this midden of
intrigue and blackmail in which, it must be said, Darlan
embroiled himself with a certain relish (while at the same
time plotting to rid himself and the Vichy regime of the
presence, influence and authority of Laval), the prime
danger to the British Chiefs of Staff seemed to be that the
two 35,000-ton capital ships, the *Jean Bart* at Casablanca
and the *Richelieu* at Dakar, would rejoin the *Strasbourg* at
Toulon.

There, together with other units of the fleet, a reformed
and powerful force would be brought up to full war
standards and then on a timely declaration of war by Vichy,
would be used against the hard-pressed Allies, or if there
were no actual declaration of war might be seized by the
Germans and Italians by stealth and the use of *force
majeure*. The threat was real. Darlan's order to scuttle and
sabotage rather than let the ships fall into enemy hands
was one thing, the skill of the German High Command in
circumventing such an order was another.

Churchill saw this danger clearly and at once invoked
the friendly understanding of Roosevelt: '. . . if the French
fleet at Toulon were turned over to Germany', he said, 'it
would be a very heavy blow. It would certainly be a wise
precaution, Mr President, if you would speak in the
strongest terms to the French Ambassador, emphasising
the disapprobation with which the United States would
view such a betrayal of the cause of democracy and

freedom. They will pay great heed in Vichy to such a warning.'

Roosevelt, who was about to send a distinguished Admiral and an old friend (Admiral Leahy) to Vichy as United States Ambassador, went into immediate action. 'The fact that a government is a prisoner-of-war of another Power', he told Marshal Pétain, 'does not justify a prisoner in serving its conqueror in operations against its former ally.' He went on to draw the Marshal's attention to the solemn assurances he had received that the French fleet would not be surrendered. Any use of that fleet in hostile operations against the British would constitute a flagrant and deliberate breach of faith with the United States government and would wreck the traditional friendship between the French and American peoples. American public opinion would react with a wave of bitter indignation against France and all American aid to the French nation would end for ever. Moreover after the war when the proper time came to return her overseas possessions to France, the United States would not support this in any way.

Churchill was delighted but still very anxious and a few days later (on 10 November 1940) hammered the message home in another of his Former Naval Person to President Roosevelt communications:

1. We have been much disturbed by reports of intention of French Government to bring 'Jean Bart' and 'Richelieu' to Mediterranean for completion. It is difficult to exaggerate the potential danger if this were to happen, and so open the way for these ships to fall under German control. We should feel bound to do our best to prevent it.

2. We conveyed a warning to French Government through Ambassador at Madrid a few days ago on the following lines: Such a step would greatly increase the temptation to the Germans and

Italians to seize the French fleet. We doubt, not the good faith of the French Government, but their physical ability to implement their assurances that they will not let the Fleet fall into enemy hands. We particularly wish to avoid any clash between British and French naval forces, and therefore hope that if they had thought of moving the ships they will now refrain from doing so.

3. As we said to French Government we should not question good faith of assurances but even if we accept assurances we can feel no security that they will in fact be able to maintain them once the ships are in French ports in the power or reach of the enemy and I must confess that the desire of French Government to bring these ships back, if this turns out to be well founded, seems to me to give cause for some suspicion.

4. It would be most helpful if you felt able to give a further warning at Vichy on this matter, for if things went wrong it might well prove of extreme danger for us both.

Roosevelt reacted dramatically to this second plea. He offered to buy the ships from the French Government if they would sell them. To this Pétain replied 'I would gladly sell them, if I were free, on condition that they be returned to us after the war and save them for France in this way' but, he explained, it was impossible under the Armistice terms, the Germans would never agree and France was under Germany's heel and impotent. They would never be used against England unless the British attacked. 'I must repeat I have neither the right nor the possibility of selling them under present circumstances.'

To this Roosevelt replied that the offer remained open but did not express his amazement that the offer itself appeared to have aroused neither surprise nor resentment. But then few people were aware at that time except very much at second-hand of what was really going on at Vichy, the way the men of Vichy thought or the pressures put upon them by their German overlords each heavy-laden day that passed.

35

Dinner at the German Embassy

The next development took place at an extraordinary dinner party at the German Embassy in Paris on 28 November 1940. The host, German Ambassador Otto Abetz, had at his side General Warlimont, one of Keitel's senior staff officers. The principal guest was General Huntziger, the French Minister of War and Commander-in-Chief of the Army at Vichy (Weygand having been eased out across the Mediterranean to Algiers as the Delegate General of the Vichy Government in North Africa, a 'victory' for Laval, on 6 September 1940). Also present were Darlan and Laval. The evening was to be what the French call 'inquiétant'.

Abetz wasted no time in coming to the point. 'We are here to discuss the basis of the joint war against Great Britain', he announced with cold precision. This was to take the form in the first place of a reconquest by Vichy forces of French Equatorial Africa, Hitler having decreed a fortnight before that the most pressing matter for the French at the moment was to protect French West and Equatorial Africa 'against England and against the de Gaulle movement'. The Fuehrer had also given out that for the present France would be a non-belligerent power. Behind this lay Mussolini's opposition to making France an 'ally' of the Axis since this would hinder the territorial claims he was making on parts of the French empire. Hitler then went on to say that France would also have to accept German military measures on her territory, particularly in the African colonies, and to back these to the best of her ability with her own armed forces.

It cannot have been a very jolly meal for Darlan. Moreover, Abetz went on to say, Hitler had decided that these 'conversations with France' were to be conducted 'outside and apart from the current work of the Armistice Commission', i.e. by von Ribbentrop (Abetz in Paris) and by the Wehrmacht (Warlimont). To make matters even more devious Pétain was *not* to be put in the picture. All such arrangements were to be solely in the hands of Laval. The Fuehrer's intention could not have been hard to grasp – Pétain was to be faced with a *fait accompli*. On top of that the French guests could not fail to notice that no mention was made of any alleviation of the systematic exploitation of the ravaged French economy by the Reich. This was no 'collaboration' Abetz was proposing to his 'friends': this was purely and simply a *diktat*. It also demonstrated the small amount of trust which Hitler placed in his ambassador. One fact alone shone clear and bright. The French were being warned.

Huntziger, however, had not conducted the long Armistice negotiations for nothing. He readily agreed with Warlimont and Abetz that the French must be and indeed were fully aware of the need to defend their African possessions and also of recapturing from de Gaulle French Equatorial Africa. But there were many difficulties, climatic and military, which had to be overcome before any steps could be taken. Nothing could be done at once. Huntziger then went on to detail some of the many reasons, already set out by the Governor General at Dakar, which prevented immediate action to regain 'territories passed into dissidence'. These included lack of resources, 'psychological disquiet' in the colonies and a further threat from the British. All these many and differing factors, Vichy had been told, required a further build-up of arms were fresh Anglo-Gaullist aggression to be effectively resisted.

While Darlan kept quiet watching it all, Laval then took up where Huntziger left off. Laval claimed he could only justify the frequent approaches he was making to the Reich provided that there would be a mitigation of the distress France was suffering. Hardships such as the non-release of prisoners-of-war, the division of the country into two halves and the enormous economic levy imposed by the conquerors – these were the areas in which he looked for relief. Laval appeared to be quite unaware that the Berlin plans to which they had just been made privy had no objective other than to make France an active partner in the German war. Indeed it was abundantly clear that the Reich would only let up in return for a yet more intensive exploitation of French resources. Although the French did not know it at the time (whereas Keitel and Warlimont certainly did), Hitler had already ordered the build-up to begin for the coming attack on Soviet Russia, at that time their solemn ally.

When Huntziger reported on this pregnant evening to Bouthillier, the Foreign Minister at Vichy, and to the rest of the anti-Laval faction, it became clear that there could now no longer be any question of merely containing the spread of Gaullism in black Africa. Now humiliated and defeated, France was to be required to join actively in the war against Great Britain. While at that time no one at Vichy believed the British could hold out for long (or if they did they kept quiet about it), to declare war on their erstwhile ally was more than even Vichy politicians could stomach. If the French were to retain any freedom of action, Huntziger continued, the result of that summons to Paris could only be interpreted as a clear signal to curb Laval. Moreover the reaction of London had to be borne in mind. There would be no alleviation of the British blockade were the 'maréchalistes' to attack the Gaullists in French Equatorial Africa. And behind Great Britain stood the United States threatening reprisals at the drop of a hat. It was certainly going to be a winter of discontent.

36

Exit Laval

The drama at Vichy now quickened. It took the plotters, that is the anti-Laval faction, a fortnight to secure the dismissal and arrest of Laval, still at that time President of the Council of Ministers in Vichy, and of Marcel Déat, leader of what Weygand had dubbed 'la bocherie' in Paris. Then, of course, all hell broke loose so far as the Germans in general and Abetz in particular were concerned.

The labyrinth of Vichy politics is not the concern of this book except in so far as it affected the Admiral of the Fleet, who was at the heart of the plot and who then became the 'Crown Prince' and effective head of the government at Vichy. This was to last until 18 April 1942. At that date the United States had been at war with the Axis powers for some four months and the American Ambassador was abruptly recalled from Vichy when Pétain under intense German pressure again caved in and restored Laval as Head of the Government which then became as deeply collaborationist as it was ever to be.

Now on 13 December 1940 Darlan found he had been plunged into deep turbulent waters, and he had no one to blame but himself. Laval had been sacked by means of a trick which Darlan and Bouthillier had proposed to Pétain at a lunch on board the battleship *Strasbourg* at Toulon on 4 December. The duplicity of this trick which incidentally Laval himself had played on the Bordeaux Government during the run-up to the Armistice, ranks high in the long-established tradition of French political intrigue. It consisted of Pétain calling a special meeting of the Council of

Ministers which, the rumour ran, would pass a decree setting up a new Ministerial team. When the Council met it was all over in twenty minutes. Pétain read from a prepared text asking for the formal resignation of each of their Excellencies. All, including the unsuspecting Laval, resigned as requested.

Pétain then left the room with these pieces of paper and a few minutes later returned to say that the only resignations he was accepting were those of Laval and Ripert, the Minister of Education. Astounded, Laval demanded to know why. He was then told in front of his peers that he no longer had the confidence of the Head of State and that he had been leading France in the wrong direction. Stupefaction turned instantly to rage and Laval, who privately described the Marshal as no more than an ornament of the mantelpiece, treated the Head of State to a lecture on his responsibilities and ended by saying: 'In separating yourself from me, the Germans will know very well that you are turning your back on collaboration.' He then flounced out and was later put under arrest.

Darlan now had his first experience of the ruthless impregnability of the Germans. These events coincided with an offer Hitler had made, in his opinion of great magnanimity, to transfer the ashes of Napoleon's son L'Aiglon, the Duke of Reichstadt, from Vienna where they had been in the Capucin crypt since 1832 to the Invalides in Paris. Hitler imagined that this chivalrous gesture made by a conqueror to the defeated would endear him to the French. The Marshal, however, did not see it that way. Pétain had no relish for the idea of going to Paris, inspecting two German battalions and then of attending a solemn ceremony at the Invalides, stage managed and recorded for the world by the Germans. The reaction of the man in the street that wretched winter was even more succinct: 'We need coal', it was said, 'and they send us ashes.'

Hitler, as might have been foreseen, took Pétain's refusal to attend the ceremony as a personal insult. However as it had all been arranged, there could be no turning back. So now with Laval out of the way, Darlan and General Laure were sent to Paris to comprise in themselves the French delegation at this lugubrious and somewhat sinister midnight ceremony at the Invalides where the coffin was solemnly passed from German into French hands between two lines of torches. When Darlan saluted von Stülpnagel and Abetz, the salute was returned with extreme frostiness and the French General and the French Admiral of the Fleet were curtly told to return to their hotel as Abetz 'had something important to say to them'.

Further humiliation was to be heaped on them the following day. Verbally abused and insulted, they were ordered to take Laval back into the government. When General Laure remarked equally coldly that Marshal Pétain as the Head of the French State was at liberty to choose his own cabinet, the German retort was to send Abetz to Vichy guarded by two S.S. outriders in uniform there to secure the immediate release of Laval who was then removed back to Paris. The frontier between the occupied and unoccupied zones thereafter became hermetically sealed. No one, not even Pétain himself, would be allowed to cross without a German *ausweis*. It was a tough start to the Darlan term of office.

37

Darlan meets Hitler

When this upheaval at Vichy became known on the other side of the Channel, the British reaction, prompted by de Gaulle, was to regard Darlan with an even more wary eye than before. De Gaulle told Churchill that in his opinion Laval hated England but would try to keep out of the war (how wrong he was in that!), whereas Darlan might well bring in the French fleet against us: 'La France ne marchera pas, mais la Flotte – peut-être.' Churchill, of course, had other things on his mind besides Darlan such as the Italian threat to Egypt from Libya, the invasion of Albania and Greece and the Battle of the Atlantic where the U-boats were really taking their toll, but de Gaulle's assessment of Darlan proved to be very near the truth. Collaboration with the Reich by Vichy had become a mangrove with encroaching roots, a growth not to be extirpated until the Liberation of France was undertaken on the Normandy beaches in June 1944.

Two years to the day bar one that he was to be assassinated in Algiers, that is on Christmas Day 1940, Darlan had his first meeting with Hitler. He had been in office a mere 12 days. Darlan took with him two letters from Pétain, one thanking the Fuehrer for the return of the Duke of Reichstadt's ashes and the other explaining at some length the reasons for Laval's dismissal and also why he could not accept Laval back into the government. The meeting again took place in Hitler's armoured train parked near a tunnel at Ferrière-sur-Epte some 40 kilometres to the south-west of Beauvais. The encounter lasted a mere 20 minutes and from Darlan's point of view was a total disaster. 'Never in my life', he confessed to Pétain's doctor, Ménétrel, on his return to Vichy, 'have I ever bawled out one of my subordinates in the way that I was abused and even then the interpreter can only have passed on a small part of that demon Hitler's vituperations.'

The Marshal's letters were tossed aside, nothing was resolved and nothing agreed. What made it even more painful was that Darlan had prepared a carefully worded statement he had intended to make to Hitler which would have enabled him to don the mantle of Laval. This is quoted here in full since it explains Darlan's real feelings and the path he was to follow in the following 15 months which, of course, included the Syrian campaign:

The Marshal envisages conferring on me an important role in the political life of France. In consequence I would like to explain to the Fuehrer my views on the situation. When the Fuehrer granted France an armistice, I was naturally confronted in my role as Commander-in-Chief of the Fleet with the question of what attitude I should take in that respect.

The fact that the Fuehrer accorded an armistice to France when he could easily have occupied the whole country seemed to me certain proof that he intended to reserve a special place for France in the reconstruction of Europe.

It is also true to say that I could well have taken the whole Fleet over to America. In that event the Armistice would have been cancelled. But because in my view the sole hope for France lay in collaborating with Germany in the framework of the New European order, I directed the Fleet to obey Marshal Pétain. This was no easy matter for the French navy which had until then envisaged a glorious battle with the Italian fleet.

However I went on ceaselessly to explain the situation to my officers and draw their attention to the gross error they would make if they opposed Germany in an atmosphere of poison and hatred which would create nothing but ruin and misery in one or other of the two countries. As Europeans the French would have to collaborate with Germany to an extent, it is true, defined by the Fuehrer. France as a defeated country – and I don't forget that for a moment – can only in effect collaborate to the degree desired and fixed by Germany.

So far as I am personally concerned, I have always favoured a Franco-German collaboration ever since I first played a role in French public life. If the Fuehrer refers to certain mistakes in French foreign policy made before the war, I answer that no Head of the Navy in France has ever been consulted by any

Government over foreign policy during the entire twenty years which have elapsed since the last war. Had this been done, events would have taken a different course. So far as my firm *personal* conviction is concerned, the health of France is to be found in collaborating with Germany. However it takes two to make a collaboration – the victor who is master of the situation must also participate. In consequence I very respectfully ask that Germany may continue to collaborate with France.

Laval could hardly have put it in a more fulsome and cringing way. These putative and 'very respectful' ideas of Darlan were not, of course, known in London at the time and only by a chosen few in Vichy. In turn Darlan was not aware that a week before, on 18 December 1940, Hitler had signed the directive for Operation BARBAROSSA, codename for the forthcoming attack on Soviet Russia. This was to be no direct concern of France but it had a part to play in the next 'set-piece' encounter between Great Britain and Vichy France in the eastern Mediterranean in the summer of 1941.

38

The French problem in 1941

Nineteen forty-one was a tough, dispiriting year for the British and their remnant allies. 'I cannot recall any period', Churchill wrote, 'when the stresses of war and the onset of so many problems all at once or in rapid succession bore more directly on me and my colleagues than the first half of 1941.' Encouraging as had been the first victorious counter-attack against the Italians in North Africa, the skies soon darkened with the arrival of Rommel and his Panzers in that theatre of war and with ensuing disasters in Greece and Crete. Occasional shafts of light such as the sinking of the *Bismarck* in May (offset by the loss of the *Hood*) did little to alleviate the gloom of the incessant blitz on the British Isles and of alarming losses of merchant shipping in the Atlantic and Mediterranean. However and despite the greater military disasters which were to befall the Allies in 1942, on 7 December 1941 the United States entered the war following the Japanese attack on Pearl Harbor. Thereafter British fortunes were to be mingled with what Churchill called the Grand Alliance.

Throughout that troubled year of 1941 the French problem – the undeclared war with Vichy and the some-times tempestuous relationship with de Gaulle – never left Churchill's mind for long. The consistent policy towards Vichy, at any rate until the Syrian campaign, remained as it had been from the start, namely that in so far as Great Britain was concerned it was never too late to mend. 'Whatever had happened in the past', Churchill wrote, 'France was our comrade in tribulation and nothing but actual war between us should prevent her from being our partner in victory.'

With Mers-el-Kébir and Dakar in mind this may not have been quite the idea in France but Darlan, Laval and the pro-German faction apart how was French opinion ever to be known? Certainly these approaches to Vichy did not suit de Gaulle who had risked his all to keep the flag flying but whose few followers outside France were woefully insufficient to comprise an effective alternative govern-ment. 'Nevertheless', Churchill went on,

we did our utmost to increase de Gaulle's influence, authority and power. He for his part naturally resen-ted any kind of truck on our part with Vichy, and thought we ought to be exclusively loyal to him. He also felt it to be essential to his position before the

French people that he should maintain a proud and haughty demeanour towards 'perfidious Albion', although as an exile, dependent upon our protection and dwelling in our midst [compare this with Darlan's attitude to the Germans] he had to be rude to the British to prove to French eyes that he wasn't a British puppet. He certainly carried out this policy with perseverance. He even one day explained this technique to me, and I fully comprehended the extraordinary difficulties of his problem. I always admired his massive strength.

Although Vichy had broken off diplomatic relations with Britain in July 1940, a Canadian representative still remained at Vichy, a Monsieur Dupuy, who served as a means of communication with Pétain. On 31 December 1940 Churchill used this channel to make a final attempt to woo the French to their old alliance:

1. If at any time in the near future the French government decide to cross to North Africa or resume the war there against Italy and Germany, we should be willing to send a strong and well-equipped Expeditionary Force of up to six divisions to aid the defence of Morocco, Algiers and Tunis. These divisions could sail as fast as shipping and landing facilities were available. We now have a large, well-equipped army in England, and have considerable spare forces already well trained and rapidly improving, apart from what are needed to repel invasion. The situation in the Middle East is also becoming good.

2. The British Air Force has now begun its expansion, and would also be able to give important assistance.

3. The command of the Mediterranean would be assured by the reunion of the British and French

fleets and by our joint use of Moroccan and North African bases.

4. We are willing to enter into staff talks of the most secret character with any military representatives nominated by you.

5. On the other hand delay is dangerous. At any time the Germans may, by force or favour, come down through Spain, render unusable the anchorage at Gibraltar, take effective charge of the batteries on both sides of the Straits, and also establish their air forces in the aerodromes. It is their habit to strike swiftly, and if they establish themselves on the Moroccan coast the door would be shut on all projects. The situation may deteriorate any day and prospects be ruined unless we are prepared to plan together and act boldly. It is most important that the French government should realise that we are able and willing to give powerful and growing aid. But this may presently pass beyond our power.

General Weygand, Commander-in-Chief at Algiers, was also sent a copy by separate hand. No answer of any kind was received from either Pétain or Weygand. So the New Year began. Weygand presumably did not answer out of loyalty to Pétain, although he was known to be mildly pro-English and strongly anti-German. To sense what Pétain really thought at any given time seems impossible to discover. Yves Bouthillier, his adviser and apologist, concludes that Pétain expected the war to end in a compromise. France might even become the mediator. 'Pétain disliked without hating the British', Bouthillier wrote, 'while he had a "veritable passion" for the United States.' His attitude could be aptly summed up in the instruction he gave to his staff: 'Concerning the British, silence; concerning the Germans, dignity.'

The first half of this ukase certainly applied to anything emanating from London; with Washington it was different. On 21 December 1940 a United States career diplomat,

Robert Murphy, who had had considerable experience in Europe (which included living across the street from Hitler) was appointed the U.S. Consul General in Algiers and had an important series of meetings with Weygand. Then on 5 January 1941, in the thick of a winter reputed to be the hardest for 90 years, Admiral William D. Leahy arrived in Vichy as the U.S. Ambassador and personal representative of President Roosevelt. One of the briefs he had been given by Roosevelt was to act as a watchdog preventing or hindering any help France might give to Germany other than that set out in the Armistice Convention. This would turn out to be an almost impossible assignment.

39

Blockade at sea

Meanwhile the Royal Navy's blockade of Europe and more pointedly of France continued as best it could, concentrating in the Mediterranean between the South of France and the French North African ports. This, of course, did nothing to increase British popularity, the more so since the immediate effects of a blockade fall first of all on the civilian population of the country being obstructed. But once again an essential weapon of war necessarily had to be employed, since the main purpose of such action, imposed at the beginning of hostilities, had been much blunted by the German conquest of most of Europe in the summer of 1940.

In maritime warfare a blockade is a declaration by a belligerent power which forbids seaborne trade with an enemy. Blockade is universally admitted to be a belligerent right to which neutral countries are bound to submit, forming as it does a part of international maritime law. In sailing ship days a blockade became virtually synonymous with investment, since a squadron patrolling off an enemy port prevented all access to that port whether in or out. The long-range gun, the mine and the torpedo, however, ended the feasibility of such a close blockade and its place was taken by a more distant watch miles out at sea on a stop-and-search basis or what became worse by unrestricted U-boat warfare when defenceless merchant ships were sunk on sight and often without warning.

So far as the situation obtained after the Armistice of June 1940, France might be said to have been struck twice by the blockade; that is, not only by the British imposing it but also by their German overlords in the conditions they required to be met before allowing maritime traffic to restart between mainland France and her overseas possessions. These requirements included three days' notice (later 14) to be given to the Armistice Commission before sailings were permitted, no stopping in the ports of any country hostile to Germany, no ships to be allowed to fall into enemy hands and finally 25 per cent of the goods carried to be handed over to Germany, an amount which the British Ambassador in Madrid, through whom most of the information was passed in the early days, considered to be more like 50 per cent.

Of course in practice things were even more complicated than the above might suggest. For instance in the French West Indies where 100 aircraft, several warships, some 20 merchant ships and 300 tons of gold had been sent for safe keeping before the Armistice, an accord with the United States, still nominally neutral, had to be worked out. By this it was agreed that the colonies would remain loyal to the metropolitan government but nothing would be repatriated to France. An American observer would also be permanently attached to Admiral Robert, the High Commissioner and Commander-in-Chief of the French West Indies. Thanks to this arrangement the Antilles were able to buy in America what they needed to subsist.

The German Armistice Commission was told only just enough of the above to allow trans-oceanic traffic to start. Naturally the British who were not party to this agreement did their best to intercept French ships off the African coast or near Martinique where the Americans did not wish them to be escorted. In 11 months of this period out of some 20 crossings in each direction six large merchant ships were captured by the British, one of which, the *Fort de France*, being sent in prize to Gibraltar with a British armed guard on board was recaptured to the west of the Canaries by the cruiser *Primaguet* and a force of destroyers from Casablanca.

The French made a point of forcing the British to admit, after being urged to make a full inspection of the French warships, that there were no Germans on board as they had been led to expect. This story, according to Admiral Auphan in his history of the French Navy in World War II, delighted the navy at Casablanca. The Admiral was perhaps a little disingenuous in overlooking the fact that early in 1941 a determined and ruthless German Commission had been fully established at Casablanca even though no Germans actually went to sea in French ships. Such deviousness perhaps is understandable when set against the plight of France but, it must be said, did continue throughout the war.

Of course a large number of ships managed in one way or another to break the blockade. In a sense this had to be or France would have starved and did indeed suffer to much the same degree as did Spain, a genuinely neutral country throughout the war. The reason for this blockade 'inefficiency', as those who support sanctions have discovered in the post-war years, lay mainly in practicalities.* The

* Talking to French naval officers who were concerned with this at that time, I found they were surprised at what they took to be British laxity or incompetence – 'They always seemed to pick on an empty ship to send into Gibraltar' – but in fact there were simply not enough ships or men for the job. After all Britain was still *fighting* a war at a desperate time with very inadequate resources.

blockade had necessarily to be on the basis of spot checks, much as customs officers will select at random travellers passing through an airport, a hit-or-miss secondary process except in so far as warships returning to Toulon were concerned, since such vessels might be used against the Allies at a later date. Moreover the War Cabinet had directed that tact and understanding should be used: no needless affront should be made which after Mers-el-Kébir and Dakar might lead to an open declaration of war by Vichy. The interpretation of this policy in a force 9 gale or in a submarine-infested area made execution of the order a different matter than the writing of it at an Admiralty desk. In addition there remained a sympathy and a fellow-feeling for the afflicted French who were whenever possible given the benefit of the doubt by those on the spot. In any case enough resentment of British 'arrogance' was caused by the incidents which did occur.

Two such incidents took place in February and March 1941. By then Italian submarines and the Luftwaffe in Sicily had closed the Mediterranean to British convoys to Alexandria and the Eighth Army in Egypt was being supplied by the long route round the Cape. On 7 February, the date Benghazi fell to the Eighth Army, Rommel was received by Hitler and given command of the Afrika Korps with instructions that Tripoli was to be held at all cost. Between that date and a week later when the first German troops disembarked at Tripoli, a British force bombarded Genoa from the sea and sweeping south on its return to Gibraltar detached a destroyer to intercept and interrogate a French convoy of nine ships from metropolitan France to North Africa. The convoy was dispersed but not before it was bombed by Italian aircraft mistaking the convoy (perhaps through the presence of a British warship) for a British convoy to Malta. Scoring a home goal was a frequent event on either side in World War II.

Then on 28 March, the same day that three Italian cruisers were sunk by the Mediterranean fleet at the battle of Cape Matapan, another French convoy from Casablanca to Oran was intercepted by the cruiser H.M.S. *Sheffield* and four destroyers in French territorial waters near Nemours on the Morocco–Algeria border. An action then took place between the French coastal batteries and the British squadron in which one of the shore batteries was destroyed with four killed and 11 wounded. After dispersing the convoy the British withdrew. It is of interest to note that the French report of proceedings states that the British were *not* the first to open fire.

40

Darlan in power

The next trial of strength between the Allies and Vichy France began on 8 June 1941. This was codenamed Operation EXPORTER. Its objective was the capture of Damascus and Beirut from the French which would then lead to the occupation and control of the whole of Syria and the Lebanon. This in turn would shift defence of the Suez Canal 250 miles to the north, relieve Turkey of anxiety for her southern border and secure essential oil supplies from Iraq where a German-inspired revolt had just taken place. Its successful completion five weeks later on 12 July 1941, when General Dentz, the French Commander-in-Chief sued for an armistice, was to end for ever the German advance towards the Persian Gulf and India, the old 'Drang nach Osten' the Nazis had inherited from the Kaisers.

EXPORTER was executed against great odds and with dangerously small, improvised forces at a crucial time in the war when Rommel had advanced to within striking distance of Egypt and the Suez Canal and the Allies had just been thrown out of Crete and Greece with grave losses of men and *matériel*. But why was this 'side show' to the main battle necessary at all?

Once again the track leads straight back to Darlan, Laval and Pétain and to understand how it all came about we have to begin with 9 February 1941 when the French Admiral of the Fleet, in addition to running the navy, became Vice-President of the Council of Ministers also taking over the portfolios of the Ministries of the Interior, of Foreign Affairs and of Information. Thus for practical purposes and for a limited time Darlan became mini-dictator of unoccupied France in the sense that he had now established himself as the highly active second in command and heir to a Head of State with powers under the new constitution theoretically exceeding even those of 'le roi soleil'. The decisive difference between Louis XIV and Pétain, however, lay in the fact that the Bourbon monarch had the resources and was acknowledged as head of one of the largest sovereign states in Europe. Pétain, on the other hand, though nominally independent had the effective powers of a warder in a prison yard.

Moreover the men of Vichy continued to be menaced by Laval now safely ensconced under German protection in Paris, furious at not being included in what came to be known as the 'Synarchie' and determined as never before to bring France into the war at Germany's side in the hope of special privileges to be granted in the event of an expected early peace.

Meanwhile the Germans kept up the pressure to get what they wanted without letting the Armistice terms stand in their way. Although Hitler himself might not be much 'bothered' about France, the German High Command on the other hand persevered in their determination to gain the use of French North and West African ports together with the active involvement of the French fleet provided some sort of deal could be done. It did not much matter what was agreed since treaties could always be abrogated or ignored. The important thing was a German physical presence where it mattered.

It was an uneasy spring for Vichy and then matters were suddenly brought to a head in an awkward and unexpected way by Rashid Ali's revolt in Iraq on 2 May 1941 when the British Air Training base at Habbaniya to the west of Bagdad was attacked by some 9000 Iraqui troops with 50 field guns. This outbreak in a sense embarrassed both the British and the Germans. General Wavell, the British Commander-in-Chief, Middle East had his hands full with Rommel on the Halfaya Pass and in addition was still reeling from the April disasters in Greece and Crete. 'I have consistently warned you', he telegraphed to Churchill, 'that no assistance could be given to Iraq from Palestine in present circumstances and have always advised that a commitment in Iraq should be avoided . . . my forces are stretched to the limit everywhere and I simply cannot afford to risk part of them on what cannot produce any effect.'

Oddly enough the Germans, too, were fully stretched, first by the immense build-up needed for the attack on Russia which was to be launched in June and secondly by their own losses in Crete of some of their most highly trained fighting men. They were further embarrassed by Rashid Ali's timing since no plans had been made to give him practical support, although the Germans had long been fomenting any sort of trouble in the Middle East and the Persian Gulf that might disconcert the British on the cheap.

So when Rashid Ali appealed urgently to Germany for help on 4 May 1941, Abetz in Paris on behalf of the German High Command in Berlin demanded the immediate use of Syrian airfields for the staging of German squadrons *en route* to Iraq. In addition he asked for the supply from French depots in the Middle East of guns, shells, machine guns, rifles and ammunition for the Iraqui revolt. Urgency was stressed. But, as Darlan was quick to spot, this was the first time since the Armistice that victorious Germany actually needed the help of defeated France. New perspectives were opening up and Darlan at once grabbed his chance. Facilities, he told Pétain, could be traded for appreciable advantages.

So with the Marshal's agreement in principle to the use by the Luftwaffe of French bases in the Middle East, Darlan with Bouthillier, Minister of Finance and the Economy, went post-haste to Paris. Once more relying like a simpleton on German good faith, Darlan anticipated the accord he was later to sign on 7 May by sending a telegram to General Dentz, the High Commissioner and Commander-in-Chief in Syria, informing him of the imminent arrival of German aircraft at French Middle East bases and directing him to provide full transit facilities.

From that moment everything turned out to be improvised and done in haste. The Admiral of the Fleet seemed to be gripped by 'intrigue fever', oblivious of the explaining he would have to do on his return to Vichy and brushing aside as 'excessive prudence' Bouthillier's advice not to rush matters. Darlan then went on to sign personally an agreement giving the Germans nearly everything they wanted *before* going on to see Ribbentrop and Hitler at the Berghof above Salzburg where he was to ask almost timidly for the concessions he wanted in return. If Hitler was ever capable of spontaneous laughter, he must have ricocheted about his Eagle's Nest at this visit of Darlan's, in the event treating the Admiral with quiet contempt, decreeing that any concessions to France would be judged by what France gave to Germany and even commenting in reply to Darlan's eulogy of 'the perfection with which the Wehrmacht, that prodigious war machine, functions', adding the tart remark that 'one sees the Admiral does not command it'.

The humiliation, though subtle, was real but must have bounced off a thickened skin because when reporting to the Vichy Council of Ministers on 14 May, Darlan claimed that Hitler had assured him that if France behaved herself, she would not be stripped of her colonial territories which naturally included Syria and that while Hitler no longer demanded direct French participation in the war, he did wish German U-boats to be based on Dakar and negotiations were under way to this effect. Meanwhile, he added, Hitler had declared that the Wehrmacht would be the master of Soviet Russia in three short weeks.

41

The Syrian campaign – I

So began the next outburst of hostilities between Vichy France and the Allies. On 14 May 1941 the R.A.F. bombed Syrian airfields at Aleppo and Palmyra. This first strike had been triggered by the arrival in Beirut on 9 May of a German diplomat by the name of Rahn accompanied by a French liaison officer (a one-time Chef de Cabinet) called Guérard. The latter carried with him a letter from Darlan to the High Commissioner accrediting him with 'exceptional powers'. They arrived in Ribbentrop's personal aircraft on which the French tricolour had been hastily overpainted.

At this point General Dentz's loyalty to Marshal Pétain must have been strained to the utmost. Yet he continued to obey and apparently never considered resigning as did Weygand in Algiers and Boisson in Dakar. However Dentz did receive the two emissaries with an extreme lack of warmth. When Guérard introduced Rahn to the High Commissioner, Dentz said: 'I am an Alsatian. My father emigrated in 1871 to avoid his two sons becoming German. I would be lying if I pretended to express any pleasure in receiving you like this, the more so since one of your colleagues who came here some months ago is the cause of the bloody struggles this country is enduring.' He might as well have saved his breath. Two days later three

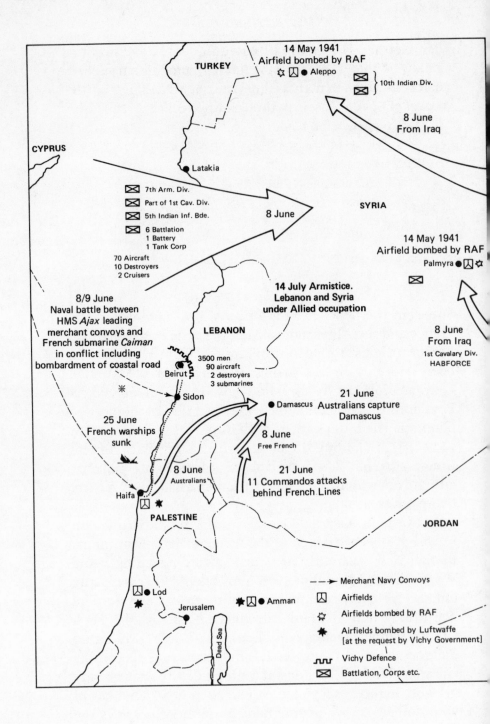

14 May 1941
Airfield bombed by RAF
☆ 🛧 ● Aleppo

TURKEY

10th Indian Div.

8 June
From Iraq

CYPRUS

● Latakia

SYRIA

🛡 7th Arm. Div.
🛡 Part of 1st Cav. Div.
🛡 5th Indian Inf. Bde.
🛡 6 Battlation
1 Battery
1 Tank Corp

70 Aircraft
10 Destroyers
2 Cruisers

8 June

14 May 1941
Airfield bombed by RAF
Palmyra ● 🛧 ☆

🛡

8 June
From Iraq
1st Cavalry Div.
HABFORCE

8/9 June
Naval battle between
HMS *Ajax* leading
merchant convoys and
French submarine *Caiman*
in conflict including
bombardment of coastal road

LEBANON

14 July Armistice.
Lebanon and Syria
under Allied occupation

3500 men
90 aircraft
2 destroyers
3 submarines

Beirut

● Sidon

● Damascus

21 June
Australians capture
Damascus

25 June
French warships
sunk

8 June
Free French

Haifa

8 June
Australians

21 June
11 Commandos attacks
behind French Lines

PALESTINE

JORDAN

● Lod

● Amman

🛧 ● Amman

Jerusalem ●

Dead Sea

- - -► Merchant Navy Convoys

🛧 Airfields

☆ Airfields bombed by RAF

✳ Airfields bombed by Luftwaffe
[at the request by Vichy Government]

ᴖᴖᴖ Vichy Defence

🛡 Battlation, Corps etc.

German aircraft wearing Italian colours landed in Syria, followed the next day by 18 more. The Germans were certainly wasting no time.

By the end of May about 100 German and some 20 Italian aircraft had staged through French Middle Eastern airfields *en route* to Iraq. In addition three-quarters of the war *matériel* assembled in Syria under the control of the Italian Armistice Commission was being transferred to the Iraquis. General Dentz's loyalty to Vichy was later to be rewarded in the High Court with the death sentence on 18 April 1945 and although this was commuted to life imprisonment on 25 October, he died stripped of his rank in the Fresnes prison hospital in December of that year. Against a natural sympathy for this fine soldier who, by his own lights and the noble tradition in which he had been brought up, was only doing his duty by the letter of the law, must be set the casualties of the Syrian campaign which amounted to some 6500 French killed and wounded and over 4600 on the Allied side.

The land attack on Syria began on 8 June 1941 under the command of General, later Field Marshal, Sir Henry Maitland Wilson. The organizing of this invading force had not been easy. All that could be mustered were the 7th Armoured Division, part of the 1st Cavalry Division, which had only recently exchanged its horses for tanks, the 5th Indian Infantry Brigade and the Free French force under General de Gentilhomme which comprised six battalions, one battery and a company of tanks. There was also the added hazard of General de Gaulle, whose demands and behaviour caused delays, anxieties and misunderstanding with the British Commander-in-Chief in the Middle East and began a crisis in London which was to simmer and occasionally come to the boil without ever mercifully spilling over until the end of the war.

The defending Vichy forces under General Dentz amounted to 35,000 men (18 battalions, 120 guns, 90 tanks), an air force of 90 aircraft with a naval force of two destroyers and three submarines based on Beirut. The

R.A.F. mustered a mere 70 aircraft at the start (the battle of Crete had only just ended on 31 May), but the Royal Navy was able to find two cruisers, 10 destroyers and some smaller support craft and thus had command of the sea approaches.

The problem with de Gaulle, whose standing had not been improved by the *débâcle* at Dakar, was that he still believed the French in Syria and the Lebanon would rally to his cause once Vichy control of the region had been broken. In the event he was again to be disappointed, as indeed were the British in their offer to Dentz, made through General Catroux (de Gaulle's 'man in the Middle East'), of both economic and military help in the event of a German attack on Turkey and, by implication, should he decide to resist by force any German military presence in Syria and the Lebanon. Both the British and de Gaulle got it wrong. De Gaulle favoured a strong anti-Vichy policy backed up by a big propaganda effort to rally Syria to the Free French, again repeating the misjudgement he had made in using these methods at Dakar.

The British still could not understand the continued loyalty of French colonial authorities and the armed forces they controlled to the decrepit Marshal who was selling them up the river or at best giving in at every point of stress to the German demands. The cards de Gaulle held in his hand were further devalued by the fact that the Americans, remarkably unimpressed by his performance to date, were still not in the war but had established listening posts in the form of Admiral Leahy at Vichy and Robert Murphy in Algiers.

The Free French at this juncture, although still supported through thick and thin by Churchill, were generally considered by the other Allies as a great pain in the neck, General Wavell even going so far at one point as to telegraph the Chiefs of Staff in London that as they appeared to be relying on the advice of Free French leaders rather than upon his own, he would prefer to be relieved of his command. It took all of Churchill's tact and Wavell's own knowledge of the proved inaccuracy of Free French information on Syria to bring him back to an even keel. All, however, were convinced, except of course de Gaulle, that Free French forces were incapable of tackling Syria alone and Churchill closed that episode in a telegram to Wavell on 23 May 1941 saying bluntly: '. . . it is your views that weigh with us and not those of Free French. You had better have de Gaulle close to you. Let me know if I can help you with him. We cannot have the Crete battle spoiled for the sake of Syria . . .'

Thus it was that when victory was achieved on 14 July 1941, General Catroux did not replace General Dentz as High Commissioner but was appointed only as French Delegate and Plenipotentiary. This in no way helped the status of de Gaulle nor did it keep him quiet.

42

The Syrian campaign – II

Except at sea, things went badly for the Allies during the first 10 days of the campaign. No one on the allied side could judge to any accurate extent in advance how the Vichy forces would react. De Gaulle kept on with the idea that only a token resistance would be offered. However the element of surprise was missing and once General Dentz realized the weakness of the forces pitted against him, he quickly counter-attacked.

The Free French were held 10 miles short of Damascus and were then threatened with being cut off from behind. The Australians going up the coast road from Haifa made slow progress over well-defended ground. Indeed at Kunaitra a British battalion was overwhelmed by a counter-attack of two Vichy battalions with tanks. After a week with little to show, Wavell decided that reinforcements must be sent in, thus further weakening his resources against Rommel on the western front. He also arranged for a brigade group of the 1st Cavalry Division, codenamed HABFORCE, which had taken part in the capture of Baghdad in Iraq, to advance on Palmyra through the desert from the south. Two brigades of the 10th Indian Division, also in Iraq, moved up the Euphrates towards Aleppo.

The Vichy side faced two main worries. One was a Commando landing behind their centres of resistance made possible by the Royal Navy's command of the sea, which in fact took place later on. The other was the loyalty and reliability of the Lebanese and Indo-Chinese troops ordered to fight for the honour of France against their allies of the previous year and also in the knowledge that the common enemy at the start of the war, namely the Germans, were up to something in Syria whatever that might be. In consequence there was a deadpan response to the Commander-in-Chief's call to arms. 'The Germans will say we do not keep our word and that we are incapable of defending our possessions', Dentz told his 'native' troops, 'if you do not fight, we shall disappear and be struck off the map of the world.' The reaction to this was inscrutable silence.

According to one military commentator, General Dentz appeared to be unaware of recent events in France and was fighting this current war on the ideas and policies of World War I. One thing Dentz did see with clarity. Any German presence constituted a danger and a threat to his own authority. Those Germans already there must go and go at once. He therefore demanded strongly and urgently that Colonel Manteuffel and his staff be instantly recalled. Otherwise, he pointed out, public opinion would without any doubt conclude that Hitler intended to take over the country. Huntziger in Vichy immediately passed this warning on to the Armistice Commission and the following day Hitler conceded this withdrawal thus, as Allied propaganda was quick to point out, justifying the Anglo-Gaullist accusations as to his real intentions. However this tactical withdrawal was immediately followed by further pressure on Pétain to turn military co-operation into co-belligerence. Hitler himself might have lost interest in the French question (the German invasion of the U.S.S.R. began on 22 June 1941), but one thing Vichy was to learn to the full was that the German High Command and the relentless civil administration the Third Reich had established in Paris never gave up.

On 11 June, three days after EXPORTER had begun, Vichy agreed to accept the help of the Luftwaffe with the proviso 'for moral reasons [sic]' that this support would come from *outside* the country, that is without the use of Syrian airfields, the targets being ships of the Royal Navy, the airfields of Haifa, Amman and Lydda and convoys between Cyprus and Haifa. General Dentz, Berlin was told, had been ordered to study the possibility of providing the Luftwaffe with up-to-date intelligence. However on 13 June Dentz refused to accept 'any major assistance from the Luftwaffe which would allow the Germans to occupy the whole of the north of Syria' with the result that on the 14th Berlin replied that in view of the flying time involved, substantial air support to operations in Syria would not be possible without the use of ground facilities. On that day, too, Vichy insisted that 'it wished at all costs to avoid the accusation that it had agreed to let Germany use the Syrian airfields', a fine example of wanting the opposite of what you proclaim, provided it can be kept secret, and of shutting the stable door after the horse has bolted.

The above double-dealing which must again be charged to Darlan is the more difficult to understand 50 years on when the attitude of the other two Governors-General concerned (Weygand in Algiers and Boisson in Dakar) is taken into account. Between 21 and 28 May 1941 what came to be known as the 'Protocols of Paris' were agreed with the Germans by Darlan and Huntziger (Minister of War) and by Admiral Platon (Secretary of State for the

Colonies). The document was in German and comprised three main protocols set out in 17 pages. The first concerned Syria and Iraq, with the results described above. The second concerned French North Africa and the third French West and Equatorial Africa. There was also a highly secret additional protocol 'of a political nature' which rounded off the three military ones and which would only come into force if the facilities it was proposed the Reich should have at Bizerta and Dakar led to open warfare with Great Britain and/or the United States.

Essentially the facilities the Germans were going to be given (a U-boat base at Dakar, the same at Bizerta plus use of the railway linking the North African ports for the transport of war materials to the desert front) added up to full military collaboration with the Reich. As soon as Weygand heard via Leahy in Vichy and Murphy in Algiers what Darlan had agreed (but which the government at Vichy had not yet ratified), he alerted Boisson in Dakar and together the two Governors-General, who were of the same mind but did not much like each other, flew uninvited to Vichy. There they proceeded to upset the apple cart. There had never been much love lost between Weygand and Darlan and this was also true of Huntziger who was intriguing to get Weygand retired.

Now Weygand brought a very unwelcome gust of fresh air into the foetid Vichy Council Chamber. Curtly and with force he told Pétain and the Council of Ministers that he was completely unimpressed by any promises the Germans might have made to Darlan. He then stated bluntly that if he were to be kept in the dark in this way he would resign and, for good measure, 'If one single German arrives in Bizerta I shall personally shoot him myself'. This 'bloody nose' given by Weygand to Darlan to the bewilderment of the Marshal in front of the Council of Ministers was backed up by Boisson in so far as Dakar was concerned: 'Not one German in Dakar' was his cry. If German armed forces were to arrive they would be fired on and 'thrown into the sea'.

The Protocols of Paris were therefore never signed, to the chagrin of Darlan and the *bochistes*, who expected an angry reaction from Hitler. Even in this they were disappointed since Hitler and Ribbentrop were fully engaged on other matters and simply lost interest in France while nevertheless ensuring that the civil demands on the country, occupation costs, etc., were enforced with even more rigour than before. On 7 June 1941 Weygand and Boisson returned to their respective pro-consulates. The following day, as we have seen, the Allied invasion of Syria began. Darlan was not having an easy run for his money.

43

The Syrian campaign III

Nor were things much brigher for those elements of the French navy based on Beirut, of which the most valuable from the Vichy point of view were the three large submarines *Caiman, Souffleur* and *Marsouin* of the 9th Submarine Flotilla. Their story began with the receipt of a cyphered signal at 0750 hours on 8 June 1941 announcing the opening of the British offensive and ordering unrestricted attack on all British warships or merchant vessels encountered. The first contact was made by the *Caiman* which picked up a British convoy of five merchant ships escorted by the cruiser H.M.S. *Ajax* and two destroyers heading for Sidon to the south of Beirut. At six minutes past midnight on the night of 8–9 June *Caiman* fired four torpedoes of which one remained in its tube and all of which missed their targets. The *Caiman* was then depth-charged for the next two hours and although damaged managed to escape.

Later that day, 9 June, the two other submarines,

Souffleur and *Marsouin*, were ordered to join *Caiman* in the sector south of Beirut. Their task was to intercept the British force attacking the French destroyers *Guépard* and *Valmy* between Beirut and Tyre, which in turn had been ordered to bombard the British columns advancing up the coast road. From the French point of view such a bombardment could only be in the nature of 'moral support' since all Vichy French ships were very short of ammunition due to the Armistice terms and in any event naval armour-piercing shells are not especially useful for bombarding open targets on shore.

The submarine *Souffleur* found herself in the middle of this confused engagement but was unable to position herself in such a way that her precious torpedoes could be fired with effect. Moreover, she was then picked up on British Asdics (the devices used in detecting submarines) and was unsuccessfully depth-charged. The French destroyer *Guépard*, however, severely damaged a British destroyer, H.M.S. *Janus*, before retiring to Beirut having used up about half of her ammunition and also having sighted a British force coming up from astern. Although *Janus* was kept afloat, her bridge was destroyed and her Captain sported a green beard for the next fortnight thanks to the colour which the French put in their shells to identify the fall of shot of individual guns.

The next day *Souffleur* spotted a British cruiser through her periscope. Ignoring the British destroyer screen, *Souffleur* positioned herself ahead of the cruiser ready to attack but was again detected on the Asdics and forced to go deep by depth-charging while the British cruiser escaped. Four hours later *Souffleur* together with *Caiman* and *Marsouin* sighted the main cruiser force with its destroyer screen and again tried to attack but all were heavily depth-charged and only just escaped. This aggressive action by the three French submarines did, however, disrupt and delay the disembarkation of Allied troops at Sidon and caused Admiral Cunningham to send reinforcements of six more destroyers and submarines.

As the French destroyers were now reduced to about 50 rounds of ammunition per gun, Darlan with the agreement of the Armistice Commission despatched the destroyer *Chevalier-Paul* from Toulon with more ammunition. This ship was expected at Beirut on 16 June but the night before was torpedoed by the Fleet Air Arm some 50 miles to the west of Latakia. The *Guépard* and *Valmy* sent to assist her arrived only just in time to see her sink and to rescue the crew.

From then on conditions steadily worsened for the French Navy based on Beirut. Overland replenishment of supplies had been blocked by Turkey in the north and replacement aircraft coming from France were obliged to stage by Brindisi and Athens. Since pride made the pilots of the 4th Bomber Squadron and 1st Fighter Squadron of the Vichy naval air arm refuse to sit down in an Italian mess and since the German regime imposed on Athens was to put it mildly 'spartan', they arrived famished in the Lebanon and a few days later lost six of their aircraft in a surprise attack by 20 British fighters. When the fighting was over and the squadrons were recalled to France, only four out of 16 aircraft remained. For all practical purposes the French Air force in Syria and the Lebanon had ceased to exist.

Damascus fell to the Australians on 21 June after three days of very heavy fighting and greatly helped by a daring raid by No. 11 Commando which landed from the sea behind the French lines. In this action its leader Colonel Pedder and all its officers were killed or wounded together with a quarter of its total strength.

From then on the pressure on Beirut intensified. Dentz sadly reported defections to the Anglo-Gaullists of numbers of his native troops and overall morale had been severely damaged by the defection of Colonel Collet, a much respected officer who had served in the Levant with General Huntziger. This, at Vichy, caused the loyalty of Dentz himself to be questioned. Huntziger was reported as saying with tears in his eyes that resistance could only be continued for another four days.

At sea the three French submarines did what they could to impede the Allied advance on Beirut and erode the Royal Navy's command of the sea. But on 25 June the *Souffleur* having been depth-charged the previous night off Beirut was caught on the surface recharging her batteries and sunk by a torpedo from a British submarine H.M.S. *Parthian*. From this disaster only four of the crew managed to swim the 4000 metres to the shore, one of whom then defected to de Gaulle which, all things considered, speaks for itself.

On 29 June three destroyers *Guépard*, *Valmy* and *Vauquelin* (from Toulon) were sent to Salonika to embark a battalion of troops who had arrived by rail from France and were headed for Tripoli to the north of Beirut. Darlan had also secured two small cargo ships and loaded them with vital materials (22 anti-aircraft guns, 80 tons of aircraft spares and 400 tons of ammunition). But one of these, the *Saint-Didier*, having survived several Fleet Air Arm torpedo attacks was finally sunk off the coast of Anatolia on 4 July. The other, *Château-Yquem*, after being similarly harassed was recalled in order to avoid the same fate. The destroyers loaded with troops were spotted by reconnaissance aircraft 200 miles off the Syrian coast. This effectively ruined any chance of their safe arrival in Tripoli so they were then ordered to turn round, refuel at Salonika and then make for Toulon. The two remaining submarines were directed to Bizerta, the rest of the shipping being interned in Turkey whence all personnel were subsequently repatriated to France.

44

The Syrian campaign – IV

At 0830 hours on 12 July 1941 General Dentz sent envoys to the Allied High Command at Acre to sue for an Armistice and this was granted with full honours of war on 14 July. Thereafter the Lebanon and Syria came under Allied occupation. Thus ended the first successful campaign Britain and her allies had waged against Vichy France. However this simple statement of fact cloaks a number of unpleasant repercussions and skeletons left in the cupboard. The principal one of these was the reaction of an angry de Gaulle who sent a telegram to Churchill on 21 July saying: 'The terms of the Armistice and the additional protocol signed by Wilson and Vichy are unacceptable to us.' This fury had been aroused because although General Catroux for the Free French had been present at the Armistice negotiations (stiffly described by the Vichy General de Verdilhac as 'correct'), the Gaullists had been unable to prevent an agreement to repatriate Vichy troops to mainland France, which the Free French privately intended to defer *sine die*, nor to have cancelled the prohibition of direct access to the troops under Dentz's command for the purpose of trying to persuade them to join the Free French forces. De Gaulle then threatened to withdraw his troops in the Middle East from overall British command.

Churchill, like Hitler, had a lot else on his mind and did not exactly welcome this latest *feu de joie* from the Free French prima donna. As John Colville, one of Churchill's private secretaries, noted in his diary: 'De Gaulle is behaving abominably in Cairo: quarrelsome and neurotic. Oliver Lyttelton seems to be treating him tactfully in order to avoid a breach . . . Auchinleck (the new C. in C. Middle East who was replacing Wavell) thinks de Gaulle is mad and consumed with personal ambition, which makes him care little for our fortunes in war. But, says A., Oliver Lyttelton has handled him very well.' The upshot was that the Armistice terms were altered and de Gaulle won that particular poker hand, being recognized as commanding in Syria and the Lebanon and with General de Larminat being given permission to 'propagandize' Dentz's officers and men to defect to the Free French standard.

De Larminat had neither a warm welcome nor much success. Between 80 and 90 per cent of the armed forces under General Dentz's command remained loyal to Marshal Pétain and were in due course repatriated to France. Altogether a mere 2500 rallied to de Gaulle, among them only about 100 officers (at the time of the Armistice Dentz had some 24,000 troops still under his command).

The Allied victory was further marred by a disgraceful and shifty trick played by Dentz on the British and Allied prisoners-of-war taken during the campaign. To their surprise and distress instead of being segregated into prisoner-of-war camps on the spot in Syria and the Lebanon, these casualties found themselves hurriedly and secretly shipped off to Vichy France whence they would later on without any doubt have been passed over into German keeping. Luckily this chicanery was discovered as soon as the ceasefire negotiations began. Since no redress was proposed, Churchill immediately directed General Wilson to take General Dentz and his staff into custody as hostages. This locking-up of a General and his staff outraged French pride once again but it did the trick. The prisoners were speedily returned to Beirut and General Dentz and the other high officers in due course released. It is strange that in French accounts of this period of the war no mention is made of this incident, but then only those who have been imprisoned or come under the control of the colonial authorities of a defeated nation know how vile are the effects of hurt pride and of resentment of a one-time ally still determined to fight on to the end.

The fine line between obedience as a virtue and the moral turpitude of 'I was only obeying orders' became all but invisible in an oasis such as Laghouat 200 miles south of Algiers where British naval officers and ratings were held between 1940 and 1942. It was here that survivors from ships and aircraft sunk or shot down in the Mediterranean and brought ashore on the North African coast were interned. And it was in such an unlikely and very apt-to-be-overlooked place that this war between the French and the British continued to be fought. This was the more distasteful because of the unexpected hostility the British prisoners found themselves facing.

As Commander Geoffrey Hare at one time the senior British officer in this wretched establishment put it:

I suppose it was Anglo-Saxon innocence but because we were casualties in a war which France and ourselves had entered as allies and which we were now carrying on alone, we expected to be welcomed as friends, perhaps luckless but still as friends. Instead it was at once made clear to us all that *we* were now the enemy and would continue to be treated as such during our unpremeditated stay in North Africa. We were not legally prisoners-of-war because no war had been declared, we were simply 'interned' so it was some time before the Red Cross could help us in any way and then very few of their parcels got through. We relied on the Protecting Power, the United States, to get us sent back to England via Tangier and Lisbon. However the U.S. Vice Consul told me he was badly overworked but would do what he could, which turned out to be nothing, and we remained half starved and under appalling conditions as 'internees' warned that if we tried to escape, the Arabs in the vicinity of the camp had been promised a reward if they killed us.*

45

Atlantic Charter to Pearl Harbor

Many great changes were to occur before the next armed confrontation took place in Madagascar in May of 1942. During this period and along 'the great highway of the war itself', there were several principal milestones. First, the signing of the Atlantic Charter by Churchill and Roosevelt on 11 August 1941. This proclaimed the joint peace aims of Great Britain and the United States (still not in the war)

*With regard to this glimpse into one of the murkier aspects of this sorry war, Geoffrey Hare sent me the obituary in the *Daily Telegraph* of Commander Dick Jessel R.N. who took over from him as Senior Officer of the Camp des Internées: 'Invalided home [from Malta where his destroyer *Legion* was sunk] Dick Jessel took passage in the destroyer "Havoc" which ran aground on the North African Coast [Cape Bar]. He was captured and shamefully treated by the Vichy French who disregarded every civilised convention for the proper treatment of P.O.W.s. Jessel as Senior Officer showed the highest degree of leadership in captivity . . . and ever afterwards had a noticeable lack of enthusiasm for France and the French.' Geoffrey Hare who is 80 years old adds: 'And that goes for me too!'

The impression which stays in the mind, however, is not really of the evil nature of those on the spot 'who were only obeying orders' but of those much higher up who gave the orders or as St Paul put it in his letter to the Ephesians 'we wrestle not against flesh and blood but against principalities, against powers, against the rulers of the darkness of this world, against spiritual wickedness in high places' of which, of course, there was a more than adequate supply in World War II.

specifically mentioning the 'final destruction of Nazi tyranny'. It might also have been subtitled 'Birth of the United Nations'.

Then in September and October the German Army took Kiev, blockaded Leningrad and advanced to within 60 miles of Moscow. The Russian Air Force had been destroyed in a matter of days, millions of prisoners had been taken in a spectacular and almost unimpeded *blitzkrieg* but the Russian winter was to save the country as it had done from Napoleon in 1812.

As to the war at sea by the end of 1941 1141 British, Allied and neutral merchant ships totalling 4,190,281 tons had been sunk, mostly in the Atlantic, the Royal Navy had lost its famous aircraft carrier *Ark Royal* and the battleship *Barham* at either end of the Mediterranean, which had been closed to through Allied maritime traffic, and was to lose its great new battleship *Prince of Wales* and the battle-cruiser *Repulse* in the Far East in December. In January 1942 two other battleships, *Queen Elizabeth* and *Valiant*, were sunk by an Italian 'human torpedoes' attack in Alexandria Harbour. The limit of pressure on the Royal Navy had almost been reached.

On 7 December 1941 the real turning point of the war was arrived at. The Japanese attacked the United States' Pacific Fleet at Pearl Harbor and by 11 December the United States had declared war on Germany, Italy and Japan. As Roosevelt put it succinctly to Churchill: 'We are all in the same boat now.' The effective combination of the whole English-speaking world in the waging of war and the creation of the Grand Alliance now made it certain, in Churchill's words, that: 'Once again in our long Island history we should emerge, however mauled and mutilated, safe and victorious. We should not be wiped out. Our history would not come to an end . . . Hitler's fate was sealed. Mussolini's fate was sealed. As for the Japanese, they would be ground to powder . . .'

This in the end was so. However the nadir of Great Britain and her Empire's progress through World War II was to be reached in the first nine months of 1942. In this the war against Vichy France played only a relatively unimportant part.

46

Vichy and Algeria

Although in this interim period from July 1941 until May 1942 only minor confrontations between Vichy France and the Allies took place, there were other developments on either side which were to affect them both. While the detailed politics of Vichy are not the concern of this book, the events of May to September 1942 in Madagascar and of November and December in Algeria and Morocco can only be understood if there is some comprehension of what provoked them during the previous year. There is little point in reading history unless a relevance can be found to whatever present is being discussed.

The French are sensitive, some would say hypersensitive, to criticism whenever their national pride is touched. Feelings must not be ruffled by Anglo-Saxon plain speaking especially in matters where those prosy Anglo-Saxons are open to criticism themselves. But facts are facts. However arrogant, haughty and self-interested the British and Americans were thought to be and in consequence resented, it is an unescapable fact that the British and the Americans have twice this century sacrificed entire generations to save Europeans from each other and in the case of France rescued the country from itself.

To ponder this fact is in no way to belittle the heroic Resistance which at this time had just begun to stir. But members of the Resistance were the tiny few and who can ever do more than guess at the real support they received from the French themselves? Today their monuments dotted about the nooks and crannies of the countryside and on plaques on the walls of towns which move one to tears are separate from official French war memorials. They are now as they were then, an *élite* of the courageous outside the main stream. Whatever individual sympathy for the Resistance there may then have been in France itself, it had perforce to be kept private. The vast majority of the nation outwardly supported Pétain until the end was already in sight. Had the Anglo-Americans at huge risk to themselves, to say nothing of the resulting casualties, not invaded first North Africa and then Normandy who knows what would have happened to France? The country had been broken in body and in spirit and there was certainly nothing to be proud of in what went on in Vichy or in French North Africa between the Armistice of June 1940 and the landings in Morocco and Algeria in November 1942.

To begin with Vichy. This was certainly a great time for Admirals in France. As Renée Pierre-Gosset remarks:

They were to be found everywhere except at sea. Darlan had three portfolios, Platon (later to be assassinated as well) was at the Ministry of the Colonies, Esteva was in Tunis, Decaux at Hanoi, Robert in the West Indies. They made Admirals into Regional and Departmental Préfets. Admiral Bard before going to Berne as Ambassador was Préfet of Police in Paris. When 'Commissaires du Pouvoir' were created and directed to see that the officials of the National Revolution acted in an orthodox manner, Admiral Gouton (late of Beirut) was put in charge. Two stories were doing the rounds in France at the time. It was said that to counterbalance the famous 'return to the soil' Vichy was going to found a League for the return of Admirals to the Sea. It was also rumoured that a controversy would take place concerning the succession to

Cardinal Baudrillart. Would it be, according to Canon Law, a Vice Admiral or a Rear Admiral who would put on the purple robe?

It was certainly jobs for the boys so far as Darlan was concerned.

Across in Algeria Weygand had Admiral Fénard (a close friend of Darlan) as Secretary of the Government Delegation to help him and the incompetent Admiral Abrial to hinder him as Governor. Weygand himself appeared to be a hotch-potch of internal conflict. His inconsistencies seemed to be made up of his patriotism, his loyalty to Marshal Pétain, his opposition to the looting of North Africa by Germany and Italy, and the requirement to say one thing in public and to suggest another in private especially so far as Robert Murphy, President Roosevelt's special representative, was concerned. Everybody was confused. When Weygand had first gone to North Africa 'people thought it could only be to prepare the revenge and to put France back into the war. The General fed the people of Algiers on this illusion with the help of marches-past of Spahis and light cavalry in their gay uniforms. We had never seen such a military display in Algiers, even before the collapse of our army. How were the crowds to know that there were more military bands than anti-aircraft batteries on the soil of Africa?'

Since the Germans listened to everything that was said, nobody took seriously the hostility to the Allies which Weygand expressed in his speeches. 'Those who reported his speeches, his partial confidences, accompanied the words with a knowing wink. But when Weygand had to act unfortunately he followed his spoken word, not his "inner thought". He allowed his police force to track down the Gaullists, he had a colonel punished who did not approve the policy of the Armistice, he let British prisoners be interned under appalling conditions.'

So the steady demoralization continued, cynically made worse by the German and Italian Armistice Commissions who bought up all the wheat, fruit, sheep and wine they could lay their hands on and shipped it all across the Mediterranean ostensibly to feed France, in reality as everyone knew for onward transmission to Germany and Italy. What rubbed in the salt was that Algeria had scarcely been touched by the first 18 months of the war which included the collapse of France and the dire Armistice terms. Life in North Africa went on very much as it had always done. Indeed Algerians did not start to suffer directly from the war until March 1941 when a mixed party of 250 Germans descended on North Africa – 'students, economists, Gestapo agents, business-men and tourists. The tourists were very numerous...' – Until then Algerians had remained confident that despite Marshal Pétain's preaching of resignation and the necessity of paying for one's sins, Algeria would continue to be a rich country notwithstanding black market prices and a great increase in the population and could persist in being self-sufficient. However, disillusionment quickly set in once the systematic plunder began.*

47

Exit Weygand

Weygand, however, did not last the course beyond the autumn of 1941. His gesture of defiance over the Protocols of Paris had sounded his own death knell or rather ensured his eventual dismissal. 'The attitude and behaviour of General Weygand in North Africa', Abetz in Paris wrote to

*By the time of the Allied *débarquement* in November 1942, as I saw with my own eyes, Algeria and Morocco had been stripped bare and the population had begun to starve.

Vichy on 25 September 1941, 'are considered by the Fuehrer, the Reich Government and the General Staff to constitute an insurmountable obstacle to the development of a constructive policy between Germany and France. The way in which General Weygand speaks of Germany in the presence of both French and foreign nationals shows that he has no intention of overcoming his hostile prejudices . . .' The German Ambassador in Paris then went on to complain about the opinions Weygand had expressed in the last month on 'the German campaign against Bolshevism' and his hopes that disaster would befall the German Army.

These attacks on Weygand suited Darlan very well. As we have seen, since being appointed Vice-President of the Council and successor designate of the Marshal in February 1941, Darlan had not had an easy time. He found himself in a continual state of frustration and bitterness caused by the many limits set to his exercise of power. In the first place the Marshal had proved to be the epitome of uselessness. He was old, uncertain, wavering and crafty. His hopelessly divided Cabinet ran on 'personal policy' lines. Without being fully in the picture, therefore, and without access to all the files, Darlan in his dealings with the Germans had been thrown back on the intrigues and passions of Benoist-Méchin, one of Vichy's more important men in Paris.

In addition Darlan's lust for power did not endear him to the various police and intelligence sources on whom he had to depend since the army, air force and navy each operated its own secret service, each autonomous and jealous of the others. Finally Darlan's *folie de grandeur* had driven him to demand of the Marshal that Brinon in Paris and Weygand in North Africa should both be yoked in under his own authority and for good measure were to swear a personal oath of allegiance to the Admiral of the Fleet. This 'childishness', as one commentator described it, was compounded by an attempt to have a decree passed putting the secret services and their funds under his personal control.

All this intrigue resulted in Pétain being subjected to

considerable pressure from Huntziger, Minister of War (later to be killed in an air crash on 12 November 1941) together with others all determined to make the Marshal refuse Darlan's demands. This in turn gave rise to a double crisis. One was Darlan's attempt to become the top dog: the other lay in the situation which developed after the Protocols of Paris (which Darlan had signed) were not ratified. This in Darlan's opinion was directly the fault of Weygand and brought the two men to a state of almost open warfare. In consequence Darlan skilfully built on well-founded German suspicions that given various reinforcements to the French Army in Africa, Weygand would turn on the Germans and Italians and redeclare for the Allies.

At last Darlan persuaded the Marshal to send for his pro-consul in Africa and between 16 and 19 October 1941 Weygand was told that the liaison he had established with the Americans and especially Robert Murphy in Algiers rendered his continued presence there impossible. Pétain hoped that Weygand would then resign and as bait offered him another nebulous appointment at Vichy. Weygand rejected this offer with contempt and refused to go unless sacked, so that it took another month for Pétain to be edged by German pressure into a decision. Reluctantly he recalled Weygand from North Africa and then placed him under a form of house arrest in the south of France. This event occurred on 18 November 1941. Thus the last opponent to collaboration with the Germans of any power and standing disappeared from public life at the age of 75, living from then on in semi-imprisonment until the end of the war and thereafter in obscurity till his death in 1965 at the age of 98.

As a corollary to this movement on the French chessboard, on 22 January 1942, shortly after the United States had entered the war, Roosevelt sent a letter to Weygand by the hand of the Secretary of the United States Embassy in Vichy. 'I am convinced', the President wrote, 'that your resolve to do all that you can for the people of France has not ended with your departure from North Africa. I also believe that France cannot but recognize now and in the future that your contribution is and has been for the future greatness of France. I am convinced that your devotion to the best interests of your country in the difficult times ahead will overcome every adverse circumstance . . .'

Blah! blah! blah! from one point of view: from another an unequivocal recognition of Weygand's status, of his resistance to Germany and of future possibilities. In this connection and most important of all the American diplomat then conveyed a verbal message from the President to the effect that 'the United States consider North Africa to be vitally important. They have the firm intention of respecting the integrity of France and her Empire and above all wish to see the French Empire in Africa remain in French hands. They have no desire to see there Americans, British or the partisans of Monsieur de Gaulle [!].' The message ended with President Roosevelt's regret that General Weygand might not be in Africa for 'certain eventualities'.

The diplomat insisted that the President's communication and indeed his visit to the villa near Cannes were to be regarded as totally secret. To this Weygand replied that he was in duty bound to inform Marshal Pétain. In point of fact, the General went on, he did not consider himself authorized to come to an understanding nor indeed to negotiate secretly at all with a foreign power. He would have nothing to do with underground intrigue. One wonders why. After all the Marshal had approved Rougier's visit to London which was understood and fully expedited by Weygand and Weygand himself had certainly been negotiating with Murphy in Algiers. One cannot help wondering whether Weygand, dapper as ever and *toujours correct*, was not just dodging the issue because in fact he had given up. At all events the offer implied by Roosevelt of taking French leadership in North Africa following an American landing there was blandly rejected. The *débarquement* of 8 November 1942 had, of course, neither been thought of nor decided upon, the United States having been at war little over a month. There was no great fount of resistance there. Whatever one thinks of de Gaulle's awkward personality, compare his courage and his firm behaviour with that of the dreadful 'complex of legality' which animated the little men of Vichy.

Nevertheless and no matter what opinions people might hold, Weygand had gone. His departure and replacement by the 'insignificant' Yves Chatel in November 1941 with General Juin as Commander-in-Chief marked the beginning of a year of madness. The last rampart against German demands in North Africa was thought to have fallen. In Pierre-Gosset's words:

> The atmosphere was quite unreal and utterly unbelievable to people who did not live through it. Enemies rubbed shoulders with each other, hundreds of plots were laid, the police were taking violent measures of repression in a musical comedy setting. Treachery, courage, ignorance, venality showed up against a background of doubt as to the morrow, of unvoiced hopes, of irresolute waiting. On this overcrowded stage, the American consuls played the main parts. In this winter of 1941 in North Africa there were dozens of them, surrounded by secretaries and others, civil servants with apparently ill-defined jobs. Usually charming in manner, sometimes erratic, they were much in view, flitting around making contacts. It was impossible to fathom the reason why they had been chosen for their jobs; thus John Boyd was a commercial man, Redgway Knight represented a firm of French wine merchants in the United States, Kenneth Pendar, amongst other accomplishments, was an archaeologist, another one was one of the main adornments of Harry's Bar in Paris . . .

Overlying it all and no matter how deplorable and chaotic the situation in North Africa might seem to be, there was little doubt that by the beginning of 1942 Darlan could justifiably claim to be the overlord both of Vichy and of the French Empire overseas, at least in so far as the command structure was concerned. Only one fly in the ointment remained and that was Laval in Paris. And before six months had passed Laval was to be the downfall to all Darlan's most cherished hopes and ambitions.

48

The French problem in 1942

The 'year of madness' which opened with Weygand's departure climaxed on 8 November 1942 with Operation TORCH, the Anglo-American invasion of Algeria and Morocco. Thus the hot war between Vichy France and the Allies began and was to end in French North Africa. However, matters in question were not to be tidied up with the ease and simplicity which that bald statement might imply. Relationships between Vichy and Berlin, between Hitler and his Axis partners, between Churchill, Roosevelt and de Gaulle, were all to develop and modify in ways which could not be foreseen following upon the entry into World War II of the United States and Japan. So although the Vichy French and the Anglo-Saxons had stopped shooting at each other by the end of 1942, it could not be said that from then on everything in the garden was lovely.

Indeed even when the fighting in Europe came to an end on 8 May 1945 (now a public holiday in France), settlements had still to be made. Civil war is the worst disaster which can befall a free nation and although Woodrow Wilson might claim, as he did in 1915, that the American Civil War of 1861–65 created something which had never existed before – 'a national consciousness. It was not the salvation of the Union: it was the rebirth of the Union' – I do not think the same could be said of France in 1945. The internal disunion of the country and the divided loyalties that resulted had not been put to rights on the Normandy beaches or by de Gaulle's arrival in Paris on 25 August 1944 in the wake of Allied troops. The contentions and disunity remained. I suspect they lurk under the surface even to this day.

However before setting out these last events of the shooting war which took place in Algeria and Morocco, the alarming success of the Japanese in the Far East during the first three months of 1942 caused the Allies to look to the security of their supply lines round the Cape of Good Hope to Egypt, India and the Gulf. Were the Japanese to drop in on Madagascar as they had surprised Pearl Harbor on 7 December 1941, they would not only acquire the fourth largest island in the world, in area nearly as large as the whole of neighbouring South Africa, but would also be able to paralyse convoys in the Indian Ocean and possibly in addition destablilize the eastern coast of the African continent.

Madagascar had been a French colony since 1896 and at the northern tip of the island the French had constructed a naval base at Diego Suarez which but for Vichy would have been of sizable use to the Allies. Now as Churchill said to Roosevelt on 7 February 1942, a week before the fall of Singapore: 'If the Japanese turned up, Vichy will offer no more resistance to them than in French Indo-China . . . we have therefore for some time had plans to establish ourselves at Diego Suarez by an expedition either from the Nile or from South Africa. But at present our hands are too full.'

This telegram had been provoked by impending discussions in Vichy, of which Churchill was informed, between the United States Admiral Leahy and Darlan which might imply a recognition of continued Vichy control of Madagascar. This naturally worried Smuts in South Africa as much as it did Churchill: 'I look upon Madagascar as the key to the safety of the Indian ocean', Smuts said, 'and it may play the same important part in endangering our security there that Indo-China has played in Vichy and Japanese hands. All our communications with our various war fronts and the empire in the East may be involved.'

These immediate fears were set at rest by Roosevelt's terse reply: 'You can be sure there will be no guarantees given about non-occupation of Madagascar and Réunion.' Fears might be lulled; the problem itself remained, the more disquieting since Leahy reported to the President that Darlan had just agreed with Italy, perhaps behind the Marshal's back, to send 200 tons of food supplies to Rommel via Tunisia each week in French bottoms plus 500 Italian trucks. He had thus committed Vichy to direct participation in the war against the Allies and having already ceded 50,000 tons of shipping in Indo-China for the 'civilian' use of the Japanese, sailing under the Japanese flag, what might his support of the Axis and his continuing hatred of England allow him to give to the Japanese where Madagascar was concerned?

The threat could only grow in intensity with the steady replacement of 'Weygand-type officers' in key military appointments overseas with others docile to Vichy. Moreover Leahy was of the opinion that Vichy would now allow the Axis any use of its shipping that might be demanded. So the problem of Madagascar, already serious, had now begun to be pressing. What to do about it was something else.

There was, of course, de Gaulle. As far back as 16 December 1941, nine days after Pearl Harbor, de Gaulle had proposed a Free French operation against Madagascar. Now on 19 February 1942 he again wrote to Churchill pressing for a decision, at the same time submitting a plan to the Chiefs of Staff for a Free French expedition with British air and naval support. But experience of working with the Free French at Dakar and in Syria made Churchill say to the Chiefs of Staff: 'Whatever happens we must not have a mixed expedition. Either it must be Free French only, once they have been put ashore, or British Empire only.' In reporting de Gaulle's proposals to Smuts, Churchill commented '. . . we are doubtful whether the necessary Free French forces are available. We are most anxious not to reject de Gaulle's plan out of hand but we cannot afford to risk a failure particularly in view of the present attitude of the Vichy Government.' He might have added that after the experiences of Dakar and Syria both the British and American Chiefs of Staff wanted to have as little to do with de Gaulle as was possible. This was not a helpful start should a joint operation perforce have to be undertaken.

The matter became more urgent in March. By then the Japanese had landed in Java in strength and both Singapore and Rangoon had fallen. There was now a very real threat to the Bay of Bengal and Ceylon. What Churchill described as the 'invaluable' harbour of Diego Suarez could not be allowed to fall into enemy hands. The rest of the island could wait but the likelihood of a Japanese submarine flotilla operating from the northern tip of Madagascar would be a nightmare.

So the decision to invest Diego Suarez was taken by the British War Cabinet on 12 March 1942. 'This rather expensive move', as Liddell Hart described it, may or may not have been essential. Hindsight however well informed is usually a false friend to historians, and to compare the taking of Diego Suarez to the sinking of the French Fleet at Mers-el-Kébir is not really to the point. Certainly to dismiss Operation IRONCLAD in one paragraph, ending with 'fear proved in the long term a bad counsellor', is to denigrate those who were obliged to make careful strategic calculations in that difficult and dangerous spring, when Allied fortunes were at their lowest ebb.

We know now that on the same day the British decision to invade Diego Suarez was taken, Admiral Raeder in Berlin reported to Hitler that:

the Japanese have recognised the great strategic importance of Madagascar for naval warfare . . . they are planning to establish bases on Madagascar in addition to Ceylon, in order to be able to cripple sea traffic in the Indian ocean and the Arabian sea. From these they could likewise successfully attack shipping round the Cape. Before establishing these bases Japan will have to get German consent [!]. For military reasons such consent ought to be granted. Attention is called to the fact however that this is a matter of great political significance since it touches on the basic question of France's relation to the Tripartite Powers on the one hand and the Anglo-Saxon on the other. Such action on the part of the Japanese may have repercussions in the French homeland and the African colonies as well as in Portuguese East Africa.

Hitler, however, disdained to pay much attention to anything Admiral Raeder might suggest (Raeder was to be replaced by Dönitz before the year was out) and merely replied that he did not think France would give her consent to a Japanese occupation of Madagascar. But Vichy could no more prevent the Japanese from landing or reinforce Madagascar than it could Indo-China. Who knows what Darlan and Laval would have done had the Japanese decided to press the point?

Once the decision to go ahead with Operation IRON-CLAD was taken on 12 March 1942, the detailed planning and the assembling of the military force under Major General Sturges, Royal Marines, proceeded with a practised speed and in complete secrecy, the first requirement of which was that no hint of the impending operation should be given to de Gaulle and the Free French. The invading force was to be entirely British or British Empire and consisted of a specially trained Royal Marine Commando, the 25th Independent Brigade and two brigades of the 5th Division which were already under orders to sail in a convoy to the Middle East. De Gaulle was no doubt going to feel aggrieved, but he had let the cat out of the bag over Dakar and his subsequent behaviour over Syria and more recently his arbitrary seizure of the Canadian islands of Saint Pierre and Miquélon 'contrary to the agreement of all parties concerned', as Cordell Hull the American Secretary of State put it, 'and certainly without the prior knowledge or consent in any sense of the United States Government', did nothing to endear him to the British and American Chiefs of Staff to whom he continued to be a pain in the lumbar regions for the rest of the war.

Roosevelt had little use for de Gaulle or for what Cordell Hull referred to as 'the so-called Free French' and it is somewhat ironic that Churchill, whom de Gaulle frequently irritated and at times insulted, alone had the understanding and magnanimity to support 'moi la France' through thick and thin. This support, however, did not include counting him in nor even putting him in the picture so far as the invasions of Madagascar, North Africa and Normandy were concerned. In matters of security it was a sad fact that the French were simply not to be trusted.

The naval problems of mounting such an expedition over 7000 miles from the United Kingdom, great in themselves, were exacerbated by the menace of the new German battleship *Tirpitz* in home waters and by the fact that under present conditions it was impossible to draw units away from the Eastern Fleet to cover the IRONCLAD landings. The whole of Force H would have to be used and this would leave Gibraltar and the western exit of the Mediterranean uncovered and at risk. Roosevelt's aid was invoked and while Churchill's first idea of replacing Force H at Gibraltar with an American task force of two battleships, an aircraft carrier, cruisers and destroyers was not accepted, the President did attach the latest United States battleship and other important warships to the British Home Fleet.

So the planning and mounting of the first British Empire large-scale amphibious assault since the Dardanelles in 1915 went into high gear and its completion in three days from 5 to 7 May 1942 was to prove to be not only a complete success but also 'in its secrecy of planning and precision of tactical execution a model for amphibious descents. The news arrived at a time', Churchill wrote, 'when we sorely needed success. It was in fact for long months the only sign of good and efficient war direction of which the British public were conscious.'

There was indeed little cheerful news to be had during the first nine months of 1942.

49

Madagascar – I

The expedition sailed on 23 March 1942. This meant that the plans had to be drafted and the four assault ships loaded in 11 days, a feat only made possible by the fact that the key personnel concerned had been training for just such an operation for the previous four months. A project to capture Diego Suarez had in fact been initiated on 23 December 1941 under the codename of Operation BONUS. For this Major General Sturges had been nominated as Joint Commander with Rear Admiral Drew and by the time BONUS was put in abeyance on 15 January 1942 draft plans had been made and a rehearsal organized which, despite the removal of the greater part of the assault troops, nevertheless took place on a reduced scale and was the first combined operation exercise since the previous October in which the naval and military staffs, the landing craft crews, the beach parties, the docks operating personnel and the naval and military signals all worked together. Lessons were learned which were to prove invaluable on Operation IRONCLAD, especially according to General Sturges, '. . . the extreme importance of close scrutiny of landing tables, so that essential vehicles had priority in

landing and that these had a high cross country performance. All units had to be prepared to make long advances
with very little transport. Although the facts were well
known to all concerned in combined operations, a new
standard was set by the difficult beaches and terrain used
in this exercise.' Such standards were to be further raised in
North Africa in November 1942, in Sicily in July 1943 and
in Normandy in June 1944.*

Rear Admiral E.N. Syfret, flying his flag in the battleship
H.M.S. *Ramillies*, then in the Indian Ocean, was nomin-
ated as Combined Commander of the expedition and
Major General R.G. Sturges, Royal Marines, as the Military Commander and second-in-command. To add to his
problems Sturges was informed that no meeting with
Syfret would be possible until the convoy in which the
expedition would sail reached Freetown. However Syfret
was to be represented by Captain G.W.A. Waller R.N. as
Chief of Staff for the operation, Captain G.A. Garnon-
Williams R.N. who had been Chief of Staff to Rear Admiral
Drew was nominated as Senior Naval Officer (Landing)
and Naval Assault Commander and Brigadier F.W. Festing
who commanded 29 Independent Brigade (the only formation trained in Combined Operations on the expedition)
became the Military Assault Commander. This small
close-knit team and its staff had four days in which to load
the ships and prepare the force for its departure.

This was a far more skilled and complicated task than
might at first sight appear, since whatever goes first into
the hold of any ship will be unloaded last at the other end of
the voyage probably in bad sea conditions or under fire.**

*Forty years on they again proved their value in the Falklands
War.
**The possibility of human error has always to be borne in mind,
vide the dental chair and equipment which was one of the first
'essential' stores to be unloaded after the assault on Algiers in
November 1942. Happily few if any such mistakes were made on
Operation IRONCLAD, although compared with subsequent
Combined Operations, the Madagascar expedition was a small-
scale affair.

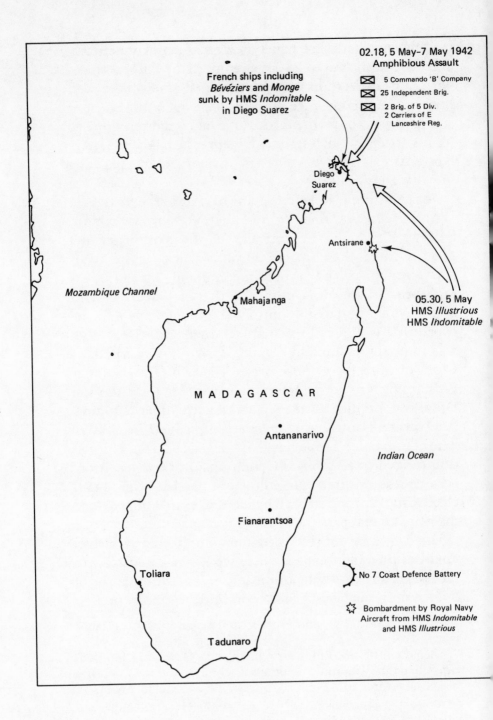

French ships including *Bévéziers* and *Monge* sunk by HMS *Indomitable* in Diego Suarez

02.18, 5 May–7 May 1942
Amphibious Assault

⊠ 5 Commando 'B' Company

⊠ 25 Independent Brig.

⊠ 2 Brig. of 5 Div.
2 Carriers of E Lancashire Reg.

Diego Suarez

Antsirane

05.30, 5 May
HMS *Illustrious*
HMS *Indomitable*

Mozambique Channel

Mahajanga

M A D A G A S C A R

Antananarivo

Indian Ocean

Fianarantsoa

Toliara

No 7 Coast Defence Battery

☆ Bombardment by Royal Navy Aircraft from HMS *Indomitable* and HMS *Illustrious*

Tadunaro

The pace at which everything had to be done can be gauged from General Sturges's operation report of the 15 June 1942 from Diego Suarez:

> On 17 March I met Major General H.P.N. Berney-Ficklin MC, Commanding 5 Division from which 17 Infantry Brigade Group was to be taken. On 18 March, I was interviewed by the Chiefs of Staff on my plans for the operation and on 19 March I met the Prime Minister. On the evening of the same day I left for my H.Q. at Melrose and on 21 March embarked in M.V. 'Winchester Castle'. On 22 March I saw Lt. General E.C.A. Schreiber DSO Commanding the Expeditionary Force which I was now leaving. On 23 March the Winchester Castle sailed.

The expedition had a mere three days at Freetown from 6 to 9 April where Sturges met his Commander, Rear Admiral Syfret, for the first time. Then at Durban between 22 and 26 April final plans were discussed and agreed, vehicles, guns and equipment checked, serviced and waterproofed, units sent on daily route marches to harden and get them fit after the voyage out and then on the 26th the slow and on the 28th the fast convoy containing all the personnel ships sailed. 'At dusk 4 May', General Sturges reported, 'the complete convoy, which now consisted of the slow and the fast elements, formed up in its assault formation and I observed with some relief that, when darkness fell, we did not appear to have been discovered by enemy air reconnaissance or surface vessels.'

Between 0218 and 0319 hours on 5 May the assault flotillas left for their three beaches by a route which the French defenders, it was subsequently discovered, considered to be impossible, and at 0430 5 Commando with B Company and two carriers of 2 East Lancashire Regiment landed at their beach unopposed. Three-quarters of an hour later they captured No. 7 Coast Defence Battery (four 6.1-

inch guns), the French garrison being found asleep and offering no resistance. By daylight all beaches were in British hands and the main landings of troops and vehicles had begun. Surprise had been complete.

50

Madagascar – II

With the assault force ashore the next requirement was to get control of the air and at first light (about 0530) aircraft from the two carriers H.M.S. *Illustrious* and *Indomitable* bombed the aerodrome some six miles south of Antsirane and also attacked shipping in the harbour. This was described in the Operation Report as 'most successful and appears to have deprived the enemy of any means of air reconnaissance or support, except for a few isolated machine gun attacks by aircraft from the south, which were promptly dealt with by the Fleet Air Arm.'

This simple statement needs a word of explanation. There were in fact only four French fighters permanently stationed at Diego Suarez. The rest of the force, 17 in all, were at Tananarive over 600 miles to the south. This meant that in order to be effective at the northern tip of the island they would have had to refuel before going into action. Moreover unlike the Fleet Air Arm the French Army of the Air was not under naval control but was independently commanded. No doubt life was more agreeable in the capital of Madagascar rather than in the 'outpost' of Diego Suarez, but it is difficult to find a good service excuse for the French Air Force not being where it was most likely to be wanted and certainly the Admiralty at Vichy in a preliminary study it issued on 21 May 1942 (based on a Reuter report for lack of direct news from the Governor at Tananarive) was forced to observe that although the four fighters did their best and 'brought down some British aircraft they had no serious effect on the troops' advance'. Nor did Vichy know if reconnaissance aircraft (Potez 63) had tried to work with the four submarines based on Diego Suarez and more particularly to discover the whereabouts of the British aircraft carriers.

Although four submarines were based on Diego Suarez, only one, the *Bévéziers*, was alongside in the harbour at the time of the attack, and she was sunk by the Fleet Air Arm before having time to get away from the jetty. The crew of the *Bévezier*, however, survived and joined the 4000 army personnel in defending the base, only surrendering during the night of 6–7 May after the submarine's Commanding Officer, Lieutenant B. Richard, had been seriously wounded by a hand grenade.

Of the other three submarines, *Héros*, *Monge* and *Glorieux*, two were at sea and one at Majunga 350 miles to the south on the west coast. Captain Maerten commanding the naval establishment at Diego Suarez immediately recalled them at the same time ordering them to 'torpedo any enemy ships encountered en route'. The *Héros*, 500 miles to the north and escorting a merchant ship to the beleaguered garrison at Djibouti, turned south and made her best speed on the surface at 17 knots. It took her the better part of two days to reach Courrier Bay by which time the fighting on land was nearing its end. She was then spotted by a Swordfish from *Illustrious*, depth-charged and sunk. Twenty of her crew were lost, the remainder being rescued by H.M.S. *Keren*, one of the assault landing ships, out of a shark-infested sea.

The *Monge*, recalled from La Réunion whither she had just escorted a convoy, also arrived off Pointe Orangea at dawn on 7 May, her arrival coinciding, unluckily for her, with a daring exploit by a British destroyer H.M.S. *Anthony* which had with considerable skill penetrated the harbour entrance during the night and had landed 50 Royal

Marines from the flagship *Ramillies* on a central quay,
then escaping under heavy fire. This brilliant and carefully
calculated dash resulted in the capture of the naval base
with its large supplies of rifles and machine guns (and 50
British prisoners-of-war). The main British fleet then
decided to anchor in the harbour of Diego Suarez and *en
route* H.M.S. *Indomitable* at 0756 hours on 8 May was
attacked by the *Monge* which was promptly sunk by
Indomitable's escorting destroyers with the loss of all
hands. This was especially tragic as Captain Maerten and
Colonel Claerebout had by then surrendered and all
fighting on land had ceased.

The fourth submarine, the *Glorieux*, made her way
north from Majunga and on 6 May was ordered to attack
the British fleet to the west of Courrier Bay. This she
attempted to do but the high speed manoeuvring of the
British capital ships and their attendant destroyers kept
them out of range. Two days later and at the point of
exhaustion *Glorieux* asked Diego for instructions but
naturally got no reply. Then during the night of 8–9 May
she received a signal from Vichy saying that Diego had
been captured and that *Glorieux* should now go south to
Majunga and later round the Cape to Dakar. In his
Operation Report Commandant Bazoche ended by saying:
'All on board felt the keen disappointment I did myself at
sighting the best target a submarine could ever be given
without also having a chance of attacking it.' Altogether
the French lost three submarines, a frigate, 171 dead and
343 wounded. British losses were 105 killed, 283 wounded
and 4 missing.

The French were accorded the full honours of war and a
protocol similar to that agreed in Syria was signed,
repatriation when circumstances permitted being promised to those who wished it. The garrison and the naval
prisoners-of-war were then sent to England where, it was
hoped, they would see sense and opt for de Gaulle. Few of
them did. Captain Maerten, however, who two years
before had lost his ship in the British attack on Mers-el-

Kébir, was now disgusted with Vichy and asked if he could join the British armed forces but, pointedly, *not* de Gaulle and the Free French. This in due course he did in the Special Operations Executive with great success and a secrecy still preserved to this day.

So Diego Suarez had been captured and the convoy routes in that part of the Indian Ocean and the Mozambique channel put firmly back under British control. The rest of Madagascar, however, remained in Vichy hands. As always over the previous two years the British hoped the Vichy French would remember that they had entered the war allied with the British and would now have a change of heart. As always, of course, that hope was forlorn.

To have taken over the whole of Madagascar at that time by force would have diverted military resources needed urgently in Egypt and in India. Nevertheless this action was strongly urged by Smuts who pointed out that 'Tamatave and Majunga, as well as other ports, have been regularly used by French submarines and can be so used by the Japanese. Madagascar authorities are violently hostile, though not the population. After capture of Diego no material resistance likely at present but if time is given to organise resistance we may have a stiff job . . .' Churchill, however, decided that while Diego Suarez should be made secure with the minimum forces, other operations in Madagascar should be abandoned for the present. Thus on 15 May he explained to Admiral Syfret who had been his Naval Secretary at the Admiralty and was a personal friend:

I want you to see clearly our picture of the Madagascar operation. It must be a help not a hindrance. It must be a security and not a burden. We cannot lock up active field army troops there for any length of time. The 13th and 17th Brigades must go on to India almost immediately. If you could take Tamatave and Majunga in the next few days they could help you in this, but they have got to go on anyhow.

Since Ironclad was conceived and executed the
Indian ocean situation has changed to our advantage.
Time has passed. The Japanese have not yet pressed
their attack upon Ceylon or India. On the contrary,
these dangers look less near and likely than
before . . .

It may be that you will think it better to let
matters simmer down and make some sort of modus
vivendi with the French authorities. Money and
trade facilities should be used . . .

To this Admiral Syfret replied: '. . . so far as our occupation of Diego Suarez is concerned, I think French will
adopt policy of live and let live. But we shall never get any
closer relations or extend our control unless we occupy
Tamatave and Majunga . . . I do not think this will ever be
achieved except by force.'

Nor was it. The Vichy Governor General remained
obdurate. So four months later when further resources
were to hand, the 29th British Infantry Brigade under the
orders of the General Officer Commanding East Africa
landed and captured Majunga on 10 September 1942, later
rounding the island and capturing Tamatave on the 18th.
A pincer movement with South African troops was then
applied to the capital and seat of government, Tananarive,
which fell on 23 September. 'Our troops were welcomed
by the inhabitants', Churchill wrote, 'but the Governor-
General and some of his staff had retreated southwards
with his troops. He was pursued, and a very successful
action on October 19 brought in 750 prisoners at the cost
of no casualties to ourselves. This was final. On November
5 the Governor-General accepted our surrender terms.
The government of the island was left in French hands.
But as a result of these operations, and at a cost of little
more than a hundred casualties, we had gained full
military control over an island of high strategic importance to the safety of our communications with the
Near and Far East.'

Three days later the Allied invasion of North Africa began. The end of Vichy as a government with any power was now close at hand.

5 I

De Gaulle's reaction

The capture of Diego Suarez without his being consulted infuriated de Gaulle, as indeed did the derisory number of French prisoners-of-war from the operation who opted to join the Free French rather than be repatriated. The bitter anger de Gaulle felt made him threaten to break with both the British and the Americans and he was only dissuaded from flouncing out by the wiser counsels of his staff with General de Larminat taking the lead. Since de Gaulle was not to be counted in on any of the subsequent Allied invasions and since this pestiferous struggle with Vichy France climaxes with and virtually dwindles away after the invasion of North Africa in November 1942, de Gaulle cannot disappear from the story without a word of explanation. Yet how in a few short sentences can a greater than life-size figure such as de Gaulle be encapsulated, the more especially when the restoration he gave to France after the war, indeed France's comparative stability, prosperity and standing in the world of today, must all in the first place be credited to this flawed but extraordinary man?

However, we are now concerned with 1942 and primarily with the Americans whose entry into the war had changed the whole balance of power. Why did Roosevelt distrust and dislike de Gaulle (even though when he met him for the first time at Casablanca in 1943 he was 'attracted by the spiritual look in his eyes')? Part of the answer could be that from the outbreak of the European war in September 1939 until the spring of 1942, the United States maintained close diplomatic relations with the legally elected French government, first in Paris and then at Vichy, and even when Admiral Leahy was recalled at the Germans' behest, a Chargé d'Affaires remained at Vichy and a diplomat with greater powers and experience (Robert Murphy) continued *in situ* in French North Africa, becoming in one sense the fulcrum on which Operation TORCH was to lever itself to success.

In other words an American presence in France and in her dominions overseas extended throughout the war and that presence influenced and was respected by the government of Marshal Pétain. In such a context de Gaulle was nothing but a dissident, an outlaw and a rebel. A rebel with a cause, perhaps, but not a cause supported by the vast majority of the French population. 'Here he was', as Churchill said, 'a refugee, an exile from his country under sentence of death, in a position entirely dependent upon the goodwill of the British government, and also now of the United States.' Churchill was well aware that de Gaulle was no friend of England,

but I always recognised in him [which Roosevelt never did] the spirit and conception which, across the pages of history, the word 'France' would ever proclaim. I understood and admired, while I resented, his arrogant demeanour . . . the Germans had conquered his country. He had no real foothold anywhere [it was that, perhaps, which put the Americans against him]. Never mind; he defied all. Always when he was behaving worst, he seemed to express the personality of France – a great nation, with all its pride, authority and ambition.

Roosevelt, on the other hand, was to write to Churchill on 12 November 1942 after the TORCH landings:

... in regard to de Gaulle, I have hitherto enjoyed a quiet satisfaction in leaving him in your hands. Apparently I have now acquired a similar problem in brother Giraud. I wholly agree that we must prevent rivalry between the French emigré factions, and I have no objection to a de Gaulle emissary visiting Giraud in Algiers. We must remember that there is also a cat-fight in progress between Giraud and Darlan each claiming full military command of French forces in North and West Africa. The principal thought to be driven home to all three of these prima donnas is that the situation is today solely in the military field and that any decision by any one of them, or by all of them, is subject to review and approval by Eisenhower. Also I think it would be well to find out before de Gaulle's man leaves for Africa just what his instructions are.

52

Laval returns to power

During the first three months of 1942 the Germans shot 237 French civilians in the France they occupied. These were hostages for the murder of a handful of the occupying force and also for the few score acts of sabotage on the railways, electric power lines and telephone installations. Among the hostages shot was the Mayor of a small village in Calvados, a father of six children, whose crime, it was claimed, was to have sheltered and succoured a wounded British parachutist for one hour.

As 1942 went on its way the terror increased. Things were not prospering for Hitler on the Russian front, the 'final solution' to the Jewish problem had started in the death camps of the Reich, the R.A.F. had begun its saturation bombing of key German cities such as Cologne, Bremen and Hamburg with over 1000 aircraft at a time, and for good measure bombed into uselessness the Renault factory at Billancourt to the south-west of Paris which was turning out tanks for the Wehrmacht. This new 'outrage' produced Vichy cries of horror in the German-controlled press.

At the same time relentless pressure was kept up on Vichy to supply a 'volunteer' labour force for German war factories. The dismantling of the Maginot line was ordered for which, of course, the French had to pay and renewed attempts were made to base U-boats on Dakar and to have the use of Bizerta as a supply port for Rommel's Afrika Korps. Meanwhile in the occupied zone the German Military authorities increasingly requisitioned what was no longer forthcoming 'à l'amiable', ruthlessly expelled inhabitants from ports such as Brest and Le Havre which they needed in the 'forbidden zone' for the construction of what would later be called 'the Atlantic wall' and in all sectors encouraged a thriving black market which added to the general demoralization of the French nation. Then in the summer of 1942, with the connivance of Vichy, the Gestapo began to operate in the so-called Unoccupied Zone. From then on all semblance of Vichy sovereignty in mainland France disappeared. The Germans did exactly as they pleased.

Such was the general situation when Laval returned to Vichy and stripped Darlan of all political power. This *tour de force*, executed with typical panache, came about in the following way.

On 24 March 1942, when Pétain returned to the Hôtel du Parc from his afternoon walk, as was his habit, he went into his doctor's room for the usual chat. Bernard Ménétrel was both the Marshal's medical adviser and his confidant. There to Pétain's surprise he found Laval's son-in-law Comte René de Chambrun. This was no accident, the chance encounter having been carefully set up with

Ménétrel's assistance. The Marshal who in a few days time would be 86 'readily accepted the idea of listening to the "serious and confidential things" that Laval wanted Chambrun to tell him.'

This first approach then led to a clandestine meeting between Pétain and Laval two days later in the Randan forest at which Dr Ménétrel was the sole witness. This rendezvous in fact was so secret that no one in the Marshal's entourage, least of all Darlan, knew that it had taken place until many hours afterwards. Laval had little time in which to terrorize the old man about the threats and horrors which were about to be forced on France and which Laval claimed to have had directly from Goering. However Laval used such little time as he had to great effect. He also played subtly on the fact that Darlan's popularity with the Marshal was on the wane.*

The next meeting was formal, open and thus common knowledge in Vichy. It took place at the luxury hotel, the Pavillon Sévigné used by the French Head of State for formal meetings. There Laval once again painted a blood-curdling picture of 'the frightful dangers that hung over France'. Three days before this meeting came about, however, Admiral Leahy who had a shrewd idea of Laval's intentions (he had been briefed by Ralph Heinzen of the United Press on the secret Laval–Pétain meeting) called on the Marshal and in the presence of Darlan warned him that 'if Laval were brought back to the government in any controlling position, the United States Government would be obliged to discontinue its aid to France and he himself would be recalled by the President'.

According to Leahy, Pétain then said it was difficult for him to take decisions which were personally unpleasant to him but in any case he was not in a hurry. He added that he

---

*The current story going the rounds was that on a visit to Toulon the Marshal rode in an open car alongside Darlan to the usual cries of 'Long live Pétain!'. Suddenly during a silence a lone voice shouted 'Long live Darlan!', whereupon the Marshal turned to the Admiral and said 'Are you a ventriloquist, Darlan?'

hoped very much that Leahy had not already begun to pack his bags. Darlan, who unknown to both Pétain and Leahy had met Laval privately on 28 March, said little at this meeting but when he and the American Ambassador were alone told him that a decision would be taken in eight days and that he personally did not think Laval had more than a 20 per cent chance of re-entering the government. This was either a direct lie or a sad miscalculation. Once again he had got it wrong.

Not only that: Darlan proceeded to compound the error. Knowing that the Germans would be only too happy to see Laval back in power and calculating, again wrongly, that Pétain would pay more attention to Roosevelt than to Hitler, he used Leahy's *démarche* to explain to von Nida (Abetz's man in Vichy) that it would not be his, Darlan's, fault if Laval were prevented from returning to the government. It would be the Americans who would be responsible. This puerile attempt to curry favour boomeranged almost at once. Von Nida telephoned Abetz who happened to be at Hitler's headquarters. Hitler was in no mood to let the Americans with whom Germany was now at war dictate whether a friend of Germany could or could not join the government of a country he had conquered. France must choose and choose quickly between Germany and the United States and Hitler made very clear what consequences to France would ensue if the wrong choice were made.

Thus just as Darlan continued to rely on intrigue, so Pétain continued to pay the bill by caving in weakly. On 17 April 1942 Laval became by Constitutional Act No. 11 Chief of the Government directly responsible to the Head of State with effective control of domestic and foreign policy. Darlan still remained nominally Dauphin to the Marshal and Commander-in-Chief of the Armed Forces, but his political power had vanished. He was curtly told he was only to attend the Council of Ministers if invited and then only to discuss purely military matters.

'Laval was imposed on me', Pétain said pathetically, 'but

I'm going to give him so much responsibility he'll collapse under it.' What a threat! One wonders if the Marshal had any real idea of the world he was living in. Laval certainly had and soon proved himself quite as bitchy as Darlan whenever he thought occasion demanded. He took immediate steps to rub the Admiral's nose in the mire of his degradation. When the new Chief of Government was officially presented to the Marshal, Darlan of course had to be there. Before a single flash bulb could light up the scene, Laval ordered all the photographers to leave the room. At the second ministerial meeting Darlan had been carefully excluded. On that occasion the event was fully recorded for the press of the world. Laval might be – and was – described as an 'ordure', he was none the less back now in absolute control, the four key Secretaries of State – Fernand de Brinon, Jacques Benoist-Méchin, Admiral Charles Platon and Paul Marion – being all directly attached personally to him, all as deeply committed to collaboration as the Auvergnat himself.

53

Giraud

It was not all jam for the Germans and their Vichy accomplices. At the very moment Laval was seizing the reins of government, a fighting French General of high rank escaped from the German fortress of Koenigstein where he was a prized prisoner-of-war. This was the 63-year-old Henri Giraud who had also got away from a similar camp in World War I and had then audaciously worked behind the German lines. Now in April 1942 despite his age and a 'gammy' leg from a badly set war wound, the General, aided by a carefully worked out and faultlessly executed French Secret Service plan, slipped down a rope 40 metres long and was spirited away to Switzerland and then on 25 April to Lyon.

This thumbing of the nose at Hitler and the whole German prison apparatus delighted the enslaved French and indeed the whole free world. Churchill, who had met Giraud in 1937 when visiting the Maginot line where Giraud commanded the main sector, immediately sensed the political possibilities and telegraphed Roosevelt on 29 April: 'I am highly interested in the escape of General Giraud and his arrival at Vichy. This man might play a decisive part in bringing about the things of which you had hopes. Please tell me anything you know.'

That same day Pétain invited the General to lunch at the Hôtel du Parc in Vichy. It cannot have been one of the better days for the old Marshal, as Giraud made it clear at once and in a totally 'undaunted' way that Germany could never win the war despite any military successes Hitler's armed forces might have. France should therefore prepare to re-enter the war relying on the United States. All Pétain found himself able to say in reply to this was that he would like Giraud to meet Laval. This was the last thing Giraud wanted, but out of loyalty as a good soldier to the Head of State he agreed to meet the newly appointed Chief of the Government.

Laval received Giraud with bustling enthusiasm and a certain respect, but did not even congratulate the General on his incredible escape. Instead he proceeded to plug forcefully his Franco-German policy with which, of course, Giraud did not agree. Laval declared himself certain of Hitler's victory and observed pointedly that his visitor had no monopoly of reliable information on the general situation.

Laval then went further. He said that the General's escape was undoubtedly a set-back to government policy and – unbelievably – asked Giraud to give himself up again to the Germans. Giraud must have found this encounter with Laval both astonishing and disgusting; however, under pressure and incredible as it may seem, the General did agree to meet Abetz at Moulins on the demarcation line between occupied and unoccupied France.

At this meeting Abetz had the nerve to produce 'a sort of protocol' for Giraud's return to Germany. This preposterous proposal was coldly rejected and it must then have been obvious even to the most benighted Vichyite that while reaffirming his loyalty to Marshal Pétain, the General had already made plans to re-enter the war on the Allied side. Six months later these plans were to mature in another amazing chain of events.

54

North Africa – the conception

The idea of taking possession of French North Africa had been in Churchill's mind a good year before the event itself took place. Moreover on 28 October 1941, six weeks before Pearl Harbor, Churchill was minuting the Chiefs of Staff to the effect that: '. . . I have received advices from America that our friends there are much attracted by the idea of American intervention in Morocco, and Colonel Knox talked to Lord Halifax about 150,000 United States troops being landed there.'

The idea began to crystallize during the visit Churchill paid to Ottawa and Washington between 22 and 28 December 1941 when the British Prime Minister gave the American President a copy of a paper he had prepared for the Chiefs of Staff because 'I felt the President was thinking very much along the same lines as I was in French North Africa. In October I could only tell him what our

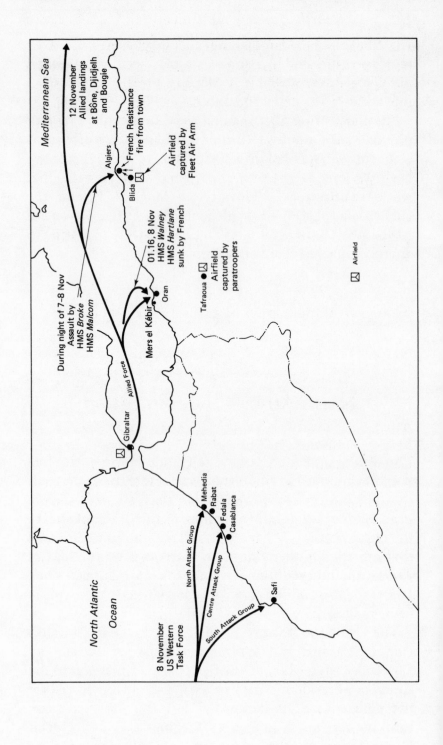

Mediterranean Sea

12 November
Allied landings
at Bône, Djidjelh
and Bougie

French Resistance
fire from town

Airfield
captured by
Fleet Air Arm

Algiers

Blida

01.16, 8 Nov
HMS Walney
HMS Hartlane
sunk by French

During night of 7–8 Nov
Assault by
HMS Broke
HMS Malcom

Oran

Mers el Kébir

Tafraoua

Airfield
captured by
paratroopers

Airfield

Allied Force

Gibraltar

Mehedia

Rabat

Fedala

Casablanca

North Attack Group

North Atlantic

Ocean

Centre Attack Group

Safi

South Attack Group

8 November
US Western
Task Force

British ideas and plans were while we remained alone. We were now Allies and must act in common and on a greater scale . . .' In this paper Churchill wrote:

> . . . we ought therefore to try hard to win over French North Africa and now is the moment to use every inducement and form of pressure at our disposal upon the Government of Vichy and the French authorities in North Africa. The German setback in Russia, the British successes in Libya, the moral and military collapse of Italy, above all the declarations of war exchanged between Germany and the United States, must strongly affect the mind of France and the French Empire. Now is the time to offer to Vichy and to French North Africa a blessing or a cursing. A blessing will consist in a promise by the United States and Great Britain to re-establish France as a Great Power with her territories undiminished. It should carry with it an offer of active aid by British and United States expeditionary forces both from the Atlantic seaboard of Morocco and at convenient landing-points in Algeria and Tunis as well as from General Auchinleck's forces advancing from the east. Ample supplies for the **French** and the loyal Moors should be made available. **Vichy** should be asked to send their fleet from Toulon to Oran and Bizerta [some hope there!] and to bring France into the war again as a principal . . . we must however reckon with a refusal by Vichy to act as we desire . . . they may help German troops to enter North Africa; the Germans may force their way or be granted passage through Spain; the French fleet at Toulon may pass under German control . . . in this case our task in North Africa will become much harder . . . our relations with General de Gaulle and the Free French movement will require to be reviewed . . . to sum up the war in the West in 1942 comprises, as its main offensive effort, the occupation and control by Great Britain and the

United States of the whole of the North and West
African possessions of France and the further control
by Britain of the whole North African shore from
Tunis to Egypt, thus giving, if the naval situation
allows, free passage through the Mediterranean to the
Levant and the Suez Canal . . .

In very general terms this was what was achieved.
However distractions happened in the first half of 1942
which threatened the whole idea and it was not until July
that the decision to mount Operation TORCH with the
maximum forces available was finally taken.

What principally militated against TORCH or GYMNAST,
as the British side of the operation was initially named,
were first the United States Navy's understandable wish to
concentrate above all on Japan and on operations in the
Pacific, and secondly clamour from 'Uncle Joe' Stalin and
the British Left for a 'Second Front Now' in Europe to
relieve pressure on the harassed Russians who, as Churchill remarked to Roosevelt, were in fact killing more
Germans than the British and Americans combined. This
drive to secure a bridgehead in Europe in 1942 which at the
time had far greater support from high and low than mere
Communist agitation suggests, became in fact a very real
threat to the successful outcome of World War II.

Just as the internal politics of Vichy, though germane,
are not an essential part of this account of our last armed
reckoning with France, so also are the higher strategies of
the global war then being waged, of which the fight against
Vichy France forms only a tiny segment. But the Anglo-
American invasion of North Africa in 1942 – so nearly
deferred or abandoned – was an operation in conception,
scale and execution which can justly be called colossal.

This first great invasion was the principal weight bearing down on what Churchill called 'The hinge of fate'
when the Allies turned from almost uninterrupted disaster
to almost unbroken success. How was it then that the
decision for TORCH was not taken until the end of July

1942? How was it that 'during this month of July', as Churchill wrote, 'when I was politically at my weakest and without a gleam of military success, I had to procure from the United States the decision which, for good or ill, dominated the next two years of the war. This was the abandonment of all plans for crossing the Channel in 1942 and the occupation of French North Africa in the autumn or winter by a large Anglo-American expedition.'

A plan already existed for an attack on Brest or Cherbourg and on 11 June 1942 the War Cabinet had decreed that SLEDGEHAMMER as it was codenamed should be vigorously pressed forward but only 'on the understanding that the operation would not be launched except in conditions which held out a good prospect of success'. This operation was further governed by two principles: first, that no substantial landing in France should be made in 1942 unless it was intended to stay, i.e. not just a daring raid such as had been made on Bruneval in February, on St Nazaire in March and was to be made, disastrously, on Dieppe in mid-August; and secondly no substantial landing in France unless the Germans were demoralized by failure against Russia.

By the beginning of July it seemed to the British Chiefs of Staff that the above conditions were unlikely to be fulfilled and on 8 July Churchill telegraphed Roosevelt saying that 'No responsible British General, Admiral or Air Marshal is prepared to recommend "Sledgehammer" as a practical operation in 1942' and then went on, 'I am sure myself that French North Africa [GYMNAST] is by far the best chance for effecting relief to the Russian front in 1942.'

This message arrived in a Washington intensely divided between General Marshall who was for Europe and Admiral King (to begin with very critical of the British) who was entirely Pacific-minded. Only the President saw it Churchill's way and in the end he alone carried the day. On 16 July he sent Harry Hopkins, General Marshall and Admiral King to London 'as my personal representatives for the purpose of consultation with appropriate British authorities on the conduct of the war', together with a directive described by Churchill as 'the most massive and masterly document on war policy that I ever saw from his hand'.

Eight days later complete accord was reached on the action to be taken and 'relations of cordial intimacy and comradeship have been cemented between our high officers' as Churchill put it. On 25 July the President cabled that plans for landings in North Africa to take place not later than 30 October should go ahead at once. GYMNAST and its variations now became TORCH, Eisenhower was appointed as the Supreme Allied Commander-in-Chief and the planning and mounting of the largest combined operation in the history of the world to that date went into high gear, the expedition being conveyed in secrecy and without loss to its three targets of Casablanca, Oran and Algiers in the greatest armada of ships to put to sea at any one time. Of this momentous decision the French, whether Vichyites or Free, remained completely ignorant. Much prudence about security had been learned since the Dakar and Syrian expeditions, the stealth in which TORCH was planned and executed being all the more remarkable when the vast scale of the operation is understood.

55

Churchill and Stalin

Just over three months were to elapse between the decision for TORCH and the actual landings in North Africa. During that time Churchill flew to Moscow and, with Averell Harriman speaking for Roosevelt, 'sold' the idea of TORCH to Stalin. This was not as simple as it sounds.

By mid-August 1942, when this visit took place, neither the British nor the Americans had been able to do anything practical on land to take the pressure off the Russian front.

Certainly the strategic bombing of Germany itself and the desperately expensive (in lives and in ships) despatch of war material to Murmansk hindered the German war effort and kept the lifelines open to Russia.

But Stalin naturally wanted a military diversion. An Anglo-American landing in France would draw back the Panzer divisions and when Churchill made it clear that for practical reasons this could not take place until the following year at the earliest, Stalin, whose understanding of sea power just about equalled Hitler's, became oppressively glum and said that 'if we could not make a landing in France this year, he was not entitled to demand it or to insist upon it, but he was bound to say that he did not agree with my arguments'.

However Churchill had not made this dangerous journey to Moscow merely to tell Stalin what could not be done:

The moment had now come to bring 'Torch' into action. I said I wanted to revert to the question of a Second Front in 1942, which was what I had come for. I did not think France was the only place for such an operation. There were other places and we and the Americans had decided upon another plan, which I was authorised by the American President to impart to Stalin secretly. I would now proceed to do so. I emphasised the vital need for secrecy. At this Stalin sat up and grinned and said that he hoped that nothing about it would appear in the British Press.

I then explained precisely Operation Torch. As I told the whole story Stalin became intensely interested. His first question was what would happen in Spain and Vichy France. A little later on he remarked that the operation was militarily right, but he had political doubts about the effect on France. He asked particularly about the timing and I said not later than October 30 but the President and all of us were trying to pull it forward to October 7. This seemed a great relief to the Russians.

I then described the military advantages of freeing the Mediterranean, whence still another front could be opened. In September we must win in Egypt and in October in North Africa, all the time holding the enemy in Northern France. If we could end the year in possession of North Africa we could threaten the belly of Hitler's Europe and this operation should be considered in conjunction with the 1943 operation. This was what we and the Americans had decided to do . . . Stalin, whose interest was now at a high pitch said 'May God prosper this undertaking' . . . this marked the turning point in our conversation.

Stalin then began to present various political difficulties. Would not an Anglo-American seizure of 'Torch' regions be misunderstood in France? What were we doing about de Gaulle? I said that at this stage we did not wish him to intervene in the operation. The Vichy French were likely to fire on de Gaullists but unlikely to fire on Americans. Harriman backed this very strongly by referring to reports, on which the President relied, by American agents all over 'Torch' territories and also to Admiral Leahy's opinion.

At this point Stalin seemed suddenly to grasp the strategic advantages of 'Torch'. He recounted four main reasons for it: first, it would hit Rommel in the back; second it would overawe Spain: third, it would produce fighting between Germans and Frenchmen in France and fourth it would expose Italy to the whole brunt of the war . . .

Of course Stalin being what Stalin was meant that what was agreed and accepted one day was overlooked, denied or begun all over again on the next. The Churchill visit in 1942 was a presage of things to come in the next half-century so far as dealing with Russia was concerned. The point is that the very first time the idea of TORCH was put to Stalin, he at once saw its merits and as Churchill reported to the War Cabinet and the President: 'Now they know the worst and having made their protest are entirely friendly; this in spite of the fact that this is their most anxious and agonising time. Moreover Stalin is entirely convinced of the great advantages of "Torch" and I do trust it is being driven forward with superhuman energy on both sides of the ocean.'

56

Robert Murphy and the Committee of Five

'The American agents all over "Torch" territories' which Averell Harriman referred to in Moscow were headed by Robert Murphy, the United States Roving Ambassador in Algiers, and it was this remarkable man's assessment of the French personalities in Vichy and North Africa which more than anything else affected the planning and outcome of TORCH.

Since the autumn of 1940 Roosevelt had kept Murphy, still under 50, as one of his 'personal representatives' with the power and requirement to communicate directly with the President. Moreover Murphy was one of the few people in both occupied and non-occupied France who could legitimately move about much as he pleased. So when Admiral Leahy was appointed Ambassador to Vichy at the beginning of 1941, Murphy was given a roving commission based on North Africa where one of the first fruits of his accreditation was an accord with Weygand, whose friend he became, for relief supplies from the United States to North Africa.

Between 1940 and 1942 it was estimated that some 200,000 Europeans, mostly French, made their way across the Mediterranean to Algeria and Morocco. These comprised people of all classes, trades and skills and their presence generated a thriving black market in everything from food to military intelligence. Murphy, who was liked and trusted by all, moved easily through this turgid mass of people, all disguising their real thoughts and feelings behind the lip service it was politic to pay to the Vichy regime.*

Conditions in the area, therefore, were well suited not only for the gathering of intelligence but also for the fomenting of particular intrigues. As Eisenhower put it:

> Mr Murphy was early taken into the confidence of the President of the United States and informed of the possibility of military action in that region. With his staff of assistants he not only conducted a continuing survey of public opinion but he did his best to discover among the military and political leaders those individuals who were definitely hostile to the Axis and occupying their posts merely out of a sense of duty to France. Affable, friendly, exceedingly shrewd and speaking French capably, he was admirably suited for his task . . . from him we learned the names of those officers who had pro-Allied sympathies and those who were ready to aid us actively . . . he told us very accurately that our greatest resistance would be met in French Morocco, where General Auguste Paul Noguès was Foreign Minister to the Sultan. He gave us a number of details of French military strength in Africa, including equipment and training, in their

*When I discussed these North African events with Mr Murphy some years later (we were both in Algiers when Darlan was assassinated on Christmas Eve 1942) I asked him how he had so easily been able to move about when Axis observers and representatives were delayed, watched and hindered at every turn. Murphy told me that the United States had a legal right to be in Morocco as the result of a treaty made with the Sultan around 1860, a right the Germans and Italians certainly did not have. Moreover the dozen or so Vice-Consulates Murphy established in the region, although understaffed compared with the 400 or so German and Italian 'observers' eventually forced upon Tunisia, Algeria and Morocco, were trusted and popular for obvious reasons whereas the Germans were feared and the Italians despised.

ground, air and sea forces. From his calculations it was plain that if we were bitterly opposed by the French a bloody fight would ensue; if the French should promptly decide to join us we could expect to get along quickly with our main business of seizing Tunisia and attacking Rommel from the rear. It was Mr Murphy's belief that we would actually encounter a mean between these two extremes. Events proved him to be correct.*

Murphy, however, went far beyond the mere collection and sifting of intelligence. He became in his way a miniature Machiavelli in actively supporting, often at much personal risk, the leadership of the anti-Vichy organization (which had no Gaullist connections). This, it was intended, should seize power in the event of an American invasion.

The leadership of this organization became known as the Committee of Five. Its head was Jacques Lemaigre-Dubreuil who had been president of one of the largest oil concerns in France (Lesieur). After Dunkirk Lemaigre-Dubreuil had made himself *persona grata* with the Germans by reopening his factories to supply their needs. This early collaboration, which would certainly have been misunderstood in London, in fact gave Lemaigre-Dubreuil an almost waterproof alibi. In Murphy's words: 'Sure of himself, speaking loudly, his angora hat at a tilt and displaying an innate taste for being observed, he moved about freely disguising his conspiracy, like Ali Baba, in so many barrels of oil.'

Number two to Lemaigre–Dubreuil and his opposite in everything except their common intent was Jean Rigault, a

---

*This was fair praise for a diplomat who had previously had little or no experience of military affairs, whose staff were woefully ignorant of Arabic and whose knowledge of naval matters could be assessed and summed up, he told me with a twinkle, as 'one or two of us with luck might be able to distinguish a battleship from a submarine on a particularly clear day'.

thin little man in his 40s, with pale grey staring eyes who had managed a pre-war right-wing paper *Le Jour Echo*. Next came the dashing Henri d'Astier de la Vigerie, nephew of a cardinal, with black feline eyes and the delicate bronzed features of a Spanish aristocrat who radiated charm. Fourth was Colonel A.S. van Ecke, nick-named 'Robin Hood', a great brusque red-headed Dutch-man of 50, with a barrel chest and rugged voice, with 20 years in the Foreign Legion behind him and who was currently in charge in North Africa of Pétain's youth movement 'Les Chantiers de la Jeunesse'. This gave him a reservoir of young, ardent and willing support which he put to good use. Finally there was a small paunchy man with a long pointed nose and a bald head. Jacques Tarbé de Saint-Hardouin was, like Murphy, a career diplomat who had been Chef de Cabinet to a right-wing Premier of France, Pierre-Etienne Flandin. Flandin, it will be remem-bered, was briefly in the Pétain government and was the only person bar Pétain himself to see the alleged protocol Professor Rougier had brought back from his meeting with Churchill in the autumn of 1940. Because of his position and status Saint-Hardouin could and did spend much time with Murphy without exciting suspicion. In addition he had a young elegant Turkish wife who ran a salon to entertain 'le grand monde' of North Africa.

These then were the Committee of Five. Lemaigre-Dubreuil was able legitimately to travel to and from the French mainland; Saint-Hardouin stuck closely to Murphy; van Ecke issued false papers and passes; d'Astier spread the plot and recruited new members on the prin-ciple of the communist cell, so that if one was blown the rest were still safe; and Rigault kept the archives which he consigned for safety's sake to a young Jesuit who hid them in the Convent of the Sisters of Notre Dame d'Afrique.

'In essence,' Murphy told Sumner Welles, his Under Secretary of State, 'their purpose is the establishment in French North Africa of a provisional government operating independently of Metropolitan France. They are searching for and hope to find shortly a military leader.' This was written before TORCH had been decided and their answer turned out to be General Giraud. Much was to happen, however, before Giraud could physically be got to the scene of action.

57

TORCH preliminaries

In the event, the TORCH landings and the subsequent Allied take-over of Algeria and Morocco proved to be an unqualified success.* The assault alone required over 200 warships, 1000 aircraft, 70,000 troops and 350 transport and landing ships, all of which had to have detailed sealed orders covering all eventualities before they sailed (although not, of course, to be opened until so ordered when at sea), the sailing of the slowest follow-up convoys having to be some weeks before the invasion took place. At one time nearly 1000 ships were at sea directly involved in the TORCH landings.

This intense planning activity raced along in London and in Washington in September 1942. An idea of the scale of the operation can be gauged from the fact that the naval orders alone were in eight parts, dictated over several days to a team of eight Wren stenographers working in spells of four on duty and four standing by and were then printed

---

*Looking back on it now after nearly 50 years – and I was with the whole thing from before it began until about four months after it was over – I am still amazed, as we all were, by the immense complications involved and by the tough security precautions which had to be rigidly enforced but which did result to everyone's surprise and relief in a complete bolt from the blue.

under the closest security by the Oxford University Press, the printers themselves being held incommunicado until the expedition had taken place. The orders were distributed 'By Hand of Officer' in Top Secret Bags between 3 and 20 October. As Eisenhower wrote: 'The tremendous pressure under which we worked is hard to appreciate for any who have not shared in the experience of planning a great allied operation in modern war.'

But getting out the operation orders in total secrecy was only one of the hazards that had to be faced. Churchill summarized the problems the Supreme Commander had to tackle as 'the immensity of the stake that was being played, the uncertainty of the weather by which all might be wrecked, the danger from Spain and above all "the complications of the French attitude."' Those were the main imperilments of which the last was perhaps the most difficult of all to assess. In these 'complications of the French attitude', General Giraud in France and Robert Murphy in Algiers played starring roles until the operation itself went through, at which point it was discovered that by an extraordinary and totally unexpected turn of fate Darlan himself happened to be in Algiers because his son Alain had been struck down by poliomyelitis and was thought to be dying.

Once the decision for TORCH had been taken and because of his considerable, up-to-the-minute knowledge of the North African scene, Murphy was recalled to Washington for a conference with the President and as a result of this was hurried on to London to brief Eisenhower. Since Murphy's unheralded presence in London and a meeting with the Supreme Commander might well have given the game away, he was provided with a fictional commission as a Lieutenant Colonel McGowan ('no one pays any attention to a mere Lieutenant Colonel'). He was then flown to the United Kingdom in uniform and the greatest secrecy. However by yet another stroke of luck – bad luck in this instance – the first person he bumped into after landing at Prestwick was Don

Coster, one of his Vice-Consuls in Africa. 'Why, Bobby, what are you doing here and dressed like that?' Coster asked, forthwith and to his astonishment finding himself arrested and, like the Oxford printers, held incommunicado until after the landings had taken place.

The procurement of General Giraud and his spiriting away from the south of France to Algeria by way of Gibraltar is an even stranger story. During the summer of 1942 and after his unfortunate meeting with Pétain and Laval, Giraud had got in touch with Murphy and the Committee of Five in Algiers. As we have seen, the Five worked mainly on the political scene but they also had strong military backing from General Mast in Algeria (number 2 to the Commander-in-Chief, General Juin) and from General Béthouart in Morocco (number 2 to the Resident-General Noguès).

It must again be emphasized that not one of these high military officers would have disobeyed or been disloyal to the Head of State to whom they had given their oath. Equally, however, none relished the increasingly disreputable collaboration into which Laval and Darlan had been dragging France in the name of the Marshal and under his nose. It therefore became politic to consider what might happen should the Americans land in North Africa. Few in authority mentioned the British except to execrate them for Mers-el-Kébir and Dakar. Such indeed was the prejudice against the British by the governing classes, with which Murphy whose background was Irish Catholic to an extent agreed, that Churchill seriously considered putting the British assault force into American uniforms and did in fact place the garrison and colony of Gibraltar under Eisenhower's command and the American flag while the expedition staged through the Straits of Gibraltar.

Great hopes were based on 'King-pin' as Giraud was codenamed. By 1942 famous French Generals who were untarnished by defeat or collaboration were thin on the ground. It was Murphy's opinion, backed by the Committee of Five and by Generals Mast and Béthouart who daily risked their lives in assisting the Allies, that could Giraud be brought to North Africa ostensibly to be present and available in the event of a provoked uprising against the Vichy Government (although not, of course, against the Head of State) there would be an immediate response. All North Africa would flame into revolt under a leader universally respected and popular.

That was the idea. In the event it proved to be dangerously wrong. Giraud turned out to be as full of pride, self-importance and narrow-mindedness as any other ranking officer of his age and in any case Darlan's presence prevented the matter ever being put clearly to the test. However in the run-up to TORCH that was how it was and also what was believed. So to clinch it, to prove his own good faith and to save unnecessary bloodshed, Murphy insisted that a high-ranking officer from the Supreme Commander's staff should go personally to North Africa for a definitive conference. This was a brilliant idea. Such a meeting, however, had to be arranged with the same secrecy as the operation itself. The dangers were patent and extreme. Any Allied officer caught in this particular act would be interned. Any French officer would automatically be regarded as a traitor by Vichy and might well be shot. Clearly Eisenhower himself could not go. Instead he sent his Deputy, Major General Mark Clark.

58

The meeting at Cherchell

The conference at Cherchell stands in the record as one of the most larky minor operations of World War II. It was also lit up by moments of pure farce. In the first place it had been difficult enough to find a suitable venue without awkward questions being asked. Early in October, however, Monsieur Jacques Tessier, a good friend of the Committee of Five, came up with his own beach villa which had several rooms, was isolated, had a garden giving on to the beach and was shielded both from the beach and the road behind by a copse of pine trees. This house had the remoteness, landwise and seawise, which such an extraordinary colloquy required, lying as it did some 60 miles west of Algiers between two rocky headlands and near the mouth of a small stream called Oued Messelman and known locally as a smugglers' haven.

By that period of the war there were no unattended small boats anywhere on the North African coastline. Moreover so many attempted escapes had been made that the French authorities had instituted an efficient system of 'douair' coastguard patrols, often alerted to anything unusual during the night by the howling of Arab dogs. In addition the police could be and were alerted through the French *concierge* system by which the caretakers in blocks of flats in towns or in country houses of any substance were required to be police informers and rewarded as such. Thus although Tessier had given his native servants three days off, this in no way guaranteed any secrecy since one or other of his staff would be almost certain to pass on this information to the police. So much for the setting.

The cover plan which Tessier carefully leaked was that he was throwing a private party for senior officials in the Administration and the American Consulate, ladies would be present and, with a knowing wink, no one in such circumstances would want to be disturbed. This was something all Frenchmen understood. The police officer in charge of that part of the coast, Lieutenant Lenen, was 'in the know' but the coastguards and the staff of the villa might still ruin it all.

In fact the visiting party were all high specialist officers from General Eisenhower's staff in London and comprised Generals Clark and Lemnitzer, Colonels Holmes and

Hamblen and Captain Jerauld Wright USN (now Admiral). They had flown secretly to Gibraltar and had then embarked in a British submarine, H.M.S. *Seraph*, under the command of Lieutenant Jewell R.N. The plan was for *Seraph* to be off Cherchell and as close inshore as was safe on the night of 20–21 October and then for the distinguished visitors to paddle themselves ashore in inflatable boats known at the time as 'folboats'.

Meanwhile the receiving party had arrived at the villa in a series of large American cars together with hampers of food and wine which it was hoped would allay local suspicions. The hosts consisted of Robert Murphy, one of his Vice Consuls Redgway Knight (described as looking like a clergyman), d'Astier de la Vigerie, van Ecke and Rigault from the Committee of Five and General Mast (Giraud's contact in Algiers). There were also three more junior officers in charge of the security of the enterprise and the owner of the villa, Jacques Tessier, there 'to look after the comfort of his guests'.

So they waited and the hours went by right through the night, the tension rising each time a messenger came back from the beach to say that there was still nothing in sight. Just before dawn, the French contingent returned in their several cars to Algiers where later in the day a coded message was received from Gibraltar saying that the operation had had to be postponed for 24 hours because compulsory (and essential) boat drills and bad sea conditions had delayed the arrival of *Seraph* at the rendezvous until 0400 hours, by which time the captain of the submarine had wisely decided it would be too dangerous to land the party before daylight.

At nightfall that same day the receiving party returned to Cherchell and the vigil began once more. This time everything went according to plan, *Seraph* duly surfaced, four boats were launched and all got safely ashore, except for General Clark who made a wet landing in the last boat which overturned in the surf. Then as soon as all were introduced discussions began on a practical plan in what one of the Committee of Five described as 'a striking atmosphere of confidence and comradeship'.

General Clark gave them the glad news that the landings had been decided upon, the scale was no longer in doubt and 'the operation will be carried out with means exceeding all understanding'. Naturally he could not reveal the date. The declaration, however, made a great impression. Although no co-operation could be expected from the French Navy – a fact already taken into account – General Mast said that given four days' notice he could guarantee that there would be little or no resistance from French military and air forces. He also guaranteed unimpeded entry into Bône, the most easterly port in Algeria and promised that General Giraud in France would co-operate to the full. At that time none of the French guessed that the TORCH expedition was already at sea or that Darlan would upset the apple cart by being unexpectedly in Algiers. Nor, for that matter, did any of them know how difficult General Giraud would prove to be.

Meanwhile, although the submarine itself had not been noticed, one of the villa servants, as had been feared, went to the Police Commissariat and 'spilled the beans' to the Commissioner's secretary. By yet another stroke of luck the secretary belonged to a Resistance group and dismissed the informer with a few reassuring words. Then another part of the farce began. The servant waited until the secretary had left and then approached the Commissioner himself. This official who was definitely not 'in the know' flew into a rage, leapt on his motorcycle and was about to investigate the matter himself when Lieutenant Lenen arrived, commented that the Commissioner looked 'quite upset' and asked where he was going. 'No wonder I'm upset', the Commissioner answered, 'I'm going to search Tessier's place. There's some dirty work afoot. Gaullists perhaps.' 'But that's my job, Monsieur le Commissaire, I'll go myself.'

So Lenen grabbed the motorcycle and set off to warn the conspirators just ahead of the raid. The conference was abruptly stopped. The French contingent disappeared in all directions: 'I never dreamed that such a dignified French

General could change his clothes so swiftly', Clark afterwards said, 'from the window I saw him making off through the garden, putting on his coat as he ran.' The visiting Americans were left to gather up all the plans and papers scattered over the table and were then bundled off into a musty cellar 'an ideal trap' Clark went on, 'we felt like rats. We could hear all that went on above. I had my revolver in one pocket and fifteen thousand francs in the other, without knowing which arm I should use if challenged. After an hour calm was restored and we could emerge from our funk hole.'*

Lenen had gone but he had left his assistant, Sub-Lieutenant Michel, to make a sort of film-set in case of a search. Cards and upturned glasses were spread over the table, empty bottles strewn on the floor – the aftermath of a night orgy had been created to perfection. Murphy and his Vice-Consul remained and agreed with the two French officers that the overseas guests should leave as quickly as possible. Murphy had offered Lenen 200,000 francs to find him a solid rowing boat but this was refused not only because such a boat did not exist but also because further suspicions would then be aroused.

So in spite of heavy sea conditions attempts were then made between 2300 and 0300 hours to get to the submarine. All failed on reaching the bar, where the surf threw them back. Finally as Clark described it: 'All eight of us took the oars after having taken off our uniforms and placed them in the bottom of the boats, together with the hundred thousand francs brought in case it proved necessary to bribe someone and, of course, all the papers. Suddenly an extra big wave capsized the boat and clothes, money, colonels, generals, plans and papers found themselves floundering about in the cold water. We lost

*One of the others in the cellar found his teeth chattering somewhat out of control. Clark stuck a lump of chewing gum in his mouth. 'But it has no taste,' the officer murmured. 'I know,' the Deputy Supreme Commander replied, 'I've been chewing it since this morning.'

everything except the most important papers. Fortunately the submarine was there to pick us up . . .' By then it was 0400.

The next morning in the police station at Cherchell, Lenen described to the Commissioner how he had surprised the United States Minister, his aides and d'Astier de la Vigerie in excellent form in the company of some 'ladies of easy virtue'. As it was clearly a private party in Tessier's house, Lenen felt it would have been out of place for him to have ordered them out; what did the Commissioner think? The Commissioner's mind was set at rest. He agreed that Lenen had done right by doing nothing, diplomatic privilege, etc., etc. There was just one thing, though: 'What were the girls like? Pretty?'

Thus it was that Robert Murphy's reputation in Cherchell was completely destroyed. The secret of TORCH, however, had not only been preserved, it was also likely that thousands of lives would not be needlessly thrown away.

59

TORCH at Gibraltar

No sooner had H.M.S. *Seraph* delivered her valuable human cargo back to Gibraltar than Lieutenant Jewell, the Commanding Officer, was sent on another similar and equally dangerous assignment. This was to pick up 'King-pin' (Giraud) off the French Riviera coast and then transfer him to a Catalina flying boat at sea for onward passage to 'the Rock' which had now become Supreme Allied Headquarters.

Accordingly *Seraph* sailed from Gibraltar on Operation

MINERVA at 2000 hours on 27 October with Captain Jerauld Wright U.S.N. once more on board and nominally in command to give the impression that the submarine belonged to the United States and not to the antipathetic British. The rendezvous was set for the small hours of 6 November, two days before the TORCH assaults were due to take place, and Eisenhower's plan was 'to get King-pin to North Africa before we land but the arrangements are dependent upon good weather to enable him to transfer from submarine to aeroplane'. This, however, was not to be.

With the TORCH landings now only hours in the future, Gibraltar had become the epicentre of the whole operation. As Eisenhower put it: 'There was no other place to use. In November 1942 the Allies possessed, except for the Gibraltar fortress, not a single spot of ground in all the region of Western Europe and in the Mediterranean area nothing west of Malta. Britain's Gibraltar made possible the invasion of north-west Africa.' Churchill wrote:

> Gibraltar's greatest positive contribution to the war was the development of its new airfield and the use that was made of it. Starting from a mere landing strip on the racecourse this was developed from 1942 onwards into a broad runway over a mile long, its western end built out into Gibraltar Bay with the rubble from the tunnelling. Here the great concentrations of aircraft for 'Torch' were made. The whole isthmus became crowded with machines and fourteen squadrons of fighters were assembled for zero hour. All this activity necessarily took place in full view of German observers, and we could only hope they would think it was for the reinforcement of Malta. We did all we could to make them think so. Apparently they did.

The rubble used for the airfield had been hacked out from inside the great Rock itself, first of all in 1940 to provide water distillation plants, vital to survival in case of another siege, then later to make caverns of war materials for the Mediterranean war and finally in 1942 to provide the Supreme Allied Commander with the safe Command Post he needed for the assault phase of the operation.

Eisenhower and his immediate staff arrived in six Flying Fortresses on 5 November after a perilous flight from the United Kingdom at 100 feet because of weather conditions which would normally have precluded taking to the air at all. Indeed the pilot of the supremo's plane remarked as Gibraltar loomed out of the mist: 'This is the first time I have ever had to climb to get into landing traffic at the end of a long trip.'

The Naval Commander-in-Chief, Admiral Sir Andrew Browne Cunningham (A.B.C. again!) and his staff, of which the author was one, had arrived five days before. They were installed in bare eerie offices deep under the Rock. The feeble lighting in the tunnels and the cold damp stagnant air combined with the constant drip, drip, drip of water through the rock seemed only to increase the tension which all felt and about which there was nothing to be done except patiently to wait and to pray.* At that time the party had no means of knowing the German staff appreciation, made as late as 4 November, which said: 'The relatively small number of landing craft and the fact that only two passenger ships are in this assembly at Gibraltar do not indicate any immediate landing in the Mediterranean area or on the North West African coast.'

'Finally', as Eisenhower wrote, 'the leading ships steamed in at night through the narrow strait and we stood on the dark headlands to watch them pass. Still no news of air or submarine attack . . .' In fact the assault forces for

---

*As I wrote at the time: 'We were all acutely aware of the whole range of disasters which could so easily happen affecting all or part of the operation. You cannot hold your breath for days on end but it felt like that and we read every signal which came through with apprehension tinged at times with alarm.'

Oran and Algiers got through into the Mediterranean without a single loss.

Before the TORCH landings began overnight and early in the morning of 8 November, General Giraud had arrived in Gibraltar. Great hopes were placed on this. The terrible disappointment which ensued is best described by Eisenhower himself who pronounced it 'one of my most distressing interviews of the war'. Eisenhower wrote:

> Because of the earnest belief held in both London and Washington that General Giraud could lead the French of North Africa into the Allied camp, we had started negotiations in October, through Mr Murphy, to rescue the General from virtual imprisonment in southern France. An elaborate plan was devised by some of our French friends and by Mr Murphy who had returned to Africa after his visit to London. General Giraud was kept informed of developments through trusted intermediaries and at the appointed time reached the coastline of southern France in spite of the watchfulness of the Germans and Vichyites. There he embarked in a small boat, in the dark of night, to keep a rendezvous with one of our submarines lying just off shore.
>
> A British submarine [the *Seraph*] commanded for this one trip by Captain Jerauld Wright of the United States navy, made a most difficult contact with General Giraud and put to sea. At another appointed place the submarine met one of our flying boats and the General, with but three personal aides and staff officers, flew to my headquarters during the afternoon of November 7. The incident, related thus briefly, was an exciting story of extraordinary daring and resolution.
>
> General Giraud, though dressed in civilian clothes, looked very much a soldier. He was well over six feet, erect, almost stiff in carriage, and abrupt in speech and mannerisms. He was a gallant, if bedraggled figure,

and his experiences of the war including a long term of imprisonment and a dramatic escape, had not daunted his fighting spirit.

The above summarizes what had happened and what was already known in London, in Washington and, presumably, by Murphy and the Committee of Five in Algiers. Now, again in Eisenhower's words, comes the incredible continuation:

It was quickly apparent that he had come out of France labouring under the grave misapprehension that he was immediately to assume command of the whole Allied expedition. Upon entering my dungeon, he offered himself to me in that capacity. I could not accept his services in such a role. I wanted him to proceed to Africa, as soon as we could guarantee his safety, and there take over command of such French forces as would voluntarily rally to him. Above all things we were anxious to have him on our side because of the constant fear at the back of our minds of becoming engaged in a prolonged and serious battle against Frenchmen, not only to our own sorrow and loss, but to the detriment of our campaign against the Germans.

Now once again our old friend 'French pride' marches to centre stage:

General Giraud was adamant; he believed that the honour of himself and his country was involved and that he could not possibly accept any position in the venture lower than that of complete command. This, on the face of it, was impossible. The naming of an Allied Commander-in-Chief is an involved process, requiring the co-ordinated agreement of military and political leaders of the responsible governments. No subordinate commander in the expedition could legally have accepted an order from General Giraud. Moreover at the moment there was not a single Frenchman in the Allied Command; on the contrary the enemy, if any, was French.

All this was laboriously explained to the General. He was shaken, disappointed, and after many hours of conference felt it necessary to decline to have any part of the scheme. He said [and here we go again in the royal third person]: 'General Giraud cannot accept a subordinate position in this command; his country-men would not understand and his honour as a soldier would be tarnished.'

Even after nearly 50 years and given the circumstances of the time, such conceit seems incredible. What sort of world did these defeated French Generals think they inhabited? It was indeed pitiful, as Eisenhower commented, to have come all that way and at such risk to all concerned to express such a pompous and self-deluding point of view. The conversation with Giraud went on, often in circles, until after midnight, the General's goodnight remark being: 'Giraud will be a spectator in this affair'.

After an uneasy night's sleep, however, the new prima donna decided that he would after all participate: '. . . on the basis we desired. I promised him that if he were successful in winning French support I would deal with him as the administrator of that region, pending eventual opportunity for civil authorities to determine the will of the population.'

Subsequent discussion, however, revealed that the General was still living in some cloud-cuckoo land of wishful thinking so far as strategy was concerned and the practical steps it would be necessary to take to effect any action at that stage of the war:

. . . it developed that there was a radical difference between his conception and mine of what at that moment should be done strategically. He was in favour of turning immediately to the attack on southern France, paying no attention to northern Africa. I showed him that even as he spoke the troops were landing on their selected beaches; that there was no possibility of providing air support for the landing he proposed and that the Allied shipping then in existence would not provide a build-up for an invasion of southern France that could withstand the force the Germans would assuredly bring against it. Finally I explained that the campaign on which we were embarking was backed up by such intricate and detailed maintenance arrangements that the change he proposed was completely impossible.

He could not see the need of North Africa as a base – the need for establishing ourselves firmly and strongly in that region before we could successfully invade the southern portion of Europe. He was not aware of the lessons the war had brought out as to the effect of land-based aviation upon unprotected seaborne craft. He had probably never assessed in terms of tactical meaning, the loss in the south-west Pacific of the two great British ships, the 'Prince of Wales' and the 'Repulse' when they were needlessly exposed to attack by land-based aviation. He assumed, moreover, that if the Allies chose to do so they could place 500,000 men in the south of France in a matter of two or three weeks. It was difficult for him to understand that we had undertaken an operation that stretched our resources to the limit, and that because of the paucity of these resources our initial strategic objectives had to be carefully calculated.

What a damning indictment of someone on whom all had set so many hopes. Worse, however, was to happen when Giraud did at last reach Algiers.

60

The TORCH assault

The TORCH landings began on time at 0100 hours on Sunday, 8 November 1942. East and west of Algiers the assault under Rear Admiral Sir Harold Burrough met with little or no opposition except on Bear Red Beach. Weather conditions were fair with a north-easterly breeze force 3. The assault on Algiers harbour itself by two British destroyers, H.M.S. *Broke* (Lieutenant Commander A.F.C. Layard DSO R.N.) and H.M.S. *Malcolm* (Commander A.B. Russell R.N.), but wearing the U.S. Ensign at the yardarm had a much trickier time.

At full speed they had to crash the booms protecting the northern and southern entrances to the harbour, place themselves alongside particular quays, land their American troops and stay there unless otherwise ordered. Although there was no blackout in Algiers, navigating into the right position in a strange harbour in the middle of the night proved to be much more difficult than had been anticipated. A 'troublesome' gunfire from the forts began and *Malcolm* was heavily hit. With three of her four boiler rooms out of action she was forced to withdraw. Just before dawn *Broke* made her fourth attempt to ram the boom, cutting through it 'like a knife through butter' and in spite of damaging fire from a French minesweeper, berthed alongside the Quai de Falaise whence American combat troops leapt ashore and captured the power station and oil installations as ordered.

The TORCH operation report reads: 'At about 0850 two French police officers and two civilians came aboard with a request that a United States officer should take over control

of the town. Captain H. St.J. Fancourt R.N. [in command of
the whole operation] at once sent an American army
officer ashore with a British naval officer as interpreter but
that party failed to get through.'

Despite the general atmosphere of Sunday calm,
tempered by an occasional 'angelus' call to mass, *Broke*
was suddenly fired on from a new quarter. This fire was
well controlled and made her position untenable. The
General Recall was sounded, although only a few United
States troops were re-embarked before the ship got under
way. As she moved out of the harbour she received
numerous hits and although later taken in tow sank the
next day in deteriorating weather.

In the meantime Blida airfield had been captured, the
first time a military airfield had been occupied by Fleet Air
Arm aircraft. In command of eight Martlets, Lieutenant (A)
B.H.C. Nation R.N. had bombed two French aircraft on the
ground and then observed airfield personnel waving white
handkerchiefs. Telling the other British aircraft to keep
watch, Nation landed and accepted a written statement
from the Station Commandant that the base was at the
disposal of the Allied armies for landing purposes. Nation
then remained at the airfield until a party of commandos
and U.S. rangers arrived.

At Oran where beach landings east and west of the port
began at 0116 hours under the command of Commodore
T.H. Troubridge, things were very much tougher and
would have been disastrous had the French not been taken
completely by surprise. Unlike Algiers the real fighting
began after the initial landings had been made and Oran
itself was not to be captured until 10 November. As at
Algiers, and in view of the known intentions of the French
Navy to resist at all costs (Mers-el-Kébir again), it had been
decided that a direct assault into the harbour itself would
be made by two ex-U.S. Cutters now renamed H.M.S.
Walney and H.M.S. *Hartland* but filled with U.S. combat
troops.

These ships and the attack itself were under the

command of Captain F.T. Peters DSO, DSC R.N. post-
humously awarded the Victoria Cross and the American
Distinguished Service Cross. The assault opened at 0245
whereupon sirens were sounded by the French and all
lights in the town extinguished. For a time the ships
circled off the entrance making announcements in French
by loud-hailer. The reply to this was hostile.

A searchlight was then turned on *Walney* and she came
under heavy machine gun fire. Followed by *Hartland* she
at once turned away northwards, coming round in a full
circle to charge the booms. At the same time the minelayer
ML 480 went on ahead at full speed, laying a smoke-
screen, but hit the outer boom and was stopped under
heavy fire half-way across it. She got off again just as
Walney at her maximum 15 knots crashed through the
booms and entered the harbour. Three canoes, manned by
special parties, were then launched but one at least was
immediately sunk by gun fire. *Walney* then continued up
harbour at slow speed being hit by a pom-pom of the Ravin
Blanc battery.

Half-way up the harbour she narrowly missed ramming
a French destroyer which raked her with two broadsides at
point-blank range. These wrecked her main engines and
she then came under heavy crossfire from the light cruiser
Epervier (later to be sunk by H.M.S. *Aurora*) lying
alongside to the south and from destroyers and submarines
to the north. According to the operation report:

> At last, blazing forward and amidships, she drifted out
> of control bows on to the jetty ahead of 'Epervier'. An
> attempt to get heaving lines ashore failed and she
> drifted once more slowly out into the harbour. Her
> guns were out of action, their crews virtually wiped
> out. Sixteen officers and men were lying dead on her
> bridge where Captain Peters alone survived.
>
> Below only five officers and men of the landing
> parties remained alive amid scenes of indescribable
> carnage. Nothing further could be done and the ship

was abandoned, her few survivors, including Captain Peters himself, being taken prisoner. Her end was near and between 0900 and 1000 she blew up and sank.

A similar fate awaited *Hartland*. With her captain temporarily blinded by a shell splinter, the French destroyer *Typhon* treated her to withering fire at point-blank range. Shells burst inside her hull, turning her messdecks full of waiting troops into a burning shambles.

Then, with fires raging fore and aft, she drifted alongside the mole. Lieut. Commander Dickey U.S.N. calling on his men to follow, at once leapt ashore to seize a trawler alongside but only one unwounded man was able to obey before the ship, caught by the wind, drifted once more out into the harbour where she anchored under heavy fire. Though her British and American ensigns were clearly visible in the lights of the flames, the French humanely ceased firing.

Despite desperate efforts to subdue them, the flames spread and expecting her to blow up at any moment, Commander Billiot ordered the ship to be abandoned. By 0410 all survivors had left and at 0525 there was an explosion on board but 'Hartland' remained afloat for some time burning furiously till she blew up with a devastating explosion which damaged buildings in a large area around the mole and left only wreckage floating on the surface of the water to mark her end.*

Meanwhile the ambitious plan to seize the airfields by means of the largest paratroop mission to date had gone

*Both Captain Peters and Commander Billiot, although wounded, miraculously survived. However by some grim irony of fate, the Catalina aircraft in which Peters was returning to England a few days later crashed on landing at Plymouth and he was killed.

badly astray. The 2nd Battalion 503rd Parachute Infantry had set out from England in 39 C.47s with instructions which relied on an unopposed landing. A later message warning them of probable French opposition failed to reach them. On top of this the formation became partially scattered by bad weather over Spain. The leading elements which reached Tafaroui encountered flak and landed at La Lourmel, where they were joined by later elements. Although the mission was technically a failure the para-troopers proved to be a valuable addition to the combat troops who captured Tafaroui airfield.

If the going had been tough in Oran, disaster came within a hair's-breadth of the Western Task Force and the Moroccan landings at Casablanca. This was a purely American operation under the overall command of General 'Old Blood and Guts' Patton. This task force had left American waters between 23 and 25 October in the greatest war fleet ever despatched from the United States. Under the command of Rear Admiral H.K. Hewitt U.S.N. it comprised some 60 warships and 40 transports and the whole armada crossed the Atlantic undetected and without incident, reaching an approach position south of Casablanca between latitudes $31°$ and $32°$ N. on 4 November.

The task force was divided into a covering group, an air group and three attack groups. The Northern Attack Group was to operate against Mehedia–Port Lyautey area, 65 miles north-eastward of Casablanca. The Centre Attack Group was to invest the Fedala–Casablanca area and the Southern Attack Group was to land in the Safi area, 110 miles south-west of Casablanca. The distances involved show the essential part communications had to play in such a three-pronged and distended operation. In the event communications were to break down almost completely.

The strategic reasons for the above plan were clear. All three landings, if successful, would secure the narrow coastal plain at the foot of the Middle Atlas mountains, through which ran all the principal roads and railways in

French Morocco. Mehedia, the nearest landing place to Port Lyautey, had the most accessible airfield in Morocco on which to base naval aircraft. Possession of Port Lyautey would secure the railway running parallel to the border of Spanish Morocco through the Taza Gap to Algeria.

In the centre, the Fedala beaches were the nearest practicable landing place to Casablanca which in turn was the only large harbour on the Atlantic coast of Morocco, housing the headquarters of the French navy plus the uncompleted battleship *Jean Bart*. This great ship was immobile but could – and did – fire her four 15-inch guns.

In the south Safi covered the native metropolis of Marrakesh, and its harbour provided the only opportunity of running Sherman tanks ashore for an assault northwards on Casablanca. The capture of Casablanca was to be the crux of the entire operation. This meant that while the northern and southern assaults might fail without jeopardizing the success of the whole operation, the Fedala landings had to succeed or disaster would be guaranteed.

Over all lay unending anxiety about the weather. A landing on any Atlantic coast has perils on a different scale from those likely to be encountered in the Mediterranean. Atlantic rollers, the tide, and surf 15 feet high are terrifying factors when any plan is executed to land heavily armed men and equipment on a hostile shore.

Then there was the U-boat threat. Luckily for the Americans one big pack of U-boats had been concentrated near Dakar and were therefore too far south to intercept the American troop convoys. The British, too, had been lucky in that another U-boat pack in the approaches to Gibraltar had been lured away by a mercantile convoy from Sierra Leone. This convoy became the sacrificial lamb which allowed the main TORCH convoys to get through unscathed. 'It looked impossible from the submarine chart', Admiral Ramsay wrote in London, 'that convoys could escape detection'.

To Eisenhower and Cunningham the strain was worse, and as Eisenhower was to write later to A.B.C.: 'I came to the conclusion that the hours you and I spent together in the dripping tunnels of Gibraltar will probably remain as long in my memory as will any other. It was there I first understood the indescribable and inescapable strain that comes over one when his part is done – when the issue rests with Fate and the fighting men he has committed to action.'

To Admiral Hewitt out at sea and nearing his objective, the problem of the weather now became acute. The Washington and London forecasts for D-Day were scarcely encouraging: 'Surf fifteen feet high and landings impossible.' These forecasts made Eisenhower consider directing the Western Task Force to abandon the Moroccan Atlantic coast and instead switch to a Mediterranean landing. Admiral Cunningham's advice, though, was to leave it to the man on the spot. In the event this was a wise decision, since at the critical moment all communication between Gibraltar and Hewitt broke down.

As was to happen 18 months later at the Normandy landings, the key decision to abandon the operation or to go ahead depended in essence on whether or not to take a chance on the weather. On board the U.S.S. *Augusta*, Hewitt's meteorologist considered the storm was moving too rapidly to have any adverse effect on the beaches (in fact it had a delayed effect after the landings had taken place). Hewitt then took one of the most courageous decisions of the war. He ordered the attack to be executed as planned. Perhaps it really is true that fortune favours the brave. At all events the meteorologist proved to be right. The weather abated sufficiently and at the right time for the landings to be made. Before dark on 7 November the Western Task Force divided itself into its three prongs and duly reached the Moroccan coast before dawn on the 8th.

All the TORCH assaults had gone through very much as planned. In general terms the vast operation had been a not-too-expensive success. But what was then the situation at the receiving end in Algeria and Morocco? What was to happen next?

61

A momentary pause

This story of England's last war with France is almost complete. With the military success of the TORCH landings, direct armed conflict between the two ancient enemies came to an end. The subsequent invasion of Normandy in June 1944 and the fighting on French soil which followed were not directed against the French nation or their government but against the one-time common enemy Nazi Germany.

The tragedy of the story so far recounted lies to my mind – and it may well be only to my mind – in the fact that the French, whom I have liked and admired all my life, had given their allegiance in overwhelming numbers to a set of men led by a dotard who gravely misled them, not, as they claim, for the sake of honour but because of a lamentable lack of moral courage, perhaps the one great human quality for which there is no substitute whatever. I know this is a grave indictment. It is a charge to which the complex of legality is but a poor defence. Certainly it is an accusation of which the brave Resistance now beginning to take off, whatever its political colour, was in no way guilty nor indeed was the misguided boy, and those behind him, who in less than two months after the *débarquement* murdered Darlan.

It is said that assassination settles nothing. I am not so sure. How many lives might have been saved had the plot to kill Hitler on 20 July 1944 succeeded? Without spelling out in words of one syllable whether Darlan was or was not a traitor, 'his murder', as Churchill wrote, 'however criminal, relieved the Allies of their embarrassment at working with him and at the same time left them with all the advantages he had been able to bestow during the vital hours of the Allied landings'.

What were those advantages and how did these circumstances come about?

62

Darlan in Algiers

The key to understanding the immensely complicated and confused situation in Algiers over the next five days from Sunday, 8 November until Friday, 13 November, when an approved agreement with the French was made personally by Eisenhower and Cunningham flying over for the day from Gibraltar, lies simply in the presence in Algiers of Darlan at the time of the landings. This again was an unforeseeable and totally unexpected act of fate. As Eisenhower wrote:

> We discounted at once the possibility that he had come into the area with a prior knowledge of our intentions or in order to assist us in our purpose. Already we had evidence, gathered in Oran and Algiers, that our invasion was a complete and astonishing surprise to every soldier and every inhabitant of North Africa except for those very few who were actively assisting us. Even these had not been told the actual date of the attack until the last minute. There was no question that Darlan's presence was entirely accidental, occasioned by the critical illness of his son to whom he was extremely devoted.

Darlan, in fact, had made a routine tour of inspection in North Africa at the end of October and had returned to France whereupon his son whom he had left in Algiers was suddenly stricken by what was then called infantile paralysis. His condition was so serious that he was administered the last sacraments. This crisis in turn caused Darlan to fly back to Algiers on 5 November.

At that time no one in North Africa except Robert Murphy had the slightest idea that the TORCH armada had long been at sea and was in fact within two to three days of executing the operation. It will be remembered that at the secret Cherchell meeting on 22 October the Number 2 military commanders (General Mast in Algiers and General Béthouart in Morocco) had said that given four days' notice they could guarantee little resistance from the French Army or Air Force. General Béthouart felt very unsure of the Moroccan Resident General (Noguès) and was prepared on D-Day to put him under arrest. Of General Juin no one had doubts and although he was not directly informed for obvious reasons, he was however in a close relationship with Murphy and undoubtedly knew of the activities of the Committee of Five and of the role it was expected General Giraud would play once he could be brought to North Africa.

Had Darlan not been in Algiers at the crucial moment and had the TORCH landings been made with the above understandings being brought into play, it is by no means clear as to the cloak of legality Generals Juin, Mast and Béthouart – indeed Giraud himself – would have been able to throw over their acts of dissidence to the Marshal, greater by far than that of de Gaulle. Would *force majeure* conveniently have justified their consciences in what would have been a clear revolt? The more one studies this French fetish of legality, the less understandable it becomes. Its face value is noble and praiseworthy but, it appears, only to the French ruling class itself. It is also convenient as an excuse for doing nothing, for that sad lack of moral courage mentioned above. It is a hard criticism to make but nations do so often get the rulers they deserve, and just as Argentina deserved and got Peron so France may have deserved the Pétain it got during World War II. Individuals must judge for themselves, bearing in mind the brave men and women of the Resistance and the subsequent restoration of France to her proper world status by General de Gaulle.

In any case during those five fateful days in November 1942 the presence of Darlan in Algiers ensured that no matter what happened, the iron curtain of legality between stage and audience had been dropped firmly into place. On the morning of 9 November, the day following the invasion, Generals Giraud and Clark, with Commodore Dick representing the Allied Naval Commander-in-Chief, went by air separately to Algiers as Eisenhower put it: 'in an effort to make some kind of agreement with the highest French authorities. Their mission was to end the fighting and to secure French assistance in projected operations against the Germans.'

What then happened is well described in the 'Record of Negotiations' which Commodore (now Admiral) Dick wrote shortly afterwards and which he has given permission to quote in full. Before doing so, however, and to set the scene it is apposite to quote what Churchill and Eisenhower wrote of this time. Churchill first:

> Our leading hope in Algiers in recent weeks had been General Juin, the French Military Commander. His relations with Mr Murphy had been intimate, although the actual date had not been imparted to him. A little after midnight on the 7th Murphy visited Juin to tell him that the hour had struck. A mighty Anglo-American army, sustained by overwhelming naval and air forces, was approaching and would begin landing in Africa in a few hours. General Juin, although deeply engaged and loyal to the enterprise, was staggered by the news. He had conceived himself to possess full command of the situation in Algiers.

But he knew that Darlan's presence completely over-
rode his authority. At his disposal were a few hundred
ardent young Frenchmen. He knew only too well that
all control of the military and political government
had passed from his hands into those of the
Minister-Admiral. Now he would certainly not be
obeyed. Why, he asked, had he not been told earlier of
zero hour? The reasons were obvious and the fact
would have made no difference to his authority.
Darlan was on the spot and Darlan was master of all
Vichy-French loyalties. Murphy and Juin decided to
ask Darlan by telephone to come to them at once.
Before two in the morning Darlan roused from
slumber by the urgent message from General Juin
came. On being told of the imminent stroke he turned
purple and said 'I have known for a long time that the
British were stupid, but I always believed that the
Americans were more intelligent. I begin to believe
that you make as many mistakes as they do.'

Darlan's fury was understandable if only for the fact that
the many mistakes he had made himself – and 'mistakes' is
a charitable word – were now coming home to roost. By an
accident of fate Darlan himself had been caught in a trap
from which there could be no escape. Either he would have
to break his oath to the Marshal, repent in biblical terms
and admit to himself that all he had done over the past 2½
years had been a ghastly error or he would become
personally responsible for an immense loss of French blood
in ordering the forces under his command to resist the
Allied invasion as he had done in Dakar, Syria and
Madagascar. He was caught and imprisoned in the most
agonizing dilemma. No wonder that he banged himself in
fury against the bars of his mental cage.

Eisenhower in Gibraltar considered that:

In Darlan we had the Commander-in-Chief of the
French fighting forces! A simple and easy answer

would have been to jail him. But with Darlan in a position to give the necessary orders to the very considerable French Fleet, then in Toulon and Dakar, there was hope of reducing at once the potential naval threat in the Mediterranean and of gaining welcome additions to our own surface craft. Just before I left England, Mr Churchill had earnestly remarked: 'If I could meet Darlan, much as I hate him, I would cheerfully crawl on my hands and knees for a mile if by so doing I could get him to bring that fleet of his into the circle of Allied forces.'

But we had another and more pressing reason for attempting to utilize Darlan's position. In dealing with French soldiers and officials General Clark quickly ran foul of the traditional French demand for a cloak of legality over any action they might take. This was a fetish with the military; their surrender in 1940, they asserted, had been merely the act of loyal soldiers obeying the legal orders of their civil superiors.

Without exception every French commander with whom General Clark held exhaustive conversation declined to make any move toward bringing his forces to the side of the Allies unless he could get a legal order to do so. Each of them had sworn an oath of personal fealty to Marshal Pétain, a name that at that moment was more profound in its influence on North African thinking and acting than any other factor. None of these men felt that he could be absolved from that oath or could give any order to cease firing unless the necessary instructions were given by Darlan as their legal commander, to whom they looked as the direct and personal representative of Marshal Pétain.

It was useless then, and for many days thereafter, to talk to a Frenchman, civilian or soldier, unless one first recognized the Marshal's overriding influence. His picture appeared prominently in every private dwelling, while in public buildings his likeness was frequently displayed in company with extracts from his speeches and statements. Any proposal was acceptable only if 'the Marshal would wish it'.*

In such circumstances it is small wonder that Giraud's welcome by the leading French commanders was icy. Eisenhower again: 'General Giraud's cold reception by the French in Africa was a terrific blow to our expectations. He was completely ignored. He made a broadcast announcing assumption of leadership of French North Africa and directing French forces to cease fighting against the Allies, but his speech had no effect whatsoever. I was doubtful that it was even heard by significant numbers.'

So with the above as an introduction here is the experience of Commodore Dick who is still alive today (he is 90 years of age) and who gave the author the report which follows – 'Record of Conferences leading up to the Clark – Darlan Agreement'.

63

The Darlan negotiations

On 9 November 1942, General Eisenhower, the Allied Commander-in-Chief, instructed Major General Clark, U.S. Army, to proceed to Algiers to come to an agreement with the French Authorities in North Africa in order to lead at the earliest possible moment to the cessation of hostilities. Major General Clark was to be accompanied by Colonel Julius Holmes [Eisenhower's principal political adviser], Captain

*During the months I was billeted on a French family in Algiers from November 1942 till April 1943 I dined every night under the eye of the Marshal while the eldest daughter of the family flashed her Croix de Lorraine behind her father's back.

Jerauld Wright, U.S. Navy [who was at the Cherchell meeting] and Commodore Royer Dick, Chief of Staff to the Naval Commander-in-Chief, Expeditionary Force [who, as will be remembered, dealt with Admiral Godfroy and Force X at Alexandria in July 1940, was of Huguenot extraction and spoke fluent French].

The party left Gibraltar in an escorted Flying Fortress at about 1400 the 9th November and touched down at Maison Blanche [the main airport to the east of Algiers] at 1600, just before dusk. As the aircraft landed, a heavy attack developed on the port and aerodrome of Algiers by a large number of Ju.88s and it was necessary to clear quickly off the airfield. Fighters took off, and the guns opened up and it was an inspiring sight to see the enemy aircraft crashing in flames in several directions, one coming down low over the aerodrome and crashing in a nearby valley. While the party was waiting in the aerodrome, an attack was made with anti-personnel bombs causing some casualties and damage. With the raid still in progress, the party left for Algiers in a Bren Gun Carrier, escorted by armoured cars, and drove at high speed to the town, as it was imperative to get into touch with the American and British Authorities as quickly as possible. Throughout the route, ditches on the roadway were lined with troops taking cover and firing at enemy aircraft, one aircraft crashing in flames within a couple of hundred yards of the cars.

The town was in an extremely disturbed state, so much so that contact had been made neither with the British Commanding General, General Anderson, or the American General, General Ryder, both of whom were out in the town taking steps to ensure the safety of their own troops since the French, recovering from the first shock of the landing and initial capitulation had begun to realise how small a force was in fact in possession of the town and that they had little equipment in the way of armoured vehicles and guns.

The French were constantly moving troops to key positions, such as barracks, forts and telephone exchanges and a most careful eye was necessary to ensure that they did not place themselves in a position of military advantage.

The position was, in fact, extremely delicate and we had not at that time a strong enough force to deal drastically with an organised resistance should it break out afresh. This, coupled with the paramount necessity of pushing on eastwards as rapidly as possible to forestall German movement in Tunisia, which was even then starting, put the Allied Forces into a position which necessarily had a dominating effect on the subsequent negotiation. Hence our hands were tied in negotiating by the initial necessity of ensuring that our forces were not robbed of the fruits of the rapid successful landing which had been achieved.

The party proceeded direct to the American Consul General's villa which is close to the Hotel St George, at that time the French naval headquarters and heavily guarded by French naval ratings. Rooms were arranged in the top corner of an annexe to the St George and in those bedrooms the party made their base both for living and as their office. Considerable care had to be taken in all discussions as at the time, the American Consul General's villa was believed to be wired, so that conversations could be overheard and recorded. Mr Murphy, the representative of the American State department who had been conducting negotiations and who was also deeply involved in the subversive movement which had failed after its initial success, arrived at the villa for discussions. He explained the uneasy situation in the town, that all his party had been arrested when the Allied Forces did not succeed in entering Algiers within the first few hours and that they, and a number of British naval ratings who had assaulted the harbour in H.M.S. 'Broke' were still imprisoned. Mr Murphy himself had to move about most circumspectly, as he had been confined to his residence for some time and had only just been released and was doubtless under surveillance.

He stated that the arrival of General Giraud had not been the rallying point of all friendly disposed Frenchmen as it had been hoped and that in fact General Giraud himself was in a precarious position, since no officer of importance except General Mast had followed his lead. Admiral Darlan was at liberty and all the leading French authorities were in a state of indecision and not one of them could be regarded as reliably attached to our cause. The most friendly probably was Admiral Fénard (in whose house Darlan habitually stayed) but he was not a man of sufficiently strong character nor was he in an important enough position to be able to sway matters sufficiently. This news was disturbing since General Eisenhower's instructions to General Clark were to direct General Giraud to use every atom of his influence to stop resistance and that if he, General Giraud, were to lead the French forces, he must have a worthwhile force on which to build up. He must urge resistance on all; that their vital interests coincided with ours; he must broadcast frequently and visit all senior commanders, and urge all Tunisian forces and leaders in particular to destroy Axis planes and resist Axis invasion. It should be emphasised at this point that fighting was still in full swing at Oran and Casablanca and that the weather had turned against us so that the unloading of stores and military material was being appreciably slowed down.

It was felt that the first thing was an immediate conference with General Giraud and he was secretly asked to come to the villa under cover of darkness. In view of the danger of discussion in the house itself, the meeting was held in darkened cars in the grounds, considerable alarm being caused when several cars with bright lights drove up in the middle of the discussion and for a moment it was feared that an attempt was to be made to arrest both General Giraud and the Allied party. However nothing eventuated. The discussion was far from satisfactory. It was evident that Giraud was bewildered at finding the almost complete lack of support with which he had been met and for the moment at any rate there was very little to be obtained. His first anxiety appeared to be whether we would implement our promise of placing him as Commander-in-Chief of the French Forces in Africa, which he appeared to wish us to do in spite of the fact that he had no following. It had to be reiterated to him that it would be folly to take such a step, as it would result in his being Commander-in-Chief in name only, whilst the antagonism of those who held the real power to stop further resistance was further aroused. The meeting then concluded and General Giraud withdrew.

Mr Murphy and party then held a conference and it was decided to hold a meeting next morning with Admiral Darlan and find out the lay of the land.

Accordingly the next morning [10 November] a meeting was held at which Admiral Darlan, General Juin, General Endipal, Admiral Fénard and Admiral Battet were present. Darlan repeatedly refused to accept the terms of the armistice which included all North Africa and he stated he would not sign them owing to lack of authority from Vichy. The meeting was somewhat dramatic as there was a company of American soldiers posted round the hotel. Inside them, however, were the French guards, and in the lobbies of the hotel, a large number of armed French officers. General Clark had orders that the party were not to carry arms and it was thus evident that if drastic action had to be taken, the process of carrying out arrests would be fraught with considerable uncertainty for those who were present at the hotel.

When, therefore, Admiral Darlan refused to accept the terms and the party got up to leave, it appeared

that there might be some shooting. General Clark got
to his feet and said that as Darlan would not accept the
terms, he must now take his own measures and we
proceeded to leave the room with the object of taking
our dispositions to effect the arrest of all concerned.
Just as the door was reached, Admiral Battet took
Colonel Holmes by the arm and asked for five
minutes' grace.

This gave us a breathing space and at the end of five
minutes, General Clark was asked to return and
somewhat to the personal relief of those concerned,
Admiral Darlan announced that he would issue an
order to all the ground, air and naval forces in North
Africa including Morocco and Tunisia, to discontinue
hostilities immediately and he there and then signed
an order to each commander which was forthwith
despatched by air in the custody of French staff
officers and the French commanders were communi-
cated with by telephone.

Meanwhile General Giraud had asked Darlan to
confer with him, but the latter had refused. However
he finally consented and the meeting was arranged for
1500 that afternoon. The meeting then broke up and
at a subsequent conference with Admiral Darlan,
General Clark asked him to issue an order to the fleet.
This conference was inconclusive except that Darlan
stated *he had instructed the fleet to be prepared to
move on notice should German troops enter unoccupied France.* He stated that in no circumstances would
the fleet fall into German hands.

The above italics are the present author's since it is
worth pausing for a moment to note that on that same day
Laval had been summoned to meet Hitler at Berchtesgaden
and that shortly afterwards German troops did begin to
move into unoccupied France. From that moment the
effective power, such as it was, of the Vichy Government
ceased to exist. 'Laval met Hitler late that afternoon [10

November]', Churchill wrote, 'The Fuehrer with his theatrical sense of history, treated the Frenchman to a discourse on past Franco-German relations, going back a long way. He also confronted him with a joint German-Italian note demanding French consent to Axis landings in Tunisia. Ciano, who was present, says Laval cut a pitiable figure. This may well be believed. Early in the morning of November 11 Laval was woken up by Abetz to be told that the Fuehrer had ordered the German Army to occupy the free zone of France. The same day the Italians occupied Nice and Corsica.'

Back in Algiers 'The first result was thus obtained', Dick's report goes on, 'a definite order for the cessation of hostilities which had been the primary object of this initial conference and General Clark felt it was of the utmost importance above all to secure this order. It will be observed, however, that a most difficult position had been reached since Darlan remained the controlling power over the forces in North Africa and General Giraud to whom we were deeply committed was no further towards obtaining his position as Commander-in-Chief, nor was there any sign, were he so placed, of the local generals obeying his orders.'

The report then gives a translation of Admiral Darlan's orders:

... Our engagements having been fulfilled, and the bloody battle become useless, order is given to all land, sea and air forces in North Africa to cease the fight against forces of America and their allies, as from receipt of this order, and to return to their barracks and bases and to observe strictest neutrality.

2. In ALGERIA and MOROCCO, the Commanders-in-Chief will put themselves in liaison with local American Commanders on the subject of terms for the suspension of hostilities.

3. I assume authority over North Africa in the name of the Marshal. The present Senior Officers retain

their commands and the political and administrative organisations remain in force. No change will be made without a fresh order from me.

4. All prisoners on each side will be exchanged.

So far so good. All concerned, however, failed to consider two factors – one being the attitude of Giraud, the other the fact that the Germans had become aware of the orders Darlan had given and immediately forced Pétain to disown him. Commodore Dick continues:

The next move started on the afternoon of the 10th with much diplomatic jostling taking place. General Giraud expressed his displeasure that Admiral Darlan had been allowed to issue the order to cease hostilities. General Giraud insisted that he should be set up immediately and announced as the Commander-in-Chief of all French forces in North Africa. This produced an awkward situation because the effect would probably be to cause Admiral Darlan to revoke his order for the cessation of hostilities. During the afternoon General Clark accompanied by General Giraud and Mr Murphy visited the Admiral at his residence and endeavoured to reach a compromise. Admiral Darlan had just received word that Marshal Pétain had disowned him. He was greatly dejected and said he would have to revoke his order for the cessation of hostilities.

General Juin was also present, and General Clark informed Admiral Darlan that he would not permit him to issue such an order. Admiral Darlan then stated that in these circumstances, he must be made a prisoner. General Clark stated that this was acceptable, and a guard was placed round the house. Admiral Darlan also gave his word of honour that he would remain there and not revoke his order. General Juin also promised that he would not issue a revocation order.

General Clark then endeavoured to get Admiral Darlan to order the French fleet to Algiers. He replied that his order would no longer have any effect. He, however, stated that he could issue a plea to the French fleet. General Clark then left the meeting and General Juin and General Giraud attempted to work out a compromise between them.

Shortly after, Admiral Fénard, a friend of Admiral Darlan and in whose house the latter was confined, informed Mr Murphy that information had been received that the Germans were about to enter unoccupied France. Admiral Darlan stated that if this were true and he received verification he would consider himself free of further moral restrictions and further would ignore the Marshal's order disowning him and the Admiral asked that Clark should go to his house again and discuss matters, including the disposition of the Fleet.

Again it should be remembered that at Oran, the headquarters of the French Navy in North Africa, the bloodiest of battles had only ceased a few hours before when the French formally capitulated to the U.S. General Fredenhall at noon that same day, 10 November. The report continues:

At 1800 that evening a conference was held with General Giraud, General Juin, Koets and Mendigal, the latter three being strong Darlan supporters. The news of the German entry into France had a profound effect, and helped matters considerably. They were informed that Admiral Darlan was to be asked to hand over the Fleet and conferences were then stopped until the next day. General Giraud was greatly moved by the news and said the time had now come for all Frenchmen to pull together.

There were spasmodic air raids during the evening but as a whole the situation was fairly quiet. A signal was sent by Commodore Dick to Admiral

Cunningham that night asking for the policy as regards the destination of the Fleet and proposing that it should be directed to sail straight across the Atlantic, stopping at Gibraltar to fuel, and pointing out that there was a likelihood that the Fleet would not obey Admiral Darlan's orders.

A signal was also received from Oran, which greatly relieved anxieties, as it stated that Oran had fallen at noon, and our troops had had an enthusiastic reception. It also stated that our prisoners had been released. This was a better situation than existed with our prisoners in Algiers [to say nothing of those at Laghouat] and Commodore Dick was obliged to go to Admiral Darlan to demand their instant release and that they should have more comfortable quarters, as they were still confined in what was little better than a large cell.*

On the morning of the 11th November, a message was received from General Eisenhower urging that all efforts should be made to get the French Fleet to sail to Gibraltar, and that since it was now confirmed by Hitler that the Germans were occupying southern France, Admiral Darlan, General Juin and General Giraud should be urged to telephone at once to Tunis urging Admiral Esteva to denounce the Axis personnel and to declare himself for us.

A signal was also received from Admiral Cunningham stating that a reconnaissance showed that the bulk of the Toulon Fleet was still in harbour, and that Admiral Darlan should be urged to do everything possible to get them to sail.

General Clark interviewed Admiral Darlan again on the evening of the 11th, accompanied by Colonel Holmes, Commodore Dick and Captain Wright USN. Admiral Darlan was interviewed in Admiral Fénard's house where he was a prisoner. However, despite all

*This was yet another instance of petty vindictiveness as had happened in Syria and makes sad reading even as a footnote.

urgings, Admiral Darlan would not issue an order to the Fleet until he was sure that Germany was moving into southern France. He stated that fighting had ceased in French Morocco. At this stage General Clark was anxious to take the guards off Admiral Darlan as it lowered his prestige locally and made negotiations difficult.

All the French Commanders were in a turmoil and some anxiety was felt about the attitude of the French naval forces to our troops and ships which were next day to land at Bône, Djidjelli and Bougie. This was particularly the case as Admiral Moreau was constantly vacillating.

The meeting was, however, cordial and it was on this occasion that Admiral Darlan for the first time offered to shake hands with Commodore Dick. The point is only of interest because previously, whilst cordially shaking hands with all the American officers, he studiously refrained from doing so with Commodore Dick, who was the only British representative. On hearing, however, that evening that Commodore Dick was Chief of Staff to Admiral Cunningham and had been with him at Alexandria he offered to shake hands, an offer which had been anticipated and which was accepted with some reluctance, for obvious reasons. However the moment was a delicate one in negotiations and it seemed best to pocket pride and do so. It was not done, however, without a sharp exchange on the subject of past history which had a surprisingly good effect, and thereafter Admiral Darlan dealt with the British representative frankly and, it should be recorded, gave and continued to give assistance in naval matters.

Next morning the battle was resumed and finally at a meeting after a hectic day of changing situations, Admiral Darlan made the following signal to Admiral de Laborde (Commander-in-Chief at Toulon):

'The protest sent by the Marshal to [Field] Marshal

von Rundstedt shows that there is no agreement between him and the German General for the occupation of France. The armistice is broken. We have our liberty of action. The Marshal being no longer able to make free decisions, we can whilst remaining personally loyal to him, make decisions which are most favourable to French interests. I have always declared that the Fleet would remain French or perish. The occupation of the southern coast makes it impossible for the naval forces to remain in metropolitan France. I invite the Commander-in-Chief to direct them towards West Africa. The American Command declares that our forces will not encounter any obstacles from Allied naval forces.

Signed Admiral of the Fleet François Darlan'

So the second round had now been won to the extent that the Fleet had been ordered to sail, though all concerned had great misgivings whether it would do so.

But an 'invitation to direct' is not an order. Once again Darlan seemed to want it both ways. He was anxious for the fleet to sail but wanted de Laborde, who detested him, to take the decision. One wonders why. In any case as Dick went on: 'Admiral Darlan himself, when told by Commodore Dick of the dispositions to cover the French Fleet when it moved westward replied: "You are more optimistic than I am in making these arrangements, I am afraid they will not come." '

It has since become known on good authority that Admiral de Laborde answered Admiral Darlan's signal with that one extremely unparliamentary French word (*merde*) which left no doubt he would pay no attention to the order or invitation. Dick again:

Meanwhile during the afternoon further agreement was reached that Admiral Darlan would become the political head in France and General Giraud would be the military commander of all French forces in North Africa. The situation was complicated by the fact that Marshal Pétain had designated General Noguès as Commander-in-Chief, North Africa because he said that Admiral Darlan was not available, being a prisoner-of-war. General Noguès was therefore summoned to a conference in Algiers the next day. The guards were removed from Admiral Darlan's house and a public announcement was decided upon for the next day, emphasising the unity of all factors for the combined effort. Admiral Darlan and General Juin telephoned Admiral Esteva [at Bizerta] to tell him to resist the Germans but Admiral Esteva over the telephone said, 'I have a tuteur [guardian] by my side', so it would appear that he was not free.

A satisfactory result of the day's work was that agreement was reached with the French to release close on a thousand British prisoners at Laghouat and Geryville. The majority of these prisoners were naval officers and men and merchant seamen and included a great proportion of the ships' companies of H.M.S. 'Manchester' and H.M.S. 'Havoc'. A report was received that the entrance to Bizerta had been blocked, but it was estimated that it could be cleared in about six days. A message was also sent by Admiral Cunningham to Admiral Esteva in the form of a personal appeal to resist the Germans [before the fall of France Admirals Esteva and Cunningham had been in close and friendly liaison] and saying that further help would be rushed to his assistance. Broadcasts were also made at intervals in French saying that Hitler had denounced the Armistice and inviting the French Fleet to sail for Gibraltar. Similar invitations were broadcast to French merchant seamen to bring their ships there and, in conformity with an order from the First Sea Lord, British naval units were told to receive the French cordially should they come over.

12th November A set back occurred early in the morning when it was discovered that the orders to the Tunisian authorities to resist the Germans had been suspended until the arrival of General Noguès and the previous agreement referred to had been approved by all concerned. It was therefore not possible to make the announcement of the fact to all French factions. A meeting was called immediately and troops were moved in order to force obedience to the agreement of the previous day. A message was also sent asking General Eisenhower to come to Algiers.

The meeting duly took place on the 12th and after a series of dramatic incidents, in which on two occasions the French had to be left to themselves to exchange vituperations, all parties agreed on the original arrangements. Our troops had meanwhile landed at Bône, Bougie and Djidjelli with little opposition and had indeed been welcomed by the French pursuant to Admiral Darlan's orders so this anxiety was removed.

Behind the above rather bland English understatement of events lay an emotional tempest entailing doors being slammed, double talk about orders being 'suspended' not 'revoked', scruples about legality being scornfully dismissed as quibbles and at one stage a threat by a totally exasperated Clark to put all the French leaders under arrest and lock them up in a ship in the harbour unless they came to a satisfactory decision within twenty-four hours. The Allied High Command which had other worries more instant than legalistic quibbling may very well have felt that dealing with the French in North Africa was like trying to put a jersey on an octopus. At all events on 13 November, Dick continues:

General Eisenhower and Admiral Cunningham

arrived in the forenoon and at a meeting held at the French Naval Headquarters in the Hotel St George, the approved agreement with the French as regards the set-up in North Africa was finally reached and agreed by all parties.

Admiral Darlan informed Admiral Cunningham that he did not think Admiral de Laborde would let the Toulon Fleet fall into the hands of the Germans, although he might not obey Admiral Darlan's orders and at the insistence of Admiral Cunningham, Admiral Darlan agreed to send a message to Admiral de Laborde telling him that the Italian Fleet were on their way north and assuring him of the support of the British Fleet. Admiral Darlan also said that he thought Admiral Godfroy would come in with him. [Both Admirals might just as well have saved their breath.] General Eisenhower and Admiral Cunningham then returned to Gibraltar . . .

where they very nearly crashed on landing and which confirmed the Supreme Commander in his previously formed intention to shift his headquarters to Algiers with all despatch.

64

Morocco and the end of TORCH

The assault phase of the North African invasion cannot be left without mentioning the situation the Western Task Force had to face after their heroic landings in French Morocco. The top Allied 'friend' in the Protectorate was General Marie-Emile Béthouart, the French Divisional

Commander in charge of the land defences of most of the Moroccan coast. The equivalent of General Mast in Algiers, Béthouart was the only senior French officer in the know as to TORCH and he in turn took into his confidence a handful of key subordinate officers.

Opposed to this small band of courageous men and, of course, completely in the dark as to the great Allied design were the Resident General Noguès at Rabat and Admiral Michelier at Casablanca. Both were totally committed to the Marshal in Vichy; both were as anti-Anglo-Saxon as they were anti-Boche and Noguès in particular was a wily and experienced politician. He was also no fool. While fully aware of what the Germans could do, once decisions were taken, he had nevertheless with Gallic shrewdness and cunning contrived for 2½ years to deny the German High Command any effective use of the Moroccan facilities he had at his disposal.

Noguès had not been impressed by British failures in Norway, Dakar, Crete and the Western Desert nor in the summer of 1942 by the disastrous raid on Dieppe. He was an astute judge of power and, unlike Darlan and Laval, sensed that once the Americans really got going, the balance was bound to change. This was where Béthouart made his first mistake. He had given the Committee of Five his considered opinion that when the landings had actually taken place both Noguès and Michelier would rally to the Anglo-American cause. Murphy was not so sure and had urged him to arrest and keep incommunicado the Resident General until the invading forces were safely established ashore. That, however, was asking too much, Béthouart said, pointing out that he had no wish to be accused of supplanting his superior officer which of course was exactly what he was proposing to do in fact. Once more it was the miasma of legalities all over again, the less comprehensible since the personal risks they were taking and had already taken were all passports to the firing squad.

Nevertheless despite their reservations, Béthouart

assembled the officers he had taken into his confidence at
2300 hours on 7 November 1942 and told them the
Americans were landing at 0500 the following morning.
The party then left Casablanca in three cars and two hours
later took over army headquarters in Rabat, the capital,
together with the General Staff and Post Office telephone
exchanges. Here Béthouart made his second mistake. Either
he did not know or he overlooked the fact that Noguès had a
secret and direct line to the commanders of the main bases
throughout Morocco. These lines remained open and
untouched.

So, when in the middle of the night Béthouart having sent
his A.D.C. to Noguès with written details of the discussions
between Giraud and Murphy and of the imminent Allied
landings, Noguès made it his first concern to discover in
what strength the invasion would be made. If it were to be
just another Dakar or Dieppe-style commando raid, it must
be thrown back into the sea or the Germans would have the
excuse they had long wanted to take over the whole of
French North Africa. If, however, the Americans were to
drop out of the sky on Rabat in great force then Noguès could
justly claim both to the Germans and to his own rather
dubious conscience that he had no option but to surrender.
Alas for them all, neither Béthouart nor anyone else in
North Africa with the exception of Murphy knew that the
TORCH plan by-passed Rabat on the advice of American
Intelligence in order not to offend Moslem opinion. This
was because Rabat was a Mohammedan religious centre
and should therefore be treated, like Rome, as an open city.

In the event the decision to by-pass Rabat and the
inexperience of the 'green' American Expeditionary Force,
which was soon apparent when the landings did begin,
justified Noguès to himself in the calculation he had made.
It also lost Patton whatever chance there had been of an
unopposed landing. In any event high drama began at this
point of decision in Rabat an hour or two before dawn. To
make sure of things Béthouart had ordered a company of
colonial infantry to surround the Residence (not, of course,

to arrest Noguès, but just as a show of strength). Noguès was naturally enraged. He promptly arrested Béthouart's A.D.C., who also happened to be his nephew, and at once rang Admiral Michelier at Casablanca on his secret line. Michelier told him there was no sign of any invasion force off the coast even though in those pre-radar days the 100 ships carrying Patton's landing force were at that moment a mere 30 miles off shore.

Very well, Noguès said to himself, that settles it. He ordered the 'Alert' and at the same time appointed Michelier as his second-in-command in place of Béthouart, then in Rabat, whose only success so far had been to place the whole of Morocco in a state of siege behind the Resident General.

At 0500 hours the American Vice-Consul in Rabat delivered a personal letter from President Roosevelt to Noguès calling on him to aid the Allies. Two hours later, after the landings had begun, Noguès informed Darlan in Algiers that he had rejected 'the U.S. ultimatum'. He then ordered Béthouart and his few supporters to be surrounded and, once Béthouart had been arrested, telephoned him to say he would also have the officers of the colonial regiment involved arrested and shot. Béthouart was tried by Court Martial two days later and was not finally released until 17 November.

Two days' hard fighting then took place and it was not until late on 10 November that Darlan's order, in the name of the Marshal, brought all naval and military hostilities to an end. Despite spirited and competent French opposition, despite the Atlantic surf (at one beach 50 per cent of the landing craft were wrecked) and despite a complete failure of communications (compounded on the spot by the U.S. Army Headquarters having forgotten to bring with them the joint code for high-grade messages, thus putting the Western Task Force effectively out of touch with Allied Force Headquarters), despite chaos on the beaches caused by inadequate training which drove General Patton himself to stay on the foreshore for some 18 hours personally heaving, shoving and pushing off landing craft and calming the nerves of G.I.s who kept faltering whenever a French plane flew over – such behaviour not being exactly the role of a Commanding General – despite each and every hazard of war which at one time or another seemed to manifest on this first great American gamble, the huge armada had successfully crossed the Atlantic unobserved, had landed the expeditionary force in a semi-hostile and astonished North Africa and had therefore arrived on the scene with a loud, resonant bang.

Thus ended the opening phase of Operation TORCH. By 11 November, only three days after D-Day, all main French bases in North and North-West Africa from Bône in the east to Safi in the west were safely in Allied hands. The political situation, however, was very far from a happy solution nor was the seizing of Tunisia by the Germans and in particular the port of Bizerta a matter for congratulation.

65

Bizerta's fate

The dithering leadership, wavering allegiance and uncertainty of purpose at the top which led inevitably to the tragic destruction of the French Navy in World War II – those and other equally grave defects – are best exemplified in the events at Bizerta during the days immediately following the TORCH landings. The two Admirals concerned were Esteva, the Resident General and overall Commander-in-Chief in Tunisia, and Derrien, the Naval Commander at Bizerta.

In March 1945, two months before the capitulation of

Germany but six months after France had been liberated, Esteva was brought to trial before the High Court of Justice in France, found guilty of treason and intelligence with the enemy and sentenced to imprisonment for life with the loss of military rank and civic rights, national degradation and confiscation of his property. Derrien, similarly accused and convicted, died in prison in 1946. Of Esteva, whom A.B.C. and Royer Dick both trusted and liked, Cunningham wrote in his *Sailor's Odyssey* published in 1951: 'In a recent letter to me from the fortress in which he is still confined, Esteva assures me that he worked for us all along the line in Tunisia. I have no reason whatever to disbelieve this statement, and it is true that he wished to remain behind in Tunis when the Axis forces surrendered in May 1943 but was forced into an aeroplane and taken away. In view of his fine record his sentence was more severe than was expected and to my mind was cruelly vindictive.' How did this tragedy come about?

Before being appointed Resident General on the formation of the Vichy Government in July 1940, Esteva had been the Naval Commander-in-Chief, South, i.e. of the whole of French North Africa. He was therefore well experienced in keeping the whole naval establishment intact, so far as that was possible, during the most difficult disarmament period when conditions imposed by the Italians were much more demanding in Tunisia than Algeria because Libya, Tunisia's neighbour to the east, was at that time an Italian colony. As Resident General in Tunis, Esteva had under his direct command General Barré for the army and Vice-Admiral Derrien as the naval equivalent.

Admiral Derrien's forces at Bizerta were negligible, consisting only of three 600–ton torpedo boats, two minesweepers and nine submarines without crews and held in reserve. It was the port itself which mattered and the use to which it could be put. Most of the coastal batteries had been disarmed and Derrien could call on a mere three battalions to man and defend the considerable perimeter of his parish, whereas 19 were thought necessary before.

Having reached the age limit, Derrien had been about to retire to Brittany the following month. In their book *The French Navy in the Second World War* Admiral Auphan (in 1942 Minister of Marine at Vichy) and Jacques Mordal record that Admiral Derrien's character is revealed by one particular trait – for the first time in his life he was about to ask a favour of the Germans through official channels and that was to be allowed to take his sword with him into retirement. The German High Command had forbidden any arms to be kept in private hands in the occupied zone, including even so useless a weapon as a ceremonial naval officer's sword. The French authors comment that this request of Derrien's indicates a disciplined irony . . .

On 7 November 1942 this 'old loup de mer', as the authors call him, was to be visited in Bizerta by a friend of long standing, General Bergeret. This General had come hot-foot from Vichy where a 'mysterious intermediary' had tipped him off about the forthcoming landings. He had then come to Tunis because he wished to be on the spot when it all began. Bound by his word of honour, which he had had to give, Bergeret had not breathed a word about this in metropolitan France. However going by way of Algiers, he had tried to alert General Juin and Admiral Darlan but without success. Derrien, whose outlook was different, lit up at the news General Bergeret gave him in confidence that the transports would begin to arrive at any moment.

Derrien was, therefore, in no way surprised when Esteva called him up in the middle of the night to say that as Resident General he had just been given a message from President Roosevelt by the hand of the U.S. Consul, Mr Doolittle, to the effect that the landings were about to begin. In reply and while making it clear to the Consul that he would of course obey any orders his superiors gave him, Esteva had declared himself sympathetic to the Allied plan and finished by saying 'But you'd better hurry up as the Germans will be here within forty-eight hours'.

All this created what Auphan and Mordal called 'une ambiance'. Indeed had any American ships arrived at Bizerta on the morning of 8 November, they might well have been welcomed with mooring lines instead of with gunfire.

Unfortunately not a ship showed up. A token force would have been sufficient to have included Tunisia in the cease-fire Darlan was to negotiate the next day. But with true French logic it was observed that a cease-fire required some shots to have been exchanged and in spite of Mr Doolittle's warning neither a ship nor a soldier had so far appeared. Among other things, and as in Morocco, this led to doubts as to the scale of the invasion. Worse still, American broadcasts announced that the Bey (Governor) of Tunis and the French Resident General had been warned, so naturally the Germans immediately took precautions of their own to secure Tunisia.

On 8 November, on orders from Darlan in Algiers, Derrien scuttled three merchant ships in the approaches to Bizerta without succeeding, because of the current, in completely blocking the channel. It is impossible to know, Auphan claims, whether Darlan was taking this precaution against the Anglo-Americans, against the Axis or simply to furnish Auphan in Vichy with an excuse for preventing the Toulon fleet from intervening on the coast of Africa.

On the 9th on orders from Wiesbaden, where the Franco-German Armistice Commission was still in session, the Luftwaffe began to land aircraft at El Aouina airfield near Tunis. By the evening of the following day, 104 planes had already arrived. 'The disciplined French troops', Auphan and Mordal continue, 'let these aircraft land because no one had ordered them not to but equally no one had said the Germans could spread out into the countryside so a strong detachment of French troops prevented the intruders from leaving the airfield.'

At midday on 10 November Derrien received orders from Algiers, as did the other Commanders in French

North Africa, to cease fire. This armistice put an end to hostilities with the Anglo-Americans, hostilities which, so far as Derrien in Tunisia was concerned, had never taken place. In spite of the immediate disavowal by Vichy both of this armistice and of Darlan himself, Derrien passed on these orders to his subordinates 'still hoping perhaps to see some battle-dress appear'. In fact the opposite happened. That evening the French Admiralty (Auphan) in Vichy informed him that the Wehrmacht would shortly be landing at Bizerta and Tunis. 'I am well aware', Auphan's signal ended, 'of the repercussions of this operation. Rest assured that like you I am only thinking of what is best for France' – which cannot have been a very encouraging message to receive. Nor indeed did it give any sort of clear lead at all.

General Barré, who had received a similar communication from the Ministry of War at Vichy, ordered his troops to avoid all contact with the Germans and to withdraw from the ports inland to the hills known as 'the Tunisian dorsal'. Thus a division opened up between the navy bound to its arsenal and ports and the army which had begun retreating to the mountains on the Algerian frontier.

On 11 November the news of the invasion of the unoccupied zone of mainland France provoked chaos in Bizerta. 'Who is the enemy?' Derrien demanded to be told by the French Admiralty, 'is it the Germans or the Anglo-Saxons?' The French Admiralty was unable to give a clear answer to this, Auphan merely replying that 'his personal advice was to be neutral to both but the Council of Ministers would decide on the matter that evening'.

Esteva in turn was called to the telephone by Darlan in Algiers. According to Auphan and Mordal the two Admirals were on intimate terms. 'Hallo, is that you, Jean-Pierre?' Darlan said, 'It's François here. Do you want to become American?' 'Bien sûr', Jean-Pierre replied, 'but the Americans had better get a move on.' It is difficult to see that brief exchange as constituting an order of any kind.

General Juin, however, was considerably more definite

than Darlan. He called Barré from Algiers and said: 'On va taper sur le Boche (fire on the Germans).' At least the army was given a lead.

That phrase 'On va taper sur le Boche' was passed on to Bizerta. 'Can I tell my men?' Derrien asked; 'Yes', said Esteva. So with immediate enthusiasm Derrien issued an Order of the Day: 'After two days of discussion and confusion, an official and precise order has just been given me designating the enemy against whom you will be fighting. That enemy is Germany and Italy. Soldiers, sailors and airmen defending Bizerta: The decision has been taken. Go to it with all your heart against the adversaries of 1940. We shall take our revenge. Long live France!'

The broadcasting of this message in the late afternoon unleashed a general exhilaration on board ship and ashore. Sailors sang the Marseillaise. In some officers' messes champagne began to flow ... However the bottles had scarcely been opened when the order came revoking Derrien's proclamation and calling in all copies. What had happened?

It seems that Derrien had read his order over the telephone to an alarmed Esteva who pointed out that when you are going to make an about-turn and fire on someone, you don't give advance warning of the fact. Moreover Esteva had just received a message from the Council of Ministers at Vichy declaring that hostilities were to continue against the Anglo-Americans. In addition, he observed, these Anglo-Americans had still failed to manifest in Tunisia. So at midnight 'with his spirit dead', Derrien cancelled his proclamation and instead ordered strict neutrality to be observed against *all* belligerents. The effect of this cold douche on the general morale can well be imagined.

The next day the fate of Bizerta was sealed. German aircraft landed at the naval air base of Sidi Ahmed and units of the Italian Navy took over the port. Tunisia was to remain in Axis hands for another six months.

66

The press outcry

The press and public outcry which followed the Darlan 'deal' rose to such a pitch in the United Kingdom and to a lesser degree in the United States that, had it occurred in peacetime, it would certainly have brought down the government. When the enabling agreements were signed with Darlan on 22 November setting up provisional arrangements for administering the North African region, British passions began to run high. People were saying such things as 'Is *that* all we've been fighting for? All this merely to compromise with the traitors of Vichy?' That at least was how the press and the Gaullists in Britain made it appear with headlines such as 'De Gaulle banned; Darlan uplifted'. How had this come about? Why was it necessary to do any deal of any kind with the men of Vichy and especially with Darlan, known to be number 2 to Marshal Pétain and who was branded and generally reviled by the fighting services and the public at large as a betrayer of the Allied cause?

Although a moment's thought would have made it obvious that the facts and more particularly the military facts could not be deployed publicly, the long-suffering public itself was not given to such moments of thought. The man in the street considered these things with his heart and the British public's heart had been thoroughly bruised. By 10 December, a month after the TORCH landings had taken place, Churchill admitting that there was a real and vivid case to be made and to be met, sought refuge in a secret session of the House of Commons. There he made one of the most significant speeches of his whole career which convinced the Commons, stopped all further Parliamentary opposition, 'quenched the hostile press and reassured the country'. But how had matters been allowed to get to such a point?

Basically the British and the Americans had once more failed to understand the French. Yet again we had got it wrong and while de Gaulle could be charged with some of the responsibility for the failure at Dakar in 1940, now two years later Robert Murphy and the sources on which Allied intelligence relied had also to admit to some wishful thinking when it came to the hard core of French colonial administration and the armed forces on which that administration depended.

Less than a week after the TORCH landings press criticism had become so severe that both Roosevelt and Churchill asked Eisenhower for a fuller explanation. On 14 November the Supreme Allied Commander replied:

I completely understand the bewilderment in London and Washington because of the turn that negotiations with French North Africans have taken. *Existing French sentiment here does not remotely agree with prior calculations* [author's italics]. The following facts are pertinent and it is important that no precipitate action at home upset the equilibrium we have been able to establish.

The name of Marshal Pétain is something to conjure with here [author's italics]. Everyone attempts to create the impression that he lives and acts under the shadow of the Marshal's figure. Civil governors, military leaders and naval commanders agree that only one man has an obvious right to assume the Marshal's mantle in North Africa. He is Darlan. Even Giraud, who has been our trusted adviser and staunch friend since early conferences succeeded in bringing him down to earth, recognises this overriding consideration and has modified his own intentions accordingly.

The resistance we first met was offered because all ranks believed this to be the Marshal's wish. For this reason Giraud is deemed to have been guilty of at least a touch of insubordination in urging non-resistance to our landing. General Giraud understands and appears to have some sympathy for this universal attitude. All concerned say they are ready to help us provided Darlan tells them to do so, but they are not willing to follow anyone else. Admiral Esteva in Tunis says he will take orders from Darlan [*but not when he was disowned by Pétain*]. Noguès stopped fighting in Morocco by Darlan's order. Recognition of Darlan's position in this regard cannot be escaped.

The gist of the agreement is that the French will do what they can to assist us in taking Tunisia. The group will organise for effective co-operation and will begin, under Giraud, reorganisation of selected military forces for participation in the war. The group will exhaust every expedient in an effort to get the Toulon fleet. We will support the group in controlling and pacifying the country and in equipping selected units. Details still under discussion.

Our hope of quick conquest of Tunisia and of gaining here a supporting population cannot be realised unless there is accepted a general agreement along the lines which we have just made with Darlan and the other officials who control the administrative machinery of the region and the tribes in Morocco. Giraud is now aware of his inability to do anything by himself even with Allied support. He has cheerfully accepted the post of military chief in the Darlan group. He agrees that his own name should not be mentioned until a period of several days has elapsed. Without a strong French government we would be forced to undertake military occupation. The cost in time and resources would be tremendous. In Morocco alone General Patton believes that it would require 60,000 Allied troops to keep the tribes pacified. In view of the effect that tribal disturbance would have on Spain, you see what a problem we have.

Whereas both the President and the British Prime Minister supported Eisenhower to the full and said so publicly, this did little to stem the tidal wave of public opinion and the resulting disquiet. Churchill said to Roosevelt three days later:

> The more I reflect on it [the Darlan arrangement] the more convinced I become that it can only be a temporary expedient, justifiable solely by the stress of battle. We must not overlook the serious political injury which may be done to our cause, not only in France but throughout Europe, by the feeling that we are ready to make terms with the local Quislings. Darlan has an odious record. It is he who has inculcated in the French navy its malignant disposition by promoting his creatures to command. It is but yesterday that French sailors were sent to their death against your line of battle off Casablanca, and now for the sake of power and office, Darlan plays the turncoat . . .

One result of this was a public statement by the President that he had 'accepted General Eisenhower's political arrangements made for the time being in Northern and Western Africa . . . (but) no permanent arrangement should be made with Admiral Darlan . . . the present arrangement is only a temporary expedient, justified solely by the stress of battle'.

This had a number of effects. It strengthened the underground opposition to Darlan led by the disillusioned Committee of Five and the plotting by other similar groups, one of which became responsible for the coming assassination. It strengthened the Vichy sentiments or rather renewed the loyalty towards the Marshal in Vichy held by 'mayors, station and post masters and other key officials' on whom the British 1st Army under General

Anderson had to rely during its advance towards Tunisia and it caused Darlan himself to write to General Clark at the beginning of December:

Information from various sources tends to substantiate the view that I am 'only a lemon which the Americans will drop after they have squeezed it dry.'

In the line of conduct which I have adopted out of pure French patriotic feeling, in spite of the serious disadvantages which it entails for me, at the moment when it was extremely easy for me to let events take their course without my intervention, my own personal position does not come into consideration.

I acted only because the American Government has solemnly undertaken to restore the integrity of French sovereignty as it existed in 1939 and because the armistice between the Axis and France was broken by the total occupation of Metropolitan France, against which the Marshal has solemnly protested.

I did not act through pride, ambition or calculation but because the position which I occupied in my country made it my duty to act.

When the integrity of France's sovereignty is an accomplished fact – and I hope that will be in the least possible time – it is my firm intention to return to private life and to end my days, in the course of which I have ardently served my country, in retirement.

67

Toulon

As the North African imbroglio of intrigue, squabbling, indecision and treachery continued to thicken its entanglements during the three weeks immediately following the TORCH landings, the Germans in mainland France wasted no time. They were not expending their valuable resources in taking over the rest of France, with all the commitments and dangers involved, out of spite or just for the hell of it. With the Allies established in North Africa in strength, the German High Command had now to secure its rear by taking precautions against a further Allied invasion, this time in the south of France.

Above all the Germans wanted the fleet at Toulon. French warships based on Toulon had increased in number from 36 in June 1940 to nearly 80 in November 1942. This represented roughly half of what was left of the French fleet and, more importantly, the most modern half. Toulon itself had for over a century been the centre of gravity of French naval power. Now it was the base for the only effective armed force the Marshal had left under his command.

The ships at Toulon had been placed in three distinct divisions:

1. The High Seas Fleet commanded by Admiral de Laborde comprising the battle-cruiser *Strasbourg*, three 10,000-ton cruisers (*Algérie, Dupleix, Colbert*), two light cruisers (*Marseillaise, Jean-de-Vienne*), 10 destroyers and three torpedo boats – all on active service,

short of fuel and ammunition, perhaps, but otherwise fully worked-up in the naval sense and ready for action.

2. The Préfet Maritime's squadron (Vice-Admiral Marquis) consisting of the World War I battleship *Provence* (flagship of the Training Division), the aircraft carrier *Commandant Teste*, six torpedo boats and eight submarines, all so organized for the defence of Toulon and of the southern coast of France.

3. Ships in reserve under the armistice terms: the battleship *Dunkerque* (damaged in July 1940 at Mers-el-Kébir but sailed to Toulon in February 1942), the cruisers *Foch* and *La-Gallissonière*, eight destroyers, six torpedo boats and 10 submarines.

The train of events since 8 November had put the naval authorities and the troops at Toulon into a rare old turmoil. The way the Americans had landed in North Africa without warning and, in the French view, 'sous un faux prétexte' reminded sailors of the previous assaults on Dakar, in Syria and at Diego Suarez, all of which had left so many gaps in their ranks. Moreover listening to the B.B.C. they had learned that losses at Casablanca had been severe.

Darlan's about-face had first astonished and then after his official disavowal, scandalized the naval world while remaining all the time cloaked by an air of mystery. Then came the German occupation of the whole of France which drove feelings to their highest pitch. Nothing could now be worse than to fall into German hands. On board certain ships anti-German demonstrations had had to be suppressed by the officers. The so-called 'neutrality agreement' for Toulon did little to lessen the tension, perhaps because this arrangement had been achieved through the personal initiative of Admirals and not by those normally responsible at government levels. On top of all that the Commander-in-Chief of the High Seas Fleet had required his subordinates, already bound by their oaths to the

Marshal, to make a further oath of loyalty to himself, thus leading all concerned into a deeper moral dilemma.

A new flood of refugees now began swirling down into what was left of the free zone. Rumour ran riot. A sloop on patrol claimed to have sunk an Allied submarine. Several army detachments arrived to shore up the defences of Toulon. These soldiers were full of resentment against the Germans, whereas the sailors dreaded above all a new Mers-el-Kébir. Unaware of Darlan and other Admirals' secret arrangements made and broken behind their backs, the local Toulon command did its ingenious best to secure the now isolated base against all foreign aggressors. This, they told themselves, would effectively cut the ground from excuses the Germans might cite to justify taking over the base themselves.

Then to make matters worse the French Admiralty on 14 November ordered the permanent scuttling and sabotage instructions to be held in abeyance for updating. What was intended by that? The next day Admiral de Laborde made a quick trip to Vichy where he was received by Admiral Auphan, the Secretary of State for the Navy (on the point of handing in his resignation), by Pétain and by Laval. That same evening Laborde issued another General Order of the Day, evidently in tune with the government, in which he assured all personnel under his command that the security of the neutralized zone of Toulon remained firmly in their hands. So far so good. Then he added: 'At such time that those in high command lose their sense of duty, you must show that Honour is not measured by gold stripes or Admirals' stars. Unflinching discipline and correct service behaviour are the ultimate duty of all . . . I myself have guaranteed your loyalty to the Marshal whom I saw today and who has directed me to say that he is counting on you to save the unity and honour of France . . .' Good fine words but in the present unsettled state of affairs what did they mean? Were their senior officers – 'those in high command' – about to lose their sense of duty? And if so how were ordinary sailors to save the unity and honour of France? No one felt able to say.

In the next few days, pressure increased. One did not have to be over-intelligent to see that the beloved Marshal was being effectively stripped of his political powers. Then Admiral Auphan resigned, so what did that imply? Each day that passed saw more and more bitter accusations and reproaches hurled at the French leaders in Africa – so where now lay the unity and honour of France? Then the German High Command began to show its hand. It ordered the additional army detachments sent in to defend Toulon to be withdrawn and on 21 November required all French Air Force formations to be stood down and demobilized.

All this created a climate of uncertainty and fear which the new Secretary of State, Admiral Abrial, endeavoured to reduce by coming himself to Toulon on 23 November. The officers remained disciplined, as always, but now they wanted to know and understand what was going on. All the minister could give them were the usual bromides. Should it be necessary to sink the ships, this should be done without capsizing them, thus leaving the after-thought that one day they might be recovered; for the rest he confirmed the dispositions taken against an attack coming from the sea in liaison with Axis troops who would now be manning the rest of the coast. The wretched Abrial's visit was not made any easier by the newly arrived *Gauleiter* in Marseilles promptly commandeering all French merchant shipping in the port except for those ships necessary for the Corsican link and by the news that French West Africa had gone over to the 'dissidents' of Algiers.

The next day German troops seized ships at Sète and Port-Vendres and German engineers occupied the naval air base at Hyères. All was then set for the Reich to renege on yet another solemn promise and to seize by surprise and by force all that was left of the French fleet. The drama now raced to its climax.

68

The destruction of the fleet

It was a very near thing. The Toulon take-over was executed by the 1st Armoured Corps of the S.S. commanded by Obergruppenführer Hausser to whom had been attached for liaison purposes a mere 50 sailors of the Kriegsmarine under the orders of Fregattenkapitan Hugo Heydel. To follow were 4500 German sailors for the occupation and running of the base, but they did not take part in the assault either because they were delayed *en route* or because Hitler could rely only on the S.S. to carry out effectively any really tough or dirty job.

So when in the middle of the night of the 26–27 November the first German units arrived in two columns from east and west of the dockyard, there was only one German naval officer, Commander Heydel, to help identify ships, personnel and targets. Here it is only fair to say that the German Navy, as we now know from their records today and like the Royal Navy at Mers-el-Kébir, had a revulsion from top to bottom at being required shamefully to break their word of honour and undertake an operation which was underhand, professionally distasteful and almost certain to fail. Indeed Commander Heydel, when asked by the S.S. General concerned what he thought were the chances of success, replied curtly: 'None whatever, if you want my opinion as the French will already have prepared a Scapa Flow just as we did in 1918.' (After the Armistice on 11 November 1918, the German High Seas

Fleet surrendered at Scapa Flow and then promptly scuttled itself.)

However the Wehrmacht intended to disarm all that remained of the French Army, as a precautionary measure, and that had to include this naval enclave which appeared to their eyes as a foreign body in their line of battle. It may also be that they thought they could teach the Kriegsmarine a lesson. The German assault forces were therefore deprived, by their own decision, of the key naval technicians who might have been able to stop or hinder the destruction which took place. In spite of all this the trust which both Vichy and Toulon continued to place in the solemn and oft-repeated promises made by the Reich resulted in the outcome being in doubt until the very last moment.

Surprise was complete. Indeed French suspicions had been so lulled that the night of 26–27 November was the first since the TORCH landings in Africa on 8 November that a small fraction of officers and men (actually an eighth part) were given leave ashore. Along the approach routes chosen by the German tanks there were only small units of the gendarmerie, unable to raise the alarm since their telephones had been cut in advance. A messenger sent by one of these posts arrived only just ahead of the German columns.

The Wehrmacht plan for Operation ANTON (their codeword for the investing of Toulon and the Fleet) envisaged a diplomatic *démarche* made at 0440 hours to Laval at home in Vichy, at which time it was hoped that the first German troops would already be on board the French ships. What in fact happened was that Vichy's subsequent telephone calls to Toulon were all too late to warn of the surprise attack or to change the pattern of events.

The first the French knew of what was to come was when German tanks suddenly loomed up at the gates of Fort Lemalgue, the unfortified barracks which housed the headquarters of the Préfet Maritime. Admiral Marquis, asleep in his bed, could do nothing but the Germans were unable to discover the whereabouts of the telephone exchange and as they ranged the corridors Rear Admiral Robin and Lieutenant Commander Le Nabec, the duty officers, were able to alert by telephone Rear Admiral Dornon in charge of the main arsenal and various other authorities. Dornon was told to warn the Commander-in-Chief of the High Seas Fleet on board the *Strasbourg* which he did at once and asked for the scuttling of the ships under his command to begin. It was 0430.

Admiral de Laborde's first reaction was one of complete disbelief in such a breaking of trust. In default of further information, he did not feel justified in doing more than alerting his command, ordering boilers to be lit and for all the preliminary steps to be taken for the scuttling without giving the definite and irrevocable order to go ahead with this terrible act.

Meanwhile Dornon in the arsenal alerted the gatekeepers at all points in the base, saying that the Germans were already there and in some cases were trying to scale the walls. He ordered them to be fired on and for as much time as possible to be gained 'en parlementant à travers les grilles'. At 0520 the Mourillon arsenal was stormed but five submarines succeeded in getting away. Five minutes later the main gate of the arsenal was smashed down by German tanks and at long last Laborde gave the general order to scuttle the fleet.

The general hell of destruction then began with the German tanks ranging the jetties in total confusion and the blackest of nights lit up by the glare of explosions in ships, docks and workshops. The Germans did not reach the Milhaud wharves where the big ships lay until 0600 and the other quays and jetties at 0620, 0720 and finally 0730 when they reached the quays where the smaller ships had been moored.

At all points they arrived too late. The demolitions and devastations had already taken place. When the giant *Strasbourg* was challenged from the jetty to hand over the ship intact, Admiral de Laborde himself replied, 'Too late. The ship is sinking', to which the German interpreter on the jetty was told to say, 'Admiral, my Colonel orders me to say he admires you'.

But as daylight came the holocaust was over and 75 warships had been destroyed or had escaped. This tally comprised one battleship, two battlecruisers, seven cruisers, 30 destroyers or torpedo boats, 16 submarines, one aircraft carrier and 18 sloops, minesweepers and smaller ships. The Germans were everywhere in the great naval port but with empty hands.

69

Immediate repercussions

The agony of self-destruction at Toulon, mercifully executed with the loss of only about a dozen lives, marks the end of the shooting war between Vichy France and the Allies. The French fleet, which in reality was what it was all about, had virtually ceased to exist with scarcely a shot fired in anger except at its former allies. The tragedy at Toulon was rounded off after the Liberation with the indictment of Admiral de Laborde who was tried and condemned to death, although this sentence was later commuted to life imprisonment.

Darlan's promise of 18 June 1940 that the fleet would never be allowed to fall into enemy hands had thus been honoured, although Darlan himself had been disowned and had lost control. He had 'invited' the fleets at Toulon and Alexandria to rally to North Africa, realizing no doubt that an 'order' from him to the Admirals in command would not be obeyed. Both invitations were tartly refused.

The little Gascon, however, had no intention of giving up. On the evening of 27 November, the man who until 19 days before had been heir apparent to the Marshal in Vichy now broadcast to the French Empire in Africa whose leaders had so recently and with such considerable misgiving rallied behind him:

Hitler has just decided to occupy Toulon and to disarm France. The Army has been dismissed. The Fleet at Toulon, after defending itself heroically, has been sabotaged or sunk. It was easy to foresee that the granting of a free zone round Toulon was a trap to retain our ships under German control. I therefore invited the Fleet to leave. The Commander-in-Chief did not listen to me. He thought he could save our ships. He has lost them and has caused the death of numerous officers and sailors. Following on the occupation of a France already cut into zones to destroy the unity of the country, after the arrest of General Weygand [which it will be remembered Darlan partly organized himself], after the restrictions placed on the powers of the head of the government, after the demobilisation of our armed forces, Germany's aim is now clear. That is to wipe out France. We shall have no mercy for all those who, deliberately or not, serve the designs of our eternal enemy [which had now become Germany once more rather than Great Britain]. No one of us must any longer hesitate to do his duty which is to crush Germany and Italy and liberate the country. French Africa is the only place in the world where our flag flies freely, where the army has its weapons, the navy flies its ensign and the air force uses its wings. We are the sole hope of France, let us show ourselves worthy of her.

When one looks back over the previous 2½ years on all that Darlan had done 'deliberately or not' to serve the designs of Germany, even allowing for the fact that he thought Germany was going to win and that he was doing it in the best interests of France, the above broadcast remains a fairly remarkable *volte-face*, with not a word about the ally (and hereditary enemy) to whom France was legally treaty-bound until the Armistice of June 1940 and certainly without a mention of de Gaulle who since that armistice had regarded himself as 'the sole hope of France'.

70

Developments in Algiers

Repercussions to the grand finale at Toulon were world wide. De Gaulle, broadcasting from London, spoke of it as a 'national reflex' and received a telephone call from Churchill expressing his 'nobly worded condolences but deep satisfaction' at what the French Navy had done. *The Times* of London wrote: 'Even those who think that the French Fleet could have been more usefully employed in the reconquest of France, must nevertheless render deep homage to the way in which the Navy has honoured its solemn promise.' The French communist paper *L'Humanité*, clandestinely published, described the scuttling as 'an act of supreme patriotism' while later claiming that 'the officers had had their hands forced by their men'.

Hitler and Mussolini were understandably furious and took their revenge in the general and brutal enslavement of France which began in 1943 and was to last for 18 terrible months until the liberation of the country by the Allies in the summer of 1944. More particularly, at Bizerta on 7 December 1942 the German General Gausse gave Admiral Derrien half an hour to turn over the ships, coastal batteries, dockyard installations and radio stations intact otherwise all would be bombed to destruction, crews would be killed to the last officer and man, and no prisoners would be taken, since Marshal Pétain had ordered the demobilization of all French forces and therefore legally (!) such troops could not be considered as regular soldiers under the laws of war. Derrien gave in to this savage ultimatum in order to save further bloodshed and Bizerta henceforth became an Axis port.

So a new era began. All fighting between Vichy France and the Allies had ceased. Metropolitan France, now totally occupied, had become no more than a German province. The French Empire in North Africa however had opted under Darlan to re-enter the war on the Allied side. The only exception to this was Force X at Alexandria where Admiral Godfroy to the great disappointment (and exasperation) of the Allies refused to recognize Darlan's authority and continued his 'letter of the law' neutrality in obedience to the Marshal, despite the fact that Pétain had become for all practical purposes a prisoner of the Reich. This obstinacy was to continue until the summer of 1943 by which time all Axis forces in North Africa had surrendered and a provisional French Government under Giraud and de Gaulle had been organized in Algiers. By then, Darlan had been dead for six months.

In December 1942 a rapid deterioration in political affairs in North Africa had begun together with a seething anarchy in civilian public and private life which, had there been no Allied military presence, could well have erupted into civil war. At the centre of this turmoil the spider-like Darlan continued to weave his web. 'Not only was there a desperate struggle against Giraud for power and recognition', Churchill wrote, 'among the recent adherents to the Allied cause, Darlan, Noguès, Boisson and others but also active discontent among those men who had helped the Allied landings in November and among the small but active group which was ardent for de Gaulle. In addition there was growing support for a movement to place the Comte de Paris, at this time living quietly near Tangier, at the head of a provisional wartime administration in North Africa in opposition to Vichy. The patchwork arrangement whereby Darlan was at the head of civil affairs and Giraud was in command of the French armed forces in North Africa came under increasing strain.'

In fact a number of sinister activities were going on while Eisenhower in the west and Alexander in the east were developing the great pincer movement on Rommel's Afrika Korps which had begun with Alamein in the east and the TORCH landings in the west and which was to culminate in total victory in May 1943. Such activities included the renewed operation of the Service d'Ordre Légionnaire (a Vichy organization of ex-servicemen) and similar Fascist groups. These continued, on a wink and a nod from the French colonial administration, to victimize those who supported the Allies, some of whom had not yet been released from Vichy-run prisons. Well-known German sympathizers, ejected when the Allies first landed, had quietly been reinstated. French soldiers were still being punished for 'desertion' because they had tried to help the Allied forces at the assault stage. All this marched with the intense Anglo-American press outrage at the 'deal' which had been struck with Darlan.

There was also a divergence between the British and the Americans in their attitude to the French which went deeper than Roosevelt's distaste for de Gaulle and the British Government's solemn treaty of support for the Free French. Churchill expressed this succinctly in the key speech he made to the House of Commons in secret session on 10 December 1942.

. . . I hold no brief for Admiral Darlan. Like myself he is the object of the animosities of Herr Hitler and of Monsieur Laval. Otherwise I have nothing in common with him. But it is necessary for the House to realise that the Government and to a large extent the people of the United States do not feel the same way about Darlan as we do. He has not betrayed them. He has not maltreated any of their citizens. They do not think much of him but they do not hate him and despise him as we do over here. Many of them think more of the lives of their own soldiers than they do about the past records of French political figures. Moreover the Americans have cultivated up to the last moment relations with Vichy which were of a fairly intimate character and which in my opinion have conduced to our general advantage. At any rate, the position of the Americans at Vichy gave us a window on that courtyard which otherwise would not have existed . . . the attitude of the United States executive and State Department towards Vichy and all its works must be viewed against this background . . . now all this may seem very absurd to our minds. But there is one point about it which is important to us. It is in accordance with orders and authority transmitted or declared to be transmitted by Marshal Pétain that the French troops in North and West Africa have pointed and fired their rifles against the Germans and Italians instead of continuing to point and fire their rifles against the British and Americans. I am sorry to have to mention a point like that, but it makes a lot of difference to a soldier whether a man fires his gun at him or his enemy; and even the soldier's wife or father might have a feeling about it too . . . all this is done in the sacred name of the Marshal, and when the Marshal bleats over the telephone orders to the contrary and deprives Darlan of his nationality the Admiral rests comfortably upon the fact or fiction – it does not much matter which – that the Marshal is acting under the duress of the invading Hun, and that he, Darlan, is still carrying out his true wishes. In fact if Admiral Darlan had to shoot Marshal Pétain he would no doubt do it in Marshal Pétain's name . . .

I must however say that personally I consider in the circumstances prevailing General Eisenhower was right; and even if he was not quite right I should have been very reluctant to hamper or impede his action when so many lives and such vitally important issues hung in the balance.

The confusion over Darlan which, in any case, was to climax in less than a fortnight could not have been better set out. No remedy was to hand but at least the circumstances could be understood. Finally and to put the Algerian entanglements into their proper perspective, Churchill ended by saying:

> I must say I think he is a poor creature with a jaundiced outlook and disorganised loyalties who in all this tremendous African episode West and East alike, can find no point to excite his interest except the arrangements made between General Eisenhower and Admiral Darlan. The struggle for the Tunisian tip is now rising to its climax and the main battle impends. Another trial of strength is very near on the frontiers of Cyrenaica. Both these battles will be fought almost entirely by soldiers from this island. The First and Eighth British Armies will be engaged to the full. I cannot take my thoughts away from them and their fortunes and I expect that will be the feeling of the House of Commons . . .
>
> I also ask them to treat with proper reprobation that small, busy and venomous band who harbour and endeavour to propagate unworthy and unfounded suspicions, and so to come forward unitedly with us in all the difficulties through which we are steadfastly and successfully making our way.

71

The beginning of the end

On the same day that the fleet at Toulon scuttled itself Alain Darlan, the Admiral's son who was recovering from polio, was flown in a U.S. Air Force plane from Algiers to Rabat in Morocco to await onward passage to Warm Springs in the United States. This was the result of an invitation from and through the direct initiative of President Roosevelt, himself a victim of the same disease. Alain was in the meantime given further treatment at the Marie-Feuillet hospital for officers while the necessary transatlantic travel arrangements were being made and these were discussed at an official lunch which the Admiral gave to the top brass both Allied and French in Algiers two days before Christmas 1942.

At that lunch General Clark, deputizing for the Supreme Commander who was away at the front at the headquarters of the British Fifth Corps at Béja, sounded out Darlan on a delicate matter. This was the Admiral's ideas about his own future. According to Pierre Ordioni, Darlan turned to Clark towards the end of the meal and said: 'Tomorrow the Axis press will report that I hosted this lunch with the muzzle of your revolver at the back of my neck'; to which Clark replied with a laugh, 'If other meals are as good as this I'm ready to threaten you with my revolver any day of the week'. Darlan acknowledged this quip with a short laugh.

Clark then brought up the question of Alain's transportation to the United States and, secretly hoping to surprise a reaction from the Admiral as to the chances of his quitting politics in North Africa, went on: 'I think it might also be possible to arrange a passage for the Admiral if he so wished.' Darlan nodded his head and said: 'Yes, I'd much like to hand over to General Giraud. He enjoys it here. I don't.' Then turning to Murphy who was also at the lunch, he drank a toast to the Allied victory and said: 'Come back with me to the office. There are one or two things I want to talk to you about.'

When, many years later, the author discussed this meeting with the former diplomat Robert Murphy in New York, his memory (he was then 82) was surprisingly clear: 'When we got to the office', he said, 'Darlan shuffled his papers around a bit and then said: "Perhaps you already know that there are four separate plots to kill me. If one of them were to succeed what would you Americans do?" He then produced from his pocket a list of his putative successors. Giraud headed this list but de Gaulle also figured on it as well. "However that would be too soon," Darlan said. "In the spring of 1943 perhaps. If de Gaulle took over now, he'd cause you a great heap of trouble." Giraud, too, he saw as no more than a good Commander-in-Chief: he was simply not interested in politics, in fact he detested them. Other names were then mentioned such as Flandin, Herriot and Reynaud but Darlan made out that for one reason or another none of them could be trusted. It was a strange meeting since Darlan seemed to be genuinely concerned but talked about his successor as if it were to do with the death of someone else and not his own. Then he shrugged his shoulders and started in on his papers again. The meeting was over and I took my leave.'

That was Darlan's last secret negotiation with the Americans. Almost exactly 24 hours later he was dead. Mr Murphy stated that he personally liked Darlan and thought his assassination quite unnecessary.*

*Murphy also said he had a high personal regard for Laval as an honest man and a patriot, an opinion I found astonishing, while about Stalin whom he met at Yalta he said: 'He was intelligent and very well informed. I liked him.'

72

The darkening scene

Since this story of England's last war with France comes to its climax with the murder of the enigmatic and legally appointed heir to the French Head of State and since those who plotted the slaying remain unknown (although suspected) to this day and are now unlikely ever to be identified with any certainty, the Algerian scene in which the event took place must be sketched if the bare facts of the drama are to be understood with any significance. Because Eisenhower was away at the front when Darlan was assassinated and because no one could assess in a matter of moments what the repercussions were likely to be, a total security blackout was immediately imposed.*

This story has been recounted so far from official records and from the reports and writings of the main protagonists in the war. What happened happened and no one can tamper with the facts. The climate in Algiers, however, during those last fateful weeks of 1942 was almost indescribable. Everyone lived in a midden of intrigue. No one was ever quite sure where he stood. No one could trust his neighbour. Families were divided against themselves.

*Although I was in Algiers at the time as a member of Eisenhower's staff, I cannot remember knowing much about it – except a feeling of dangerous tension and that anything might happen – until the 20-year-old assassin, Bonnier de la Chapelle, had been court-martialled and executed by firing squad, his coffin having been ordered before the court martial sat. We were all in the dark and so far as the French and native population of Algiers were concerned, perhaps this was just as well. Who was to know what might happen next?

Rumour ran like quicksilver, espionage was rife and no one knew whom or what to believe.

One reason for this was that the deal with Darlan, made five days after the landings, while it secured a cease-fire and no further loss of blood, left the worst Vichy men in power, 'from Governor Châtel and the Préfet Temple down to the lowest of sub-Légionnaires. The Allies', Renée Pierre-Gosset observed,

> trusted them almost to the point of naiveté and it was with good cause that General Catroux on General de Gaulle's staff in London one day exclaimed 'I would not feel safe if I had to fight with Admiral Darlan at my back.'
>
> For weeks the 'protected' Mogador Post Office through which all essential military communications between the Allies passed was directed by Colonel Merlin, the man Laval had placed there after consulting the German-Italian Armistice Commission. The entire staff had been chosen by the Gestapo. The Gaullists, the 27 Communist Deputies, all the political internees remained in prison or in camps . . . 'and when a member of Darlan's staff was questioned about this matter, he replied "What? Free political prisoners? But we surely cannot do that. What about the problem of finding housing accommodation? Where would these unfortunate men find room in Algiers?" Indeed as late as 16th December when Darlan told a Press conference of Allied War Correspondents that "the High Commissioner [i.e. himself] has already granted complete and entire amnesty to those who have been arrested because of Allied sympathies" the assembled War Correspondents knew to a man that this was a direct lie and that thousands were still languishing in French concentration camps in Algeria and Morocco.
>
> At that same conference a journalist asked a precise and embarrassing question "Could the Admiral tell us

why he collaborated with Germany?" Darlan, who had lit his pipe and was doodling on a writing pad, looked his questioner squarely in the face. "Collaboration was imposed on me by force" he said, "Yes, the Germans had me by the throat. All my movements, all I said or wrote, everyone I spoke to was closely watched by them. I was constantly surrounded by spies." Then he stood up and brought the conference to an end. The general impression was disastrous.

Renée Pierre-Gosset added a footnote, saying: 'This assertion caused an angry reaction in France. Fernand de Brinon, Paul Chack, Philippe Henriot violently attacked Darlan. "Was it under constraint", wrote de Brinon, "that you spontaneously wrote to the Germans offering them your advice regarding naval war against England and handing over to them secret British documents in your possession?"'

However successful Darlan appeared to be in the official wheeling and dealing he was able to do in the Marshal's name, his popularity with the man in the Algiers trolley-bus continued to wane. This culminated with the serious blow to his prestige struck by the scuttling of the Toulon fleet. The Admiral might prate of 'French honour being gloriously saved', but ordinary folk saw it in plainer terms. It was clear to them that Darlan was covering up yet again. Quite simply he had not been obeyed by the very men from whom he could have expected the most loyalty and understanding. When the Germans began occupying the whole of France, the fleet should have sailed and this view was sadly confirmed when sailors from the submarines *Casabianca*, *Marsouin* and *Le Glorieux* arrived in Algiers after escaping from Toulon. Even as far back as 11 November, these sailors said, the fleet could have sailed if only their leaders had given the order. There had been enough fuel for 10 days. Several destroyers were alleged to have sailed but had been called back at the last minute. People were ashamed. The fleet should have sailed and the fact that it never did was blamed on the officers in general and on the Admirals in particular. The leaders of France were rotten at the top, and this in no way increased Darlan's popularity during the few weeks in which he reigned in Algiers issuing edicts which began: 'We, Admiral Darlan, by virtue of the power given to us by the Marshal of France, Chief of the French State . . .'

Moreover and despite the censorship clandestine copies of the Gaullist paper *Combat* got through, being passed from hand to hand and eagerly read. The paper's criticism of Darlan intensified by the day with statements such as 'Darlan must give way. This "comédie" has lasted quite long enough. His historic mission is finished. He can no longer serve any useful purpose', or again, 'Where can this government be found? Who shall we have instead of Darlan whose days are numbered?'

One morning at breakfast, according to Renée Pierre-Gosset, the Admiral found a copy of *Combat* sent to him in a white envelope: 'It contained but a single dreadful indictment: "François Darlan, what have you to say in your own defence?" The Admiral gave instructions. In future his secretary was to sift the post more carefully. But Madame Darlan who having first trembled for the health of her son, now trembled for the life of her husband, repeated again her daily reminder "You will end by being assassinated". The Admiral's secretary told this authentic story in the presence of several people who spread it around. I myself noted it in my diary on 30 November. I was to be reminded of it again around a coffin . . .'

73

The assassination of Darlan

At 3 o'clock in the afternoon of 24 December 1942 Admiral Darlan returned from lunch to the Summer Palace, the Moorish building in which the High Commissioner had established his office and the Commissariat. The admiral was accompanied by his A.D.C., Commander Hourcade. A young man calling himself Morand and who was in reality Bonnier de la Chapelle had an appointment to see Admiral Darlan 'for personal reasons' and had been sitting in the adjacent waiting room for half an hour.

Commander Hourcade stepped aside at the door of his own office to let his superior officer pass and Darlan continued down a dark, narrow corridor to the High Commissioner's room. As he reached the door he heard a noise behind him and turned to see the young man. At point blank range the assassin fired two revolver shots. One hit the Admiral in the mouth, the other in the chest. Darlan tottered and then slid limply to the floor up against the open door of his office.

The young man then tried to escape but found the window he had intended to use barred on the outside. He was trapped. He then turned on the A.D.C. who had rushed to the Admiral's assistance and fired two more bullets one of which hit Hourcade in the thigh and the other in the ear. By this time the High Commissariat had been fully aroused. Admiral Battet, Darlan's Chief of Staff, and another Commander rushed on the scene and while one tried to help Darlan, the other arrested the young man who gave up his revolver without resisting and was then led away.

Now not a moment was lost. Admiral Battet, helped by orderlies, carried Darlan to his own car and drove him to the nearby Maillot hospital. The Admiral was almost lifeless and never spoke. At the hospital he was X-rayed and a bullet found in his lung. Madame Darlan arrived as a priest was giving the last rites to the dying man. Extraction of the bullet was attempted, although the doctors knew it could not succeed. Without regaining consciousness and recognizing no one, François Darlan, Admiral of the Fleet, Commander-in-Chief of the French Armies and High Commissioner of France, met his death.

Allied Headquarters immediately put Algiers into a state of emergency. Total censorship of the news was imposed – American war correspondents having to make their Christmas broadcasts about Christmas trees, toys and parties for the troops when one of the biggest scoops of the war had just happened virtually in front of their eyes.

American, British and French troops were at once confined to barracks and held at the ready in case order in the town might have to be restored. A lot had been learned since 8 November and strategic points in the town were put firmly under military control. General Eisenhower and General Giraud were both recalled from the Tunisian front, taking 30 hours of non-stop driving through rain, snow and sleet to reach Algiers.

Meanwhile the murderer was being interrogated. Police Commissaire Garinacci was faced by a youth no longer inspired by savage zeal, a youth without any defence and who seemed to be astonished at being imprisoned after his act of liberation. At that moment he was willing to confess everything and he did, giving names. Then a strange thing happened. Commissaire Garinacci read through this confession which the young man had signed and was so appalled by what this revealed that in a moment of panic he seized the document and burned it.

Bonnier de la Chapelle was placed in solitary confinement and a court martial hurriedly arranged for the following day – Christmas Day. At the next questioning by

Divisional Commissaire Esqueyré, the young man had retreated into himself and now insisted that he had acted alone with no accomplices. He had borrowed the gun. He had been loaned the car and a driver in which he hoped to get away but these friends had not been in the plot. He did however talk of a 'mysterious protector' who would grant him mercy. But that was all he could be forced to say.

Bonnier de la Chapelle continued to be unmoved right through the Court Martial which was convened at 6 o'clock in the evening of Christmas Day. After short deliberation this Court Martial declared him guilty and condemned him to be executed. Then later that evening his assurance began to melt away. Would his 'mysterious friends' never show up and save him at the last moment? He spoke about the 'pretence of an execution' but was he merely deceiving himself?

On the morning of the 26th, abandoned and unaided, the young man realized he had been hoodwinked all the way through. Now when he knew he had to die, he wished to make a further confession. He asked for sheets of paper but the prison chaplain in his cell had neither paper nor pencil. So Bonnier de la Chapelle wrote his final confession on a visiting card he had on him which in a few words revealed the existence of a monarchist plot and the names of those who, in one way or another, had suggested to him the idea of murdering Darlan to clear the way for the Pretender to the Throne. These names included the enigmatic Abbé Cordier, a priest who worked with the French Secret Service and who procured plans of the Summer Palace and the revolver. It was small wonder, then, that Commissaire Garinacci had burned the first and full confession. The name printed on the visiting card was Henri d'Astier de la Vigerie, Secretary General of the Police.

74

Requiem

Repercussions to the Darlan assassination were instant. The Axis propaganda machine immediately churned out stories claiming the murder as the work of Allied Intelligence Services. Vichy newspapers, promptly copied by the Paris, Rome and Berlin press, revealed the last words of the Admiral spoken in the car (slightly reminiscent of Nelson in reverse): 'Nothing more can be done for me . . . England has attained her goal.' In fact, of course, Darlan went into a coma from the moment he was shot and never uttered a word till he died.

Eisenhower, too, reacted with equal speed. He ordered the most searching investigation to be undertaken at once and said that if this revealed the slightest British or American complicity in the plot, he would ask to be relieved of his command. In fact, because of the destruction of Bonnier de la Chapelle's first full confession and then his own immediate execution, it was impossible to prove anything which would stand up in a court of law and after many months of following up lead after false lead, rumour upon rumour, nothing definite could be established with any certainty and the process was quietly allowed to run into the sands.

Perhaps the kindest personal requiem was given a few weeks after the admiral's death by Commander Dupin de Saint Cyr, one of Darlan's immediate entourage during his last days, who said:

It was the kind of end the Admiral would have wished

for. The moral crisis through which he was passing during these last weeks after he had realised how great was his unpopularity was a source of constant distress. He courted risks, provoked them, walking unescorted through the most populous parts of the town, where attempts on his life were most probable. He recalled bitterly the dream which was never to come true and which was so dear to him: to end his days as Senator of the Département of the Lot-et-Garonne.

Of those who, like Darlan himself, made history – the British and American leaders who were first allies or friendly neutrals, then adversaries and finally allies once more, such as Churchill, Eisenhower and Cunningham – all tried to comprehend the agonizing dilemma in which Darlan spent the last 2½ years of his life. These great men were all generous to him in their judgement, more generous in fact than many of his own countrymen. This is understandable in itself but it was Churchill, as so often in World War II, who best summed up the character and life of this principal French personage in the perfidious war which had now ended with Darlan's assassination, and as always Churchill did it with clear and outspoken magnanimity.

Few men have paid more heavily for errors of judgment and failure of character than Admiral Darlan. He was a professional figure and a strong personality. His life's work had been to recreate the French Navy and he had raised it to a position it had never held since the days of the French Kings. He commanded the allegiance not only of the Naval Officer Corps but of the whole Naval Service. In accordance with his repeated promises, he ought in 1940 to have ordered the fleets to Britain, to the United States, the African ports, anywhere out of German power. He was under no treaty or obligation to do so except assurances which he had voluntarily given. But this was his resolve until on that deadly June 20, 1940 he accepted from Marshal Pétain's hands the office of Minister of Marine. Then, perhaps influenced by motives of a departmental character, he gave his allegiance to Marshal Petain's government. Ceasing to be a sailor and becoming a politician, he exchanged a sphere in which he had profound knowledge for one where his chief guide was his anti-British prejudices, dating from the Battle of Trafalgar, where his great-grandfather had fallen.

In this new situation he showed himself a man of force and decision who did not wholly comprehend the moral significance of much that he did. Ambition stimulated his errors. His vision as an Admiral had not gone beyond his Navy, nor as a Minister beyond immediate local or personal advantages. For a year and a half he had been a great power in shattered France. At the time when we descended upon North Africa he was the undoubted heir of the aged Marshal. Now suddenly a cataract of amazing events fell upon him. By a strange chance the illness of his son had drawn him to Algiers, where he fell into Anglo-American power.

We have recounted the stresses which he underwent. All French North and West Africa looked to him. The invasion of Vichy France gave him the power, and it may be the right, to make a new decision. He brought to the Anglo-American Allies exactly what they needed, namely a French voice which all French officers and officials in this vast theatre, now plunged in the war, would obey. He struck his final blow for us, and it is not for those who benefited enormously from his accession to our side to revile his memory. A stern impartial judge may say that he should have refused all parley with the Allies he had injured, and defied them to do their worst with him. We may also be glad he took the opposite course. It cost him his life, but there was not much left in life for him. It seemed obvious at the time that he was

311

wrong in not sailing the French Fleet to Allied or
neutral ports in June 1940; but he was right in this
second fearful decision. Probably his sharpest pang
was his failure to bring over the Toulon Fleet.
Always he had declared it should never fall into
German hands. In this undertaking before history he
did not fail. Let him rest in peace, and let us all be
thankful we have never had to face the trials under
which he broke.

75

End-piece

So the reluctant war changed once more into an equally
recalcitrant alliance. This lasted through the remainder of
World War II and, it might be said, continues today with
France, the odd man out, no longer a member of N.A.T.O.
yet still unquestionably on the western side. Nearly half a
century has passed and the events, politics and opinions
of this ensuing period are no part of the story which has
just been told and which came to an end with Darlan's
disappearance from the scene. The aftermath to those
unwilling hostilities climaxed in the ascendancy of General de Gaulle and the restoration of France to her proper
position as one of the great world powers and, as she had
always been, a fount of civilization.

But this aftermath also proved to be fraught with
contention, distress and what amounted to civil war –
cruel, vindictive and bitter even when blood is not actually
being shed. This was set out and foreseen by de Gaulle
three days after Darlan's death when he sent a message
through the American Embassy in London to General

End-piece

Giraud who had been unanimously chosen to step into the Admiral's shoes:

> The assassination at Algiers is an indication and a warning: an indication of the exasperation into which the tragedy of France has thrown the mind and soul of Frenchmen; a warning of the consequences of every kind which necessarily result from the absence of a national authority in the midst of the greatest national crisis of our history. It is more than ever necessary that this national authority should be established. I propose, mon général, that you should meet me as soon as possible on French soil, either in Algeria or in Chad, in order to study the means of grouping under a provisional central authority all French forces inside and outside the country and all the French territories which are in a position to struggle for the liberation and the salvation of France.

Thus the regeneration of France began. The French Empire overseas and the armed forces on which it depended now had the painful task of coming to terms first with themselves and their hitherto Vichy-orientated leaders, secondly with the Gaullists no longer dissidents but instead somewhat arrogant brothers-in-arms and thirdly with the British and Americans to whom alone they owed the enormous debt of their liberation and whom, after the first flush of joyous relief, they often regarded with resentment, disdain and dislike.

It was not an easy time for Giraud, Châtel, Noguès and Boisson and those leaders of the armed forces who had been hidebound in their oaths of loyalty to the Marshal which were theoretically freely given but in fact had virtually been compelled. Only the fighting French under Generals de Gaulle and Leclerc, who were to blaze such a glorious trail for the rest of the war, had the unity of spirit which animated the rest of the Allies outside metropolitan France.

End-piece

In France itself, now totally enslaved, the immensely courageous Resistance alone kept the soul of the country alive. That in itself was no easy task since the initially incoherent Resistance suffered not only from infamous denouncement by some of their pro-German countrymen, resulting at once in the torture and persecution of the Nazi overlords, but in addition was rent by the internal struggle for power of those in its ranks.

All such matters, however, although they naturally followed on, as did the great invasion of Normandy in 1944, are not the concern of this story of the last tragic war between the English and the French which I have tried to recount and which, I venture to believe, can never happen again, any more than the Scots will fight the English or the Confederates the Yankees. Our children will have other problems to solve.

76

Coda

In essence, what was it all about and *could* it ever happen again? In the course of this narrative I have said some hard things about the French whom I have liked and admired all my life and in whose lovely country I now spend most of my time. I began by quoting Philippe de Commynes who said that God created neighbours the exact opposite of each other, so that each would hold the other in fear and humility. But the Second Commandment tells us we should love our neighbours as ourselves. This is no easy thing to do.

In 1942 Churchill put it differently to the House of Commons: 'The Almighty in His infinite wisdom did not see fit to create Frenchmen in the image of Englishmen . . .

Coda

but it would be very foolish not to try to understand what is passing in other people's minds and what are the secret springs of action to which they respond.'

The freedom in which our two great nations now live has been bought at the heavy price of two world wars in this century alone. I make bold, however, to think that one huge result of this purchase is a permanent improvement in the regard we now have for each other. We have moved on some little way from both Philippe de Commynes and from Churchill. The French and the Anglo-Saxons, while still wary of one another, are more friendly and understanding than they have ever been in history and provided we continue to keep our leaders under some sort of control this peaceful and agreeable appreciation can only increase. Deep differences in character, outlook and the way we lead our lives will always, indeed should always, remain but the fear, distrust and hostility have now very largely melted away into the mists of time.

I have a notion, unprovable now as it was wishful thinking then, that the ordinary people of both countries never for a moment wanted to be at war with each other. Yet at war they were. This arose because of the low quality of leadership, the weakness, the treachery and the ill-advised cheating and bargaining which was all that the aged French Head of State and his craven advisers could set against the monstrous demands of the Nazi demon and his Fascist Italian side-kick. That said, how was it possible for them nevertheless to carry the defeated nation with them into even deeper distress? The answer, I think, lies in the highly legalistic habit of mind which the French prize as a quality and the English consider as an offence against common sense when taken to the limits which it was in that terrible crisis. As Churchill put it:

In a state like France which has experienced so many convulsions – Monarchy, Convention, Directory, Consulate, Empire, Monarchy and finally Republic – there has grown up a principle founded on the 'droit

315

administratif' which undoubtedly governs the action of many French officers and officials in times of revolution and change. It arises from a subconscious sense of national self-preservation against the dangers of sheer anarchy. For instance, any officer who obeys the command of his lawful superior or of one whom he believes to be his lawful superior is absolutely immune from subsequent punishment. Much therefore turns in the minds of French officers upon whether there is a direct, unbroken chain of lawful command and this is held by many Frenchmen to be more important than moral, national or international considerations. From this point of view many Frenchmen who admired de Gaulle and envy him in his rôle nevertheless regard him as a man who has rebelled against the authority of the French State which in their prostration they conceive to be vested in the person of the antique defeatist who to them is the illustrious and venerable Marshal Pétain, the hero of Verdun and the sole hope of France.

To my mind that is the nub of the matter, but each must judge for himself. If Colonel A gives a patently ridiculous order, Lieutenant B is blameless in carrying it out. Taken to its logical conclusion, the murderers and their accomplices who ran the Nazi concentration camps – and for that matter their clones in France and French North Africa – should never have been put on trial. Thank God they were. Thank God too that the events of this last reluctant war are very unlikely ever to occur again in so far as the two friendly neighbours of Great Britain and France are concerned. Let us continue, nevertheless, to bear in mind with Othello that

> To mourn a mischief that is past and gone
> Is the next way to draw new mischief on.

SELECT BIBLIOGRAPHY

Antier, Jean-Jacques, *L'aventure Héroique des sous-marins français*, Eds. Maritime et d'Outre-mer 1984.

Amouroux, Henri, *La grande histoire des Français sous l'Occupation Vols 1–7*, Laffont 1976–87.

Aron, R., *Histoire de Vichy*, Fayard 1954.

Aron, R., *Nouveaux Grands Dossiers de l'histoire contemporaine*, Perrin 1964.

Auphan & Mordal, *La marine française pendant La Seconde Guerre Mondiale*, Hachette 1958.

Bouthillier, Yves, *Le Drame de Vichy*, Paris 1950.

Boutron, Jean, *De Mers-el-Kébir à Londres 1940–44*, Plon 1980.

Carré, Paul, *Les Lévriers de la Mer*, Eds. France-Empire 1953.

Colville, John, *The Fringes of Power – Downing Street Diaries*, Hodder & Stoughton 1985.

Churchill, Winston, *The Second World War Vols II, III & IV*, Cassell 1951.

Cooper, Dick, *Aventures of a Secret Agent*, Muller 1957.

Cunningham of Hyndhope, *A Sailor's Odyssey*, Dutton 1951.

Eisenhower, Dwight, *Crusade in Europe*, Heinemann 1948.

Godfroy R.E., *Aventure de la Force X à Alexandrie*, Plon 1953.

Hough, Richard, *The Longest Battle – the War at Sea 1939–45*, Morrow 1986.

Jannen, Hervé, *Marin de Guerre*, Pen-Duick 1984.

Leahy, William, *I was There*, Plon 1950.

Liddell Hart, B.H., *History of the Second World War*, Pan 1973.

Bibliography

Lottman, Herbert, *Pétain: Hero or Traitor*, Viking 1985.

Maggiar, R., *Les Fusiliers Marins de Leclerc*, France-Empire 1984.

Marder, A.J., *Operation Menace*, Oxford 1976.

Ordioni, Pierre, *Le Secret de Darlan*, Albatros Paris 1974.

Paillat, Claude, *L'Occupation – Le Pillage de la France*, Laffont 1987.

Pierre-Gosset, R., *Algiers 1941–1943*, Cape 1945.

Plimmer, C. & D., *A Matter of Expediency*, Quartet 1978.

Rome, Contre-Amiral, *Les Oubliés du Bout du Monde*, Maritime & d'Outre-mer 1983.

Spears, Edward, *Pétain: de Gaulle*, Presses de la Cité 1966.

Taillemite, E., *L'histoire ignorée de la Marine française*, Perrin 1988.

Tute, Warren, *The Deadly Stroke*, Collins 1973.

Tute, Warren, *The North African War*, Sidgwick & Jackson 1976.

Voituriez, A.J., *L'Affaire Darlan*, Jean-Claude Lattès 1980.

Watson, J.A., *Echec à Dakar*, Laffont 1968.

INDEX

Index

329

Index

Index

Index

Royal Navy, 15, 19, neutralizes French Navy, 16; strengths, 27; Mers-el-Kébir, 28–30; in Alexandria, 30–9, 70–4, 75–9; blockades German coast, 59; takes over French ships in British ports, 65–70; Dakar expedition, 88, 90–2, 99–127; and the 'liberation' of Libreville, 145; blockades France, 161–5; Syrian campaign, 172, 174, 175, 177–80; severe losses, 185; and Madagascar, 199–207; North African campaign, 229

Rubis, 49, 58–62, 67–9, 81

Rufisque, 118

Rundstedt, Field Marshal von, 268

Rushbrooke, Commander, 105–6

Russell, Commander A.B., 244

Russian Air Force, 185

Ryder, General, 258

Safi, 248, 249, 275

Saint-Didier, 180

Saint-Hardouin, Jacques Tarbé de, 228

St Nazaire, 221

Saint Pierre, 199

Salonika, 180

Sartine, 21

Savorgnan-de-Brazza, 145

Scapa Flow, 290–1

Schmidt, Paul, 135, 137

Schreiber, Lieutenant General E.C.A., 203

SCIPIO, Operation, 88

SEALION, 92, 93, 128

Senegal, Dakar expedition, 84–92, 96–130

Seraph, H.M.S., 234, 237–8, 240

Service d'Ordre Légionnaire, 297

Sète, 289

Sevestre, Lieutenant J.M., 50, 52–3, 55–7, 59

Shaw, George Bernard, 15

Sheffield, H.M.S., 165

Sicily, 164, 201

Sidi Ahmed, 280

Sidon, 177

Sierra Leone, 105, 249

Singapore, 197

SLEDGEHAMMER, Operation, 221

Smuts, Jan, 195–6, 197, 207

Solvaersboen, 61

Somerville, Vice-Admiral Sir James, 30, 78, 101, 102, 108

Souffleur, 177–8, 180

Sousse, 50–1

South Africa, 195–6

Southampton, 66

Soviet Union, 93, 128, 132, 151, 157, 167, 169, 185, 220, 222–5

Spain, 100, 127, 129, 134–5, 163, 224

Spears, General, 84, 87–9, 90, 97, 111

Spears Mission, 107, 109

Special Operations Executive, 207

Sprague, Lieutenant Commander, 70

S.S., 290

Stalin, Joseph, 65, 220, 222–5, 301n.

Strasbourg, 146, 152, 286, 292–3

Stülpnagel, General von, 113, 129–30, 154

Sturges, Major General, 198, 200–3

Suez Canal, 108, 165

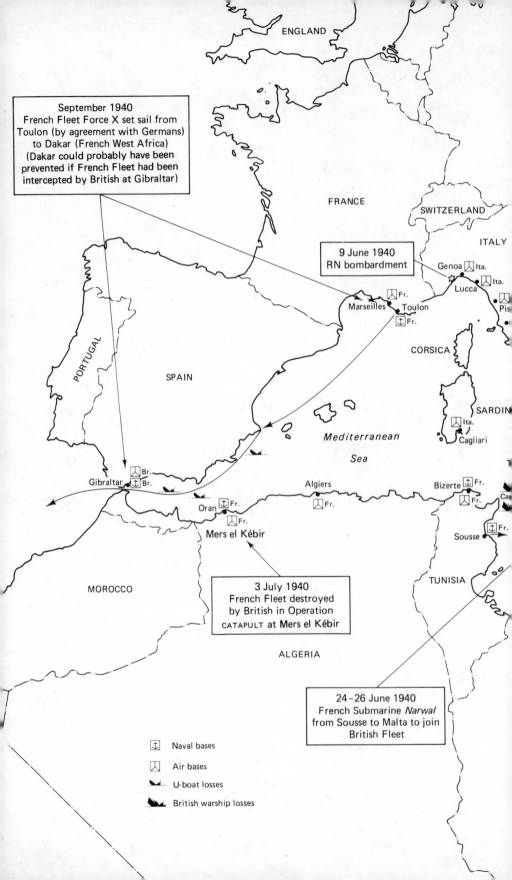

ENGLAND

September 1940
French Fleet Force X set sail from
Toulon (by agreement with Germans)
to Dakar (French West Africa)
(Dakar could probably have been
prevented if French Fleet had been
intercepted by British at Gibraltar)

FRANCE

SWITZERLAND

ITALY

9 June 1940
RN bombardment

Genoa ⚔ Ita.
⚔ Ita.
Lucca
Pis

Marseilles ● Toulon ⚔ Fr.
⚓ Fr.

CORSICA

PORTUGAL

SPAIN

Mediterranean
Sea

SARDIN

⚔ Ita.
● Cagliari

Gibraltar ⚔ Br.
⚓ Br.

Algiers

Bizerte ⚓ Fr.
⚔ Fr.
Ca

Oran ⚓ Fr.
⚔ Fr.
Mers el Kébir

⚔ Fr.

⚓ Fr.
Sousse ●

MOROCCO

3 July 1940
French Fleet destroyed
by British in Operation
CATAPULT at Mers el Kébir

TUNISIA

ALGERIA

24–26 June 1940
French Submarine *Narwal*
from Sousse to Malta to join
British Fleet

⚓ Naval bases

⚔ Air bases

U-boat losses

British warship losses